ROARING '20S FASHIONS
DECO

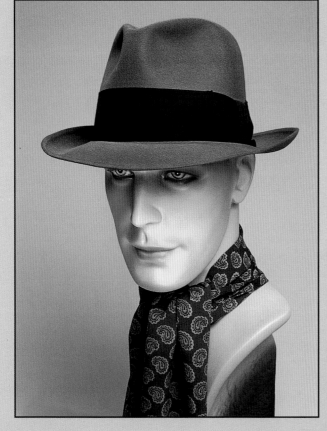

Schiffer Publishing Ltd

4880 Lower Valley Road, Atglen, PA 19310 USA

SUSAN LANGLEY
WITH PHOTOGRAPHY BY JOHN DOWLING

Dedication

This book is dedicated to my husband, Joe,
with my thanks for all his help and support.

Acknowledgments

Heartfelt thanks to my family and friends, fellow antique clothes lovers, and history buffs. Thanks to Steven Porterfield, Ken Weber, Janet Swartz, Doris Butler, Mrs. John E. Dowling, Amanda Bury, and T.W. Conroy, for loan of their lovely items; and to June Lang, Patricia St. John and Lee and Jeannine Seely, and my aunt Dot and uncle Leon. Thanks to Lorenzo State Historic Site; to Decoeyes for their splendid job of mannequin restoration; to Emmanuel Voucher for French translations; and to Karl at Microtech for helping a computer illiterate. Thanks to my excellent editors, Donna (Book I, Jazz) and Jeff (Book II, Deco); to John for his marvelous layouts and Colin for his wonderful covers, and of course, to Nancy and Peter Schiffer.

And last, but not least, thanks to the original creators of the clothes—and the flapper owners who wore them with such panache!

Library of Congress Cataloging-in-Publication Data:

Langley, Susan.
  Roaring '20s fashions : deco / Susan Langley ; with photography by John Dowling.
    p. cm.
  ISBN 0-7643-2320-2 (hardcover)
1. Clothing and dress—History—20th century. 2. Fashion—History—20th century. 3. Decoration and ornament—Art deco. 4. Nineteen twenties. I. Title: Roaring twenties fashions. II. Dowling, John. III. Title.

GT596.L36 2006
391'.009'04—dc22

2005022137

Copyright © 2006 by Susan Langley

Designed by John P. Cheek
Cover Design by Bruce Waters
Type set in Bodoni Bd BT/Aldine 721 BT

ISBN: 0-7643-2320-2
Printed in China
1 2 3 4

Published by Schiffer Publishing Ltd.
4880 Lower Valley Road
Atglen, PA 19310
Phone: (610) 593-1777; Fax: (610) 593-2002
E-mail: Info@schifferbooks.com

For the largest selection of fine reference books on this and related subjects, please visit our web site at
www.schifferbooks.com
We are always looking for people to write books on new and related subjects. If you have an idea for a book please contact us at the above address.

This book may be purchased from the publisher.
Include $3.95 for shipping.
Please try your bookstore first.
You may write for a free catalog.

In Europe, Schiffer books are distributed by
Bushwood Books
6 Marksbury Ave.
Kew Gardens
Surrey TW9 4JF England
Phone: 44 (0) 20 8392-8585; Fax: 44 (0) 20 8392-9876
E-mail: info@bushwoodbooks.co.uk
Free postage in the U.K., Europe; air mail at cost.

Contents

Introduction

Our companion book, *Roaring '20s Fashions: Jazz*, covered the events that influenced the times and mores of this fabulous decade through the first half of the twenties—including the coming of Prohibition, Silent Films, The Automobile, Women's Emancipation, and of course, Jazz! People of this new decade felt that with the end of World War I, a CELEBRATION was in order, and what a celebration it was! F. Scott Fitzgerald would write of it as "The Greatest, Gaudiest Spree in History," and in this second volume, *Roaring '20s Fashions: Deco*, you'll see the "celebration" heat up to its most Hedonistic!

As *Roaring '20s Fashions: Jazz* ends in 1924, preparations were well under way for the Exposition des Arts Decoratifs in Paris—the electrifying exhibition that would give "Art Deco" its name and influence every aspect of "modern" twentieth century life, including, of course, fashion.

In *Roaring '20s Fashions: Jazz*, we followed the emergence of the "simple" chemise or tubular frock to its apex in 1924; in *Roaring '20s Fashions: Deco*, we'll witness new feminine curves emphasized via such methods as skirts' fuller "flare" and the sensuous "bias cut"—as skirts rise to the knees. By the end of the decade, in 1929, we'll see a dramatic change in fashion as longer skirts and natural waistlines return to usher in the clothes of the Tantalizing Thirties.

The Art Deco Exposition
of 1925

The Art Deco Exposition was held from April to October 1925 in the heart of Paris—along the Seine from the Pont Alexandre III to the Pont de l'Alma. Its purpose was to showcase the Decorative Arts of the "streamlined" new century—extremely modern designs influenced by the art of many countries. The Art Deco Expo evidenced a new willingness to accept different cultures as it shaped the spirit of its era. *Vogue* noted the impact of Art Deco, proclaiming: "A New Style is Born... rejecting elaborate curves of Nouveau in favor of Cubist and rectilinear lines!"

The French spared no expense—the grounds were enchanting, with the various pavilions surrounded by "attractive gardens with their own specially designed fountains and statues...". In addition to the pavilions' displays, there were plays, parades, ballets, fashion shows, beauty contests, and concerts—including Jazz concerts by black American musicians. At night, Paris truly became The City of Light as countless electric lights transformed the grounds into a wonderland; the Eiffel Tower alone was lit with over 25,000 light bulbs, courtesy of Citroen. Spectacular fireworks added to the excitement.

Artists whose names have become synonymous with Art Deco displayed their most "moderne" creations at the Expo. Rene Lalique's incredible crystal fountain became a favorite meeting place. In the shape of an obelisk, it was fourteen meters high with some 140 figures—lit from within, fine jets of water sparkled like a waterfall, shimmering in the lights. Lalique decorated his own pavilion with stunning low relief glass panels; also on display were his exquisite lamps, vases, and perfume bottles. The magnificent glass dining room he designed for the Sevres Pavilion won raves. Another of the Expo's highlights was Edgar Brandt's riveting Art Deco screen, fashioned of wrought iron and gilded bronze.

Of the all the Expo's pavilions, none was more startling (or controversial) than architect LeCorbusier's *Pavillion de L'Esprit Noveau*—an "ideal" ultra modern house or "machine for living"!

In *Le Pavillion d'un Collectionneur* (the Pavilion of a Connoisseur of the Arts), Ruhlmann exhibited his fabulous furniture—"veneers of rare woods encrusted with ivory...". Another focal point in this pavilion was artist Jean Dupas' spectacular Art Deco panel, *Les Perruches (The Lovebirds)*.

No wonder *Vogue*, after visiting the Expo, advised its readers:

> *It is like a city in a dream... bold experiments... enormous fountains of glass play among life size Cubist trees... cascades of music; electric lights turn the Expo into a fantastic spectacle.*

Haute couture, of course, received proper homage—as the Exposition's official catalog exclaimed, "It is right that fashion should take a privileged place among the decorative arts displayed in the Grand Palais, **for fashion is essentially an art**". Among the exhibitors were Lanvin, Vionnet, Patou, Jenny, Lelong, Paquin, Worth, Callot Soeurs, Doeuillet, and Lemmonnier; displays by Coco Chanel and Sonia Delaunay/ Jacques Heim included stockings, shoes, hats, gloves, and lingerie. Couture fashions were exhibited in several areas: at the *Pavillion de l'Elegance*, in the *Grand Palais*, and in boutiques along the Pont Alexander III. Paul Poiret exhibited on three barges moored along the Seine. *Gazette du Bon Ton* published a special edition in honor of the Expo, and *Art Gout Beaute* had their own pavilion.

Le Pavillon de l'Elegance housed couture creations with *le Stand* (displays) by Lanvin, Callot, Jenny, and Worth. The stands were decorated by Jeanne Lanvin; settings included bronze furniture by Rateau and lacquer screens by Jean Dunand. Haute couture gowns were shown on stylized Art Deco wax mannequins by Andre Vigneau of Siegel's—described by one *Vogue* commentator as "STRANGE SILVER LADIES FROM

Artist Tony George Roux's cover of the April 8, 1925, issue of *L'Illustration - Exposition des Arts Decoratifs*, a magazine promoting the Parisian Exposition that gave "Art Deco" its name.

MARS"! Two full pages of the September 1, 1925, issue with photos by Man Ray were devoted to the mannequins: "Modern Art and the new Siegel Mannequins... interesting examples of a modern expression of art at the Expo of Decorative Arts in Paris are the mannequins used by the great couturiers in the *Pavillon de l'Elegance* and the *Grand Palais...*".

Paul Poiret named his three extravagant barges *Amours* (Loves), *Orgues* (Organs), and *Delices* (Delights); they were decorated by his famed studio, *Atelier Martine*. *Amours* showcased Martine's latest interior designs—a seductive boudoir display featured Rosine perfume bottles, and a special "Perfume Piano" sprayed Rosine perfume when the keys were pressed! On *Orgues*, Poiret displayed his latest couture creations, complimented by a background of fourteen spectacular toile wall hangings by artist Raoul Dufy with scenes in-cluding Paris by air, a bridge game at a casino, Longchamp races, a circus, a dance hall, and a reception. The Expo's official catalog featured a Poiret sequin evening gown on a Siegal mannequin, and a summer day dress in Martine fabric against matching Martine wallpaper. His last barge, *Delices*, was a gourmet restaurant.

Boutiques lined the avenues—*Revillon Furs* exhibited at Boutique No. 11 at Pont Alexandre III, and artist Sonia Delaunay, collaborating with couturier Jacques Heim, exhibited at the *Boutique Simultanee*, also on the Pont Alexandre III. Delauney was famous for her cubist-themed fabrics called *"Simultanes"*—bold geometric patterns in vivid primary colors that were the antithesis of the fantasy fabrics of Dufy and Seguy. Delauney's creations were designed to compliment the wearer in motion.

Elegant fabrics were displayed in the *Pavillon du Tissu*. The Expo's magazine praises the exhibit of Rodier in particular, noting their fine woolen fabrics woven as border prints (*à disposition*). Four great department stores exhibited along the *Invalides*; the most exciting, *Le Pavillon des Galeries Lafayette*, with its marble facade and Deco sunburst, and theme of "*La Vie en Rose.*" The legendary Mario Fortuny displayed fabrics that took one's breath away along the Pont Alexandre III.

There were daily fashion shows, and a "*Fashion Extravaganza*" was held at the staircase of the *Grand Palais* on June 16, 1925! It featured hundreds of models, musicians, and dancers—including almost nude dancers from the Folies Bergere in Erte-style in feathers and sequins! Highlights included "*Vision of the East,*" French gowns in Oriental motifs, and a show-stopping parade of models descending a staircase in extravagant ermine coats with long trailing trains. In 1926, some of the Expo's creations were displayed in New York.

This large sheer silk scarf is printed in the Cubist or "*Simultaneous*" designs typical of Sonia Delaunay; it's labeled: *Made in France*. 150-$250

A rare "fantasy" pattern silk scarf, in an Art Deco print similar to those of Dufy and Seguy. This charming version combines Ancient Egyptian themes with "moderne" street scenes. $100-$200

Twenties BLACK IS BEAUTIFUL!

As Harlem Renaissance poet Langston Hughes wrote, "We younger Negro artists who create now intend to express our individual dark-skinned selves without fear or shame... we know we are beautiful...".

In 1925, beautiful American dancer Josephine Baker became the toast of Paris—the Queen of the Folies Begeres! *Vogue* describes the amazing Miss Baker as "a woman possessed... a shining machine 'a danser' ...all joint and no bones"! When she opened her own nightclub, one interviewer reported: "...the length of her graceful body which is light sealskin brown is swathed in a blue tulle frock with a bodice of blue snakeskin... her hair is brilliantined to her head as if painted on..."! Josephine tooled around the streets of Paris in her brown Voisin auto—upholstered in brown snakeskin.

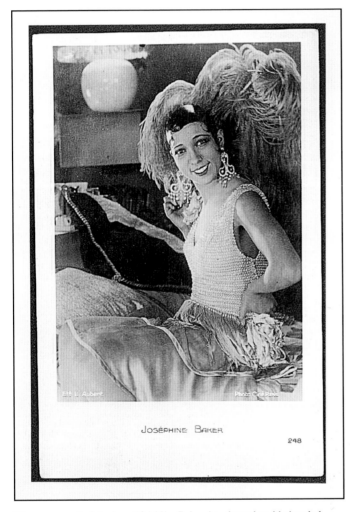

Photo postcard of the beautiful Miss Baker, be-plumed and bejeweled. Note her very short brilliantined hair.

Josephine Baker opens at the *Casino de Paris* in *"la Grande Revue."* Poster, ca. 1925.

Jazz and Dancing

By mid-decade, "The Party of the Century" was well underway—pulsating to the sounds of the Jazz music that was its heartbeat. By 1925, American Jazz had spread across the seas—the whole world was caught in its spell! It would be impossible to exaggerate the impact of Jazz... there was an insatiable appetite for this compelling new sound that set the whole body shakin'... even formerly staid socialites coaxed Harlem musicians to Park Avenue to give "authentic" Black Bottom and Charleston lessons.

Louis Armstrong

Jazz greats Louis Armstrong and Duke Ellington had become icons. For the millions unable to hear the them in person, the magic of their music spread like wildfire via radio, gramophone recordings, and sheet music.

Sheet music to Louis Armstrong's best selling *St. Louis Blues*, recorded in 1925 with Bessie Smith. Bessie electrified audiences as she belted out: "I hate to see de ev'nin' sun go down... Cause my baby, he done lef dis town..." Louis got the nickname "Satchmo" when he told audiences he had a big "satchelmouth"—a British journalist thought it suited, but shortened it to "Satchmo." Born in poverty in New Orleans, young Louis sang for pennies in the streets of New Orleans, and later played in small saloon bands. His mentor, King Oliver, encouraged him, and in 1922 Oliver invited him to Chicago to play with his band, King Oliver's Creole Jazz Band. Satchmo later performed at New York's Roseland Dance Hall with Fletcher Henderson's Black Swan Troubadours; then he returned to Chicago to form his own band, Louis Armstrong and His Hot Five (later Hot Seven). In November of 1925, he starred at Chicago's famed Dreamland, with his wife Lil's band—billed as "The Jazz Coronet King who just got in from New York". By 1928, Louis was back in New York thrilling throngs at Harlem's Savoy Ballroom; he also appeared with the legendary Fats Waller in Broadway's *Hot Chocolates*. The Savoy Ballroom, The Cotton Club, and Roseland Ballroom were New York's HOTTEST jazz spots.

The Savoy Ballroom, "The Home of Happy Feet," opened March 12, 1926; it took up the entire second floor of a block long building that ran from 140th to 141st Streets in Harlem. Many jazz greats performed there, and both black and white fans were included in the audience—the only criteria being how well one could DANCE! The Savoy was such a hot spot that the floor was completely replaced every three years. According to jazz legend, George "Shorty" Snowden introduced The Lindy Hop, the first Swing dance, there in September 1927—four months after Lindbergh's famous flight.

The Cotton Club opened in 1920 as the Club Deluxe; in 1922 it was taken over by Owney Madden, who changed its name to the Cotton Club. In the twenties, the Cotton Club was located at 664 Lenox Avenue and West 142nd Street in Harlem. It featured the world's best black jazz musicians, but in the twenties, audiences were white high society.

Roseland Ballroom opened on New Year's Eve, 1919. Located at 239 West 52nd Street, it was a favorite twenties hotspot—performers included Fletcher Henderson's band, Louis Armstrong, Duke Ellington, and, during the Swing era, Benny Goodman and the Dorsey brothers.

This dynamic snapshot of Harlem's famous Cotton Club was taken ca. 1929-35. You can almost feel the electricity of the era through the billboards, compelling you to step through time and into the Cotton Club of the twenties—the great Duke Ellington is performing! Originally from Washington, D.C., The Duke moved to Harlem in 1923 with his band, Duke Ellington and the Washingtonians. His big break came in 1927, when he was booked into the Cotton Club, where his performances were broadcast nationally... "Live From the Cotton Club"! Duke Ellington was a composer as well as bandleader and pianist—a handsome man and very sharp dresser, his friends nicknamed him "The Duke."

Houghton's Jazz Bandits. Inspired by such greats as Armstrong and Ellington, many small jazz bands formed during the twenties—like the Houghton's Jazz Bandits, which included drums, banjo, saxophone, and piano. The pretty flapper pianist may have doubled as a singer. Photograph, ca. 1925.

To be elegantly attired for a Night of Jazz, *National Style Book* advocates "Our Young Chap's Jazz Suit"—in all wool flannel for $22.98! (1924-25 issue).

Dances

During the second half of the decade, the most popular dances were the Black Bottom, and, of course, The Charleston—a dance so popular it would become synonymous with the twenties.

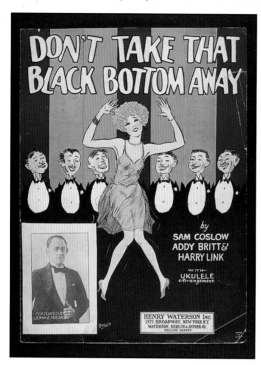

DON'T TAKE THAT BLACK BOTTOM AWAY! In this wild and witty illustration, a red-headed flapper gyrates to the famed Black Bottom... cheered on by tuxedoed Sheiks with slicked hair and lecherous leers! The fascinating chorus goes:

*Every time I do that dance I lose my self control
It has taken full possession of my very soul —
So just take everything you can — You can even take my man
But don't take that Black, Black, Bottom away
Hey! Hey! Hey!*

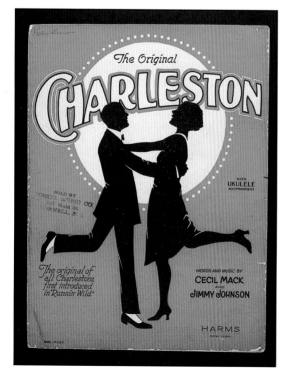

It was, in fact, danced so enthusiastically that in 1925 Boston police reported the collapse of The Pickwick, a Boston speakeasy—caused, they claimed, by the "excessive shaking and wild gyrations of the Charleston dancers."

Naturally, the Charleston was condemned by members of the clergy. It was so frenetic one minister declared: "Any lover of the beautiful will die rather than be associated with the Charleston. It is neurotic! It is rotten! It stinks! Phew, open the windows!" One might wonder where he was when he witnessed this scandalous dance.

Mirroring the cover of the Charleston sheet music, this couple shows how to "cut the rug"! Photo postcard, ca. 1925.

Charleston sheet music (copyright 1923); at bottom left a banner proclaims it's "The Original of all Charlestons, first introduced in *Runnin Wild*" (a 1923 all-black Broadway musical). Partial lyrics:

*Charleston! Charleston! Made in Carolina
Some dance, Some Prance,
I'll say, there's nothing finer than the Charleston, Charleston—
Lord how you can shuffle
Ev'ry step you do Leads to something new—
Man I'm telling you It's a La-pa-zoo—
Buck dance, Wing dance, will be a back number—
But the Charleston, the new Charleston—
That dance is surely a comer—
Sometime You'll dance it one time,
the dance called the Charleston - Made in South Caroline!*

Lively flappers, clad in bathing suits, rolled stockings, and high heels, dance a mean Charleston—the two gals at left do the famous "Bees Knees"! At the bottom of this rather risqué photo postcard is printed: "Eight reasons why the Navy likes San Diego!"

On the back cover of *The Original Charleston* sheet music are "Dance Directions" for the uninitiated. Note her sexy ankle bracelet!

"Flaming Youth" —
Sheiks and Shebas!

Collegiate gals and guys became "Sheiks and Shebas"(in homage to Valentino's smoldering desert films)—they became fashion's new trend setters, and styles set at ivy league colleges were soon adopted by all.

Going to college was one of "Flaming Youth's" main goals—not just to acquire an education, but for FUN! Silent movies depicted college life as an endless round of mad dancing, petting parties, and football games, complete with ukuleles and hip flasks—and the collegians did their best to live up to their on-screen counterparts. *The Collegians*, Universal Studio's popular comedies that debuted in 1926, expounded on collegiate goals: "You go there to learn things—how to drink, how to pet, how to win the big game, and, above all, how to meet people who will be useful to you when at last the four years of hedonistic freedom are over and you have to put your nose to the grindstone and make your pile." Woodrow Wilson, a former President of Princeton University, once described it as "The Best Country Club in America."

F. Scott Fitzgerald, in *This Side of Paradise*, memorialized his undergraduate days at Princeton:

> *Evening after evening the senior singing had drifted over the campus in melancholy beauty, and through the shell of his undergraduate consciousness had broken a deep and reverent devotion to the gray walls and Gothic peaks and all they symbolized as warehouses of dead ages... "Damn it all," he whispered aloud, ... "Next year I Work!"*

This *Life* Commencement Number cover by L.J. Holton pictures a cute collegiate couple illustrating the decade's favorite fads. Note the Sheik's wide Oxford bags, ukulele, and pipe—and Sheba's short skirt, rouged knees, cloche hat, and long cigarette holder! As they clutch their new diplomas, they ask "Now what shall we commence?"(*Life*, July 7, 1927)

Sheiks

By 1925, WIDE Oxford Bags are all the rage—a necessity for any college man. *National Style Book* offers wide trousers, "Styled on English Lines," noting they "...will appeal to the up-to-the-minute man." The cuffs are a full 20-inches wide.

Plus Four Knickers and "Whoopee Hats"

Knickers were the college man's sporty alternative to Oxford bags; they're often paired with Argyle sweaters and two-tone spectator "co-respondent" oxfords (see also pages 95, 96).

This quintessential "Sheik"—with his slicked back hair, plus four knickers, Argyle sweater, and spectator wingtips—must have made many a Coed swoon! Snapshot, Brown University, 1926.

Bellas Hess urges: "Buy yourself a Whoopee Hat. The bright colors are all the rage! The Whoopee comes in eye-popping colors like red, royal blue, and purple..." and "you can roll it up and put it in your pocket without doing it a bit of damage." (1929)

"RAH, RAH, ZIZ BOOM BAH!" Out for a lark, Yale men and their dates bundle up in Raccoon coats. *YALE PROM 1926* is noted on the reverse.

The Raccoon Coat

Another symbol of the decade, the raccoon coat was a must for both Sheiks and Shebas—especially when icy north winds blew over the campus. As *Vogue* advised college-bound readers: "There is always a good word to be said for the Raccoon Coat for campus, since nothing bears up under any wear and any weather as it does..." (1925). It was popular throughout the twenties and into the thirties—though *Men's Wear* observed that at the 1929 Princeton-Yale game, the snappy camel's hair coat had edged into first place.

This jazzy sheet music, "Doin' the Raccoon" (copyright 1925) exhorts:

> *College men - knowledge men - Do a dance called "Raccoon"*
> *It's the craze now-a-days—And it will get you soon.*
> *Buy a coat and try it—Bet you'll be a Riot!*
> *(chorus) Oh they wear them down at Princeton—And they share them up at Yale—Oh they eat in them at Harvard—And they sleep in them in jail!*

Note that snappy "WHOOPEE" fedora!

Raccoon coats are similarly styled for men and women. *National Style Book* offers a snazzy raccoon coat in two lengths; note the huge convertible shawl collar, and contrasting placement of the fur at collar, cuffs, and hem. (Fall/Winter, 1924/25)

13

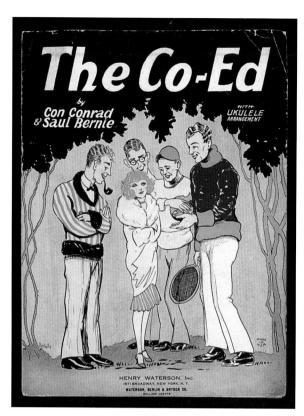

Shebas

Sassy, Sexy College "Co-Eds" — "VAMPERS on the College Campus"!

"The Co-Ed" sheet music ("with ukulele arrangement," naturally) pictures a Clara Bow-ish red haired coed surrounded by admiring college men—one wearing a Frosh beanie! (1925). Partial lyrics:

Stranger, if you're fearing danger—
Keep away from Co-Eds on a Moonlight Night.
Vampers on the College Campus
—always make me foolish when I hold them tight.
(Chorus) Fair Co-Ed, I love you, with your cheeks powdered up and a ring on each finger of your hand. Rare Co-Ed it's for you—that my lips pucker up when we dance to the music of the band. It's not the knowledge you gained at college that makes you famous throughout the land—It's the red in your head knocks 'em dead, sweet fair Co-Ed...

These "Vampers" are off to college in a very jazzy sports coupe—note their short skirts and "Clara" bobs! Left to right are: (illegible), Christine Peterson, Cordora Diggs, Mildred Hayton, Hilda Floe, (illegible). Snapshot, ca. 1925-29.

The news photo notes: "An Episode in a School Girl's Life... Prides Crossing, Mass.—Girls of Kendall Hall, an exclusive school on the North Shore near Boston, toasting marshmallows before a wood fire on the beach in front of the school on an autumn day—*Wide World Photos*, Boston Bureau, 11-26-26." Note the girl second from right, wearing a striped blazer—a must for both Sheiks and Shebas!

Vogue offered the college girl the following fashion advice:

Simplicity is the soul of college chic... a girl arrives at college to be judged first by her appearance; an adequate wardrobe is exceedingly important... Semi-sport clothes, versatile ensembles that can be interchanged are recommended. Frocks with youthful lines—an informal air, are a perfect expression of the well-dressed college girl... Sweater, blouse and pleated skirts have long been a college uniform; sweaters are now considered part of a complete ensemble and should be chosen to coordinate accordingly... For dinner, the college girl changes from a semi-sports frock into one slightly more formal... One smart town outfit is necessary for trips to New York or Boston for the matinee or dinner. One evening dress is essential—a georgette crepe or light metal cloth... or a picture frock. They should be simple, a beaded dress should never be chosen... an evening wrap is a necessity... (9/25)

Cosmetics of the Second Half of the Decade

Cosmetics in one form or another have been used since before recorded history. Around 60 B.C. Cleopatra, one of the most famous beauties of all time, was outlining her eyes with kohl and staining her lips and cheeks with a paste of red ochre. During the Renaissance, Catherine deMedici introduced the art of "face painting," using cosmetics made of white lead and vermilion. In Marie Antoinette's day, towering hairdos were powdered as well as the face, and cheeks were heavily rouged—and as a finishing touch, "beauty mark" patches of various shapes were liberally applied.

Though using makeup was not considered "Ladylike" in Victorian and Edwardian times, by the twenties there was no longer any stigma attached to a "painted face." Cosmetics had become so popular that *Vogue* observed: "The every hour act of powdering and lipsticking is performed with such concentration and indifference to spectators as can only flow from a sense of deep importance of the act...". "Lipstick" as we know it (in a push-up tube container) was first mass-produced ca. 1915.

Encouraging women to follow Tallulah Bankhead's advice, "One can never use enough lip-rouge!", twenties cosmetic firms offer such novelties as Cupidsbow-Self-Shaping lipstick, and KISS-PROOF-Waterproof lipstick. (Tallulah starred in 1925 in the stage version of Michael Arlen's *The Green Hat*).

"You will never know how beautiful you really are until you are *KISSPROOF*," avows Delica Laboratories of Chicago, Illinois. (*Harper's Bazar*, October 1926)

CUPIDSBOW Lipstick by Helena Rubinstein, "A lipstick that forms a perfect Cupidsbow as you apply it!" As this delightful ad illustrates, women can have "Perfectly curved lips with professional deftness"... in Red Raspberry, or Red Geranium. (*Harper's Bazar* October 1926)

"It Girl" Clara Bow exhibits her irresistible Cupidsbow lips! The sassy Miss Bow is the idol of millions... flappers henna their hair red and paint their lips vermillion as they imitate her sexy, devil-may-care ways! Hand tinted photo postcard, ca. 1925.

Morals

By the second half of the decade, old-fashioned Victorian morals had gone the way of the starched collar and the cruel corset... and panicky parents, faced with a phantasmagoria of short skirts, low necklines, sexy jazz music, wild dances, bathtub gin—and even petting parlor cars—were fighting a losing battle. And, as if all this wasn't enough, the controversial new theories of Dr. Sigmund Freud indicated that "Sexual repression may lead to neuroses!"

The right to vote won at last, young women now aimed to be "just one of the guys"... and they smoked, drank, swore, and loved accordingly! Men were often referred to as "pals" or "chums"—*women's* equals.

"Oh Say! Can I See You To-Night?" was sung by Ruth Gillette, a tempestuous canary with seductively kohled eyes and Cupid's Bow lips! Just one generation ago, a girl calling a guy to suggest a date would have been unthinkable... and now girls were calling guys to arrange unchaperoned assignations!

This vintage photo, taken ca. 1925, advertises the "Petting Parlor on Wheels... An example of back porch love in an auto—this new type offers all the comforts of your home back porch. It has reversible back seat and curtain to draw for obvious reasons!" Ready for a night of love, this amorous guy is dressed in a tuxedo, while his gal wears a short satin frock that shows plenty of leg.

"Oh Say! Can I See You To-Night?" inquires a fringed flapper of her guy via candlestick telephone! Partial lyrics:

Today her people went away—
So she called him on the telephone to say
Oh say! Can I see you tonight
There'll be nobody home—We'll be there all alone
Call around about nine—Everything will be fine... (1925)

Prohibition

Prohibition, in effect for five years by mid-decade, was considered a nuisance by many fun-loving folks, and by 1925 there was much talk of repeal. Booze was flaunted as the Party of the Century heated up.

In the late twenties, when she was just eighteen, my husband's mother, Teresa, decided to throw a party. She asked friends for recipes for bathtub gin, bought the ingredients, and literally mixed them up in her bathtub. She was a bit afraid to try the bubbling brew herself, so when her boyfriend Bob stopped in to see how things were going, she asked him to sample it. Bob thought it was DYNAMITE; then he said he had to leave, but would be back in time for the party. Soon after, Teresa's father came in and said that he thought Bob had left. Teresa said he had—and her father replied, "...but his car's outside!" They went looking for Bob—and found him chattering in a tree and about to leap from the branches—he told them he was a squirrel. Teresa's father finally coaxed him down with some party nuts. Teresa vowed this was a true story... and many bathtub concoctions *were* potent enough to blind people—or turn them into squirrels!

Foremost among The Crusaders to Repeal the 18th Amendment, this perky gal leaves no doubt as to her feelings on the subject...

This fun-loving flapper asks, "Where's the Party?" as she swigs her hootch... after all, why wait to get to the party when you can have fun en route? Vintage snapshot, ca. 1925.

The Party in Full Swing... Revelers, snapshot ca. 1925.

How This Book is Illustrated

This charming trio guides us on our odyssey through the
Deco years of the late 1920s:

Vintage Photos

Snapshots, studio portraits, and photo postcards charmingly depict the lifestyles as well as the fashions of the decade with unerring accuracy.

This marvelous vintage photo brings the late twenties to life! (See page 141.)

Professional Photos of Existing Garments

John Dowling's combination of artistic talent and technical skill are evident in his photos of these existing twenties garments. John was a photographer for the Syracuse newspapers for many years before opening his own studio; he has a Master's Degree in photojournalism from Syracuse University.

In John's photo of this spectacular original Chanel evening gown, you can almost reach out and touch its splendor! (See page 26.)

Artists' Illustrations

These have been culled from many period magazines, including exclusive French pochoir* publications, American fashion magazines, and pattern magazines.

Pochoir magazines depict the finest haute couture creations; the most famous are *La Gazette du Bon Ton*, published from 1912 through 1925, and *Art Gout Beaute*, published monthly by the French textile firm of the Successors of Albert Godde et Baude from 1920-1933. Pochoir plates resemble exquisite water colors; they're made from a series of finely cut stencils, hand colored to reproduce the exact colors and textures of the artist's original painting. Each color had a separate stencil cut from very fine zinc or copper or thin oiled card. Colors were applied with a brush or textured sponge, and each print involved up to thirty-two stencils.

Fashion magazines like *Vogue* and *Harper's Bazar* kept American women abreast of the latest fashions, with articles on the latest in French couture and the news from exclusive New York shops. In 1909, Conde Nast took over a small American magazine called *Vogue*, and it quickly became one of the leading arbiters of fashion. Published bi-monthly, it cost $6 a year for twenty-four "Numbers" in 1920. *Vogue* appealed to everyone, offering articles on dressmaking and "Dressing on a Limited Income," as well as haute couture. *Harper's Bazar*, first published in 1867, was a popular monthly. In the late 1890s, its readership declined, however it was rejuvenated in 1913 by William Randolph Hurst and during the teens and twenties it was in the forefront of fashion. During the twenties, *Harper's* featured Erte covers and illustrated articles; its cost was $.50 a copy or $4 for a yearly subscription. Pattern magazines, very helpful as they describe the cut of the clothing and the terms used, include *Butterick Quarterly, Ladies Home Journal Fashion Quarterly, Delineator, McCalls, Pictorial Review Fashion Book*, and *Vogue Pattern Book*.

* It's interesting to note that in the twenties, the fashions shown in fashion magazines were quite similar to the fashions worn by women in vintage photographs. Today, however, even on the streets of New York, dress is much more casual.

Values

Values in this book are based on consultations with dealers (including websites), auctioneers, and appraisers from around the country. Also taken into consideration are such factors as:

Location – where the item was purchased. Prices vary greatly among antique shows, auctions (including Internet auctions), small shops, large antique malls, flea markets, and local tag sales.

Condition – If an item is torn, soiled, untrimmed or trimmed recently with inappropriate material, its price would be accordingly less.

Rarity – Of course, the harder an item is to find, the higher the price.

Trends – In the field of antique clothing, items that are currently "trendy" bring higher prices. For example, "car wash" beaded flapper dresses and lavish twenties lingerie are currently hot items.

Labels – Labeled items are most desirable, with haute couture of course, being the ultimate goal of discriminating collectors.

This wonderful pochoir illustration for the cover of Pierre Imans' 1927 wax mannequin catalog truly captures the spirit of the twenties! (See page 129.)

Chapter One
1925 Women's Fashions

Timeline

By 1925, the Charleston dance craze has swept the nation, and "Everybody's "Doin' It"!

January 3: Mussolini and his Black Shirts seize power in Italy.

July 4: Boston police report the collapse of a speakeasy caused by "excessive shaking and wild gyrations of the Charleston dancers... The Pickwick Club, which collapsed on the morning of July 4, came crashing down on 200 dancers, 41 of whom have been brought out... some dead, others dying outside. Firemen, police and private volunteers are now hard at work clearing away the wreckage trying to get the rest of the bodies out. Sixteen others are injured, and alive."

July 10-21: The famous Scopes Monkey Trial is held in Dayton, Tennessee. John T. Scopes, a biology teacher, was arrested for teaching Darwin's Theory of Evolution. William Jennings Bryan appeared for the prosecution and Clarence Darrow for the defense. On July 21, Scopes is found guilty of teaching evolution; he's fined $100. The trial will later be the basis for one of the most famous movies of all time, *Inherit the Wind*, starring Spencer Tracy as Clarence Darrow, Frederick March as William Jennings Bryant, and Dick York as John Scopes.

October: Investors discover to their horror that land they purchased in Florida from Charles Ponzi is worthless... his name will forever be associated with "Ponzi Schemes".

Collapse of Boston's Pickwick speakeasy due to wild Charleston dancers

On the Silent Screen

Warner Bros. produced *Bobbed Hair!* a popular comedy; Lon Chaney chilled in *Phantom of the Opera*; Charlie Chaplin shined in *The Gold Rush*. Norma Shearer tantalized in *Lady of the Night*. Unrestrained hedonism was the theme of *The Golden Bed*, which featured the notorious "Candy Ball"—an extravagant affair given by the wife, which caused her husband's ruin. A Midwest housewife won a $500 prize in *Movie Weekly's* contest to rename "Lucile LeSueur"—who, as the new *Joan Crawford*, stared in that year in MGM's *Sally, Irene, and Mary*. A newcomer, Gary Cooper, appeared in Westerns as a bit player, and Clark Gable was an extra in *Merry Widow*.

On Broadway, Fred Astaire and his sister, Adele, were a sensation in George Gershwin's *Lady be Good*. Everyone was humming its favorite tune, *Tea for Two*. Michael Arlen adapted *The Green Hat* for the stage—it opened September 2 at the Adelphi Theater, starring a scantily clad Tullulah Bankhead as the tempestuous Iris Storm, and lingerie sales skyrocketed!

Favorite New Recordings

Hit records included "Charleston" by the Paul Whiteman orchestra and "If You Knew Susie" by Eddie Cantor—also Ethel Waters' two hits, "Dinah" and "Sweet Georgia Brown." "Everything is Hotsy Totsy Now" by the Coon Sanders Nighthawks was also a hot new recording.

In Literature

Fitzgerald's classic novel of the twenties, *The Great Gatsby*, was published. Young Anita Loos' marvelous comedy, *Gentlemen Prefer Blondes*, was a huge success. Theodore Dreiser's *An American Tragedy*, based on the Adirondack murder of Grace Smith by Chester Gillette, was a bestseller. Other popular titles included *Arrowsmith* by Sinclair Lewis and *In Our Time* by Ernest Hemingway.

In Fashion 1925 – Feminine Flares and Shorter Skirts!

The stage was set for distinctive changes in the fashion silhouette as the second half of the decade began. The long, tubular chemise had reached its pinnacle in 1924, and "it was impossible to grow much longer or straighter." New trends appeared as couturiers evolved the tube to a shorter, more graceful, feminine look, a look that fluttered and flared—a look that was in motion.

Couture Trends

Frocks flared anywhere and everywhere—fronts, backs, and sides. As *Vogue* observed, "The flared silhouette... has come upon us gradually, but, while it was second choice to the straight silhouette in the spring, it is now the first fashion alternative." (September 1925). *Harper's* noted: "Flair at the back is the strongest new note... front flair is here too, in clever versions, showing fluidity of silhouette by means of pleats and underlays". Flair was achieved as "an intrinsic part of the cut"—bias cuts, godets inserts, and circular-cut sections were often used to provide the essential "Motion." Practical pleats were popular for sports—they were narrow, wide, and every combination thereof. Chanel's new "inverted" or "kick" pleat made headlines, and Lanvin created a sports skirt that was pleated only on one side.

"Skirts are a Great Deal Shorter Than They Were Last Winter!", trumpeted the January 1925 *Harper's Bazar* as skirts began their notorious climb to the knees. In 1925, most fashion photos and illustrations were showing skirts one to two inches below the knee. *Vogue* cried, "Legs are as popular as complexes!" as legs become one of fashion's new erogenous zones.

Vionnet, pioneer of the famed bias cut, paved the way to the more feminine silhouette. *Harper's* raved, "Any garment made by Vionnet will be so cunningly contrived that only the most ingenious person could discover the secret of a similar cut." Vionnet and Patou accented the natural waistline while Chanel, Lanvin, and Worth utilized uneven waistlines—higher in front, and curving low in back. Décolletage was a must for evening; gowns featured both front and back décolletage (generally lower in back than in front). Lamés, crepes, and satins "are all the mode." Fashion favored long, luxurious fringes, beaded georgettes, and lavish laces. There were printed velvets "in riotous colors" and "cut-out velvets on transparent grounds" (known as burnout, voided velvet or cut velvet today).

The Art Deco influence was seen not only in the cut of the clothing, but in bold printed designs as well. As *Harper's* noted: "Last year modernistic art lived inside frames in picture galleries; this year it paints its cubes and triangles and fantastic figures on sports wear and accessories". *Vogue* observes "designs as a whole are geometrical and modernistic... small all-over designs of weave, of color or both in dots, chevrons, squares and diagonals...".

At the Paris Exposition's *Pavillon de l'Elegance*, Lanvin awed audiences with a magnificent *robe de style*, lavishly appliquéd with flowers, on a "very striking mannequin made of grey wax" by André Vigneau of Siegel's. Also shown were frocks with features that would be very popular over the next few years—a frock with a low, draped tight girdle from Cheruit, and a metal lace frock with the modish new cape back.

For daywear, the versatile ensemble costume reigned supreme. *Harper's* advised: "The ensemble exercises control over every smallest detail... No single accessory should be purchased until the coat and frock are chosen, then accessories should be given utmost consideration; the time spent in selection will be repaid by the infallible chic they bring to the costume." Completely sleeveless dresses for day were now accepted as "Sleeveless frocks sway the Mode"—they were often worn under the ensemble coats. Scarves continued with their "...vivid touches of chic and debonair ways of being worn!"

Noting this plethora of new fashion features, *Vogue* cautioned: "In this season of changing mode, shops display a bewildering array... the wise woman knows how to pass by these new and often transient fancies."

Shops and Catalogs Interpret the Mode for the "Average Woman"

Though catalogs by necessity were somewhat conservative, many trends were adapted with amazing speed and acumen. *Bellas Hess* offered a Patou "inspired" evening gown that featured the new emphasis at the natural waist, described as

"Slightly modified at the waistline by fine pintucking at either side". For day, the ensemble suit was quickly adopted; *National's* noted: "The world is wearing the ensemble suit—so ultra smart... and so very, very practical—it can be used for almost any purpose from early morning till dinner time." In their Spring/Summer 1925 catalog, they advised: "There are two distinct silhouettes; the slim, arrow straight and sporty, and the new flared fullness for dressier day, afternoon and evening".

Saluting couture's new "In Motion" edict, *Butterick Quarterly* noted "Frocks Tie the Collar, Fly the Jabot, Flare the Skirt!" They also observed that "The hipline is the only point where fashions of today fit snugly... the hipline is the present waistline"; and "the new fullness frequently runs to the hip, often falling flat in pleats and draperies that spread and flutter in motion". They pictured the new floating Jabots "...that are beginning to play a graceful role in the new summer fashions"—center jabots, side jabots, and even jabots that extended from collar to hem were all very modish. *Butterick* recommended: "An ideal daytime wardrobe for the average women... might be based on two day frocks and two day coats, with one color scheme so as to be able to use the same accessories."

For day, surplice wraps, vestee bodices, jumpers with deep v-necks, and caped coat dresses were shown. Frocks often featured skirts draped on one side (or both), ruffled and/or flounced hems, and tunic effects. Circular apron-effects or panels flared from lowered waistlines—and deco-ish "Zig-zagged triangular waistlines are strong for afternoons." Another favorite was the scalloped waistline (and/or hem). On a great many frocks, narrow self belts that tied in back or at one side emphasized low waistlines. Chanel's name was frequently mentioned in catalog descriptions. *Bellas Hess* noted: "This skirt shows the popular Chanel kick pleat, which makes a pleasing variation from the perfectly straight silhouette of other seasons." *National's* recommended the "Chanel inverted pleats" for ease of motion, and also raved over the "very important Chanel collar"—a narrow band which extended to tie in a bow or the long ties were simply left hanging as streamers (see pages 84, 86, 87).

For afternoon and evening, the Spanish Shawl still held sway. *National's* exclaimed: "Right now the 5th Avenue shops are just flooded with exquisite Spanish Shawls in gay colors and richly embroidered. Few women will resist this opportunity to secure one of these handsome shawls for $9.98!"

College Girls

Special "College Departments" were now featured in many shops and catalogs. New York's trendy Stewart's store advertised "College Club Fashions" that were clever couture replicas:

Chanel created this College Club two piece frock, here 'expressed' in canton crepe, smartened with Paris hand-embroidery and rows of novelty bone buttons; the skirt favors the Chanel kick pleats. In Lanvin Green, Hazelnut, Pencil Blue, Bordeaux red, $18.50. And, Lanvin's youthful two piece frock is particularly appealing when interpreted in this College Club mode... The Lanvin side pleated skirt is a new fall feature and the blouse shows the Lanvin boyish collar, silk tie and patch pockets, $15.75 (Advertised in *Vogue*, September 1925)

Vogue, noting that "Simplicity is the soul of college chic," advised:

Chanel type frocks with their youthful lines, their informal air, their debonair simplicity are a perfect expression of the well-dressed college girl. Semi-sport clothes are advised, versatile ensembles that can be easily interchanged. Sweater, blouse and pleated skirt have long been a "college uniform," but sweaters are now considered part of the complete ensemble, and should be chosen accordingly.

Of course, "GALOSHES belong in every college wardrobe...!" *Vogue* also suggested "a smart town outfit for trips to New York or Boston for matinee or dinner"—and for a reception or formal afternoon tea, "a dressy afternoon dress is called for". As college dining was more casual, "One formal dinner dress will suffice for the season... a georgette crepe, light metallic, or simple picture frock... an evening wrap is a necessity."

By the second half of the decade, emancipated young women had developed more independent attitudes towards fashion—and marriage! Commentator Olga Dahlgren noted:

Most women would go back to political slavery with less protest than they would endure its livery of a heavy trailing skirt, tiny pinched waist, rigid corset, boned collar, stuffy coiffure with—no, we can't call it a hat—millinery perched atop a perilous pompadour... Having flung away the upholstery and steel girders from their clothes, women, logically, began to do the same with their minds, and there is slowly emerging as a result, the emancipated woman, with no corsets on her soul, no hairpins in her imagination, "Free at Last" from the narrow prejudices and stifling codes of the Victorian era...

She continued, declaring that even:

Old Maids are extinct; like the dinosaur and pterodactyl, they have passed away, let us hope forever... In her place the new bachelor woman has arisen, no longer an object for pity and derision, but a shimmering creature, iridescent and fascinating, who puzzles and intrigues, surrounded by mystery and respect... Her hair is shingled, her clothes are smart, her cat has been replaced by a career and other interests. The unmarried lady has usurped all the rights, privileges and prestige that formerly belonged to the debonair bachelor and become a "bachelor woman"—her success nowadays depends on more than her ability to procure a husband... Let us all thank heaven for her and wish her luck, and may she never again lapse into her former fearful state. (*Vogue*, June 1926)

Perfect for a Party – The Sensuous Spanish Shawl

With long, long fringe that swings, sways, and plays leg peekaboo—these lovely embroidered shawls were Chinese (made for export)—though during the twenties they were known as "Spanish Shawls." They'd shocked and delighted audiences in the *Four Horsemen of the Apocalypse*, the 1921 silent film that catapulted Rudolph Valentino to stardom. In one of the early scenes, Rudy and his partner danced a tempestuous tango; she dressed only in a strategically draped Spanish Shawl, its long fringe swaying hypnotically as she danced. Both the tango scene and the shawl created an indelible impression, and by mid-decade the Spanish Shawl had become the rage—the avant-garde wore them with nothing else *a la* the famous Tango Scene.

A poignant portrait of a very young Hollywood starlet, Miss Mimi D'Amoi. This photo was found in a box of film memorabilia from a Los Angeles estate, along with some files labeled *Savage and Barbaric*, *Serpentine Temple Priestess*, and *Voluptuous Feline Oriental Leopardess*—and several passionate love letters from ardent admirers. A simple strand of pearls compliments Miss D'Amoi's Spanish Shawl, and she wears the latest "spike" heeled T-strap pumps.

Proving that his Arrow Shirt man can emote as erotically as Rudy, artist Leyendecker portrays him admiring his lady's seductive Spanish Shawl—with a look of barely controlled passion! Note her Spanish mantilla haircomb and bangle bracelets... (1922).

The former owner of this shawl vowed it had been worn to a Hollywood party by an aspiring starlet—with nothing beneath! The embroidery and shading are so detailed that the flowers seem three-dimensional. The erotic fringe border is 20 inches long (including 5 inches of macramé).

Closeup of the shawl's exquisite embroidery, pink-to-red peonies, and blue forget-me-nots. The embroidery is so fine it's hard to tell the back from the front. $500-$800 (The finer the embroidery, the more expensive the shawl.)

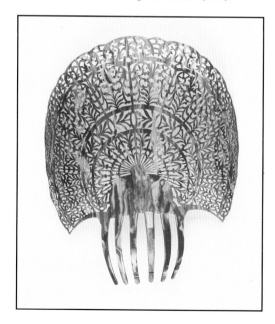

This huge mantilla comb, very intricately pierced, is a perfect foil for the Spanish Shawl. It's faux tortoise (celluloid), and measures one foot wide and one foot high (including the teeth). $75-$125.

Note that by mid-decade period catalogs offered less expensive embroidered shawls in the "new" synthetic, rayon. As the 1925 *National Style Book* advised: "Right now the Fifth Avenue shops are just flooded with exquisite Spanish Shawls in gay colors and richly embroidered. Few women will resist this opportunity to secure one of these handsome shawls for $9.98. In apple green, yellow, Chinese red or black." Today these inexpensive versions range around $75-$150.

Blue Fringe Dance Frock

In keeping with fashion's new "In Motion" concept, dresses also flew with fringe—imagine it swaying to the steps of the Charleston!

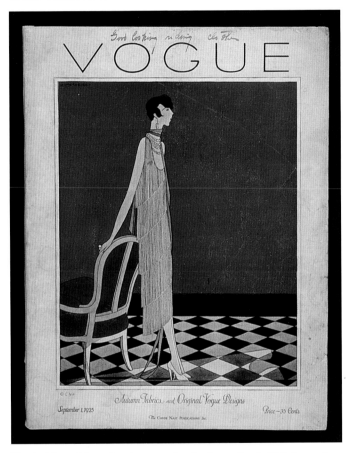

Harriet Meserole's enchanting cover for the September 1, 1925, issue of *Vogue* pictures an evening frock composed of tiers of asymmetrical fringe. Ropes of pearls, dangling earrings, and spike-heeled pumps complete her ensemble, and long red and blue ribbons drape round her neck to trail along the floor. Note that the skirt length is noticeably shorter.

A perfect accent to our fringed dress—silver dance slippers! Their Mary Jane straps continue on to the quarters (sides) as an applied Art Deco decoration. They feature the new, more rounded toe popular during the second half of the decade and the latest "Half-Spanish" heels. Mary Jane straps are favorites for dancing as the wild gyrations of the Charleston require secure fastenings. Stamped on the inner soles is: "*Grossman's Quality Shoes—Genuine Hand Turned*". Then, around $20 in better shops; now $150-$200

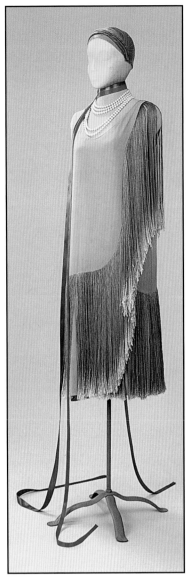

Closeup photo of the side and back; note that the fringe placement accents a natural waist.

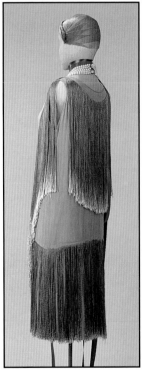

Fabulous from front—or back! This tubular light blue silk georgette dress features long silk fringe that's designed to swing and sway to the beat of jazz music! This ombreed silk fringe shades from royal blue to light blue as it accents the low waist—then climbs the left shoulder to dip in the popular cape effect across the back. Ropes of pearls and a blue turban headdress complete the ensemble, and long trailing ribbons of red and blue salute Miss Meserole. A matching underslip is attached at the shoulders. Although this dress has no label, it may have been inspired by the Chanel design that follows—the lines are quite similar. Then, party frocks like this might be priced between $40-$60 at upscale New York shops. Now, collectors may pay between $600-$800.

Chanel Original Evening Gown

"I feel the invisible presence of a master-mind, which takes the form of Mme. Chanel..."

—Baron De Meyer, *Harper's Bazar*

Both DeMeyer and Howard noted the new Rodier fringes—De Meyer stated: "The new Rodier fringes are found on both day and evening gowns." Howard noted: "The new evening gowns... drip with fringes, especially new Rodier fringes called 'perlic' of which Chanel has made a feature... their fabrication is a trade secret." (*Harper's Bazar*, October 1926)

Reynaldo Luza illustrates a stunning fringed frock created by the "High Priestess of Chic"—Coco Chanel! *Harper's* comments: "Chanel's blue georgette evening gown has a long strip of *'franges Perlics'* in degrade blue around the skirt, with a long end attached at one hip to be draped as one chooses." Note the slightly bloused back that hints of feminine curves, and the fringe placement that points to the natural waist. (*Harper's Bazar*, October 1926) Note that a Chanel dress with very similar lines was featured in the Metropolitan Museum of Art's recent exhibit, "Chanel." As they dated this dress to 1926, perhaps this was the dress that Luza illustrated for Harper's Bazar's October 1926 issue!

An extremely rare CHANEL evening gown in gold lamé so spectacular it rivals the rising sun! This tubular dress is metallic gold lace encrusted with thousands of red rhinestone "rubies" in a *Hindu* motif. Swagged tiers of electric pink *Rodier?* beaded fringe (the topmost at the natural waist) suggest feminine curves. A matching gold lamé underdress is attached at the shoulders, and the Chanel label is basted on the inside at back. Note the very low décolletage—both back and front. The turban headdress is formed from period silk and metallic gold lace. $15,000-$20,000. *Courtesy of Steven V. Porterfield.*

In this photo of the back of the gown, you'll note the seductive LOW back!

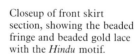

Closeup of front skirt section, showing the beaded fringe and beaded gold lace with the *Hindu* motif.

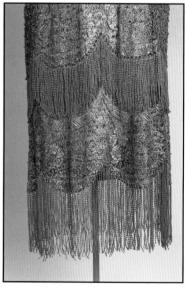

The gown's original Chanel label.

A spectacular georgette dance frock in "Lanvin Green"—beaded with emerald, bronze, and crystal bugle beads in a fabulous Art Deco motif of stylized flowers, diamonds, circles, scrolls, and vertical parallel lines! Smocking at the sides of the low waist provides "slight fullness over the hips." The wide bateau neck and armholes are self-piped, and there's a snap closure at the left shoulder continuing down to the waist. $800-$1000

This dress has been shortened at the hem rather hastily by about two inches... perhaps its flapper was in a hurry to get to the Speakeasy! The evening bandeau from period materials including a lamé Deco flower; faceted crystal rope necklace.

The 1925 *Bellas Hess* catalog offers a similar "Hand Beaded All Silk georgette" dress over a separate slip—with this tantalizing description:

"How very Frenchy," you will say when you see this elaborate creation of beautiful quality All Silk Crepe georgette, heavily Hand Beaded in handsome design. "And why wouldn't it be Frenchy?" we answer, knowing that IT IS AN EXACT COPY OF AN ORIGINAL PARIS MODEL WHICH WAS RECENTLY IMPORTED BY A FASHIONABLE FIFTH AVENUE DRESSMAKER! And (a fact) $100 wouldn't buy the original!... The beading which form a panel down front and back, is entirely done in crystal and colored beads... the round neck and slit Kimono sleeves are finished with piping of self material and narrow self-sash ties in bows at each side. Colors, Pencil blue, Lanvin Green or Moonbeam Grey... $14.98!

Closeup of the dance frock's exquisite beadwork!

The Flapper Dress of the Twenties

This classic beaded silk georgette dance frock is what most people think of when they hear "Flapper Dress." To find one in excellent condition is rare as the glass beadwork is heavy, and the silk crepe georgette very sheer.

The beadwork was done with a type of tambouring stitch, which left an easily unraveled chain stitch on the reverse (thus these dresses often have a row (or rows) of missing or hanging beads). It was a painstaking, time-consuming process—the bead worker attached pre-strung beads, one by one, with a hand-held device.

Many flappers, eager to show off their shapely legs as styles grew ever shorter, took up their favorite beaded frocks at the hemline; or if the hemline was scalloped or fringed, it was taken up with a tuck at the waistline. For modern repair purposes, note that extra beads can often be found in hems, tucks, and seams.

Beaded dresses were available ready made in shops and catalogs—and for home sewers, pre-beaded fabric lengths were available by the yard.

Though this dress is a vertical tube, feminine curves are saluted via the adjustable ties at the hips. Period catalogs often showed sleeveless styles accompanied by separate short sleeves, noting the dress "May be worn as a sleeveless model or with the short sleeves that come separate...". Note that though this dress has a wide bateau neck, the separate slip is cut straight across.

These very slippers danced their way to the Grand Prize at the *Rainbow Gardens Dance Contest*! These wonderful green silk dance slippers are still glamorous, though a bit worn as one would expect after a challenging night. Note the devastating Art Deco rhinestone and "emerald" buckles, and the new 3 1/4 inch Spike Heels! Kid lined and labeled: *I. Miller - DeLuxe Shoes*. $200-$300 (worn, with provenance).

The large silver-plated trophy is engraved: "Rainbow Gardens ★ Dancing Trophy—Grand Prize won by—Miss Careyne Thurman—Mr. Herman Weisheit—Ocean Park, Cal". Parched after their winning exhibition, Miss Thurman and Mr. Weisheit promptly filled it with champagne and drank to their victory!

Lavender Lace Gown

"... Much of the gold would be lace, like cobwebs touched by Midas; and the silver might have been woven by Jack Frost on a windowpane—delicate, fragile, moonlit lace!" (*Vogue*, September 1, 1925). Metallic lace in silver, gold—or a combination of both—is a popular choice for evening...

Left:
A lovely lady views her colorful fantail fish in this beautiful pochoir from *Art Gout Beaute*. She wears an enchanting blue evening dress, the uneven hem embellished with a deep border of gold lace. (Metallic gold paints are used in this pochoir, ca. 1925-28)

Right:
This stunning evening frock utilizes many of fashion's latest methods to achieve its fabulous new flair! It's cut so that as the wearer moves—or dances—various sections glow when the light hits them. Horizontal strips of both silver and gold metallic lace, embroidered in amethyst and deep purple silk floss, form the overdress; these lace bands are connected with gossamer hemstitching that's as fine as a spider web. At the center of the low waist is a spectacular appliquéd diamond with Art Deco amethyst beadwork. The famous "inverted pleat," often attributed to Chanel, provides both interest and ease of motion—it's bordered with panels of contrasting lace, which continue up the center of the bodice. The essential flair is achieved by a complicated cut: center front and back are cut straight, while bias folds flare gently at the sides. The bodice is cut in one piece with no side seams, to center back where two triangular pieces, part of wide band at the waist, provide interest and subtle shaping. The overdress is a slip-on style, with snaps inside at the shoulders to hold its matching amethyst lamé slip in place. The slip is a bit more formfitting and has a snap closure down the left side. $700-$900

Closeup view of the skirt's fabulous lace and gossamer hemstitching.

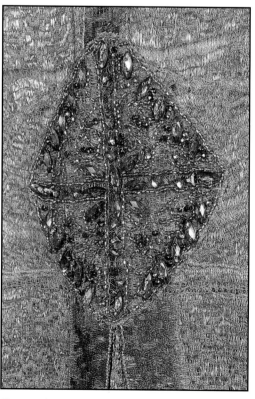

Closeup of the diamond-shaped amethyst beadwork.

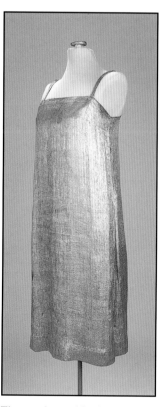

The gown's matching lamé slip.

Black Lace and Silver Lamé Frock

For late afternoon through early evening this "Spanish" dress is so soignee!

Left:
A stunning pochoir with a Spanish flavor from the July 1925 issue of *Art Gout Beaute*! This black lace dress, entitled *Fugitive*, was designed by Doucet, one of the oldest and most revered couture houses. This enchanting frock is short and sassy, as the new mode demands. It features a short-tiered skirt and bloused bodice over a matching vestee; long sleeves fall full from the elbow. Note her Deco belt, pendant necklace, and earrings—and her ultra chic Eton crop!

Right:
A delightful evening frock with circular trellises—the leaves worked in metallic silver and black lace on a transparent georgette ground. Its silver lamé underdress shines seductively through the sheer georgette, and the low waistline is accented with a wide lace girdle (belt). The bodice's long, flowing sleeves compliment the skirt's floating side panels. The chic v-neck has a small, wired standup "*Medici*" collar (a Renaissance touch that was also very popular during the teens). Shown with a jet necklace and turban bandeau formed of period materials—black velvet with an Art Deco flower of silver lamé. $500-$600 *Courtesy of Mrs. John E. Dowling.*

Ever-so-chic Art Deco evening slippers in black satin accented with silver kid! The vamps are a checkerboard pattern of tiny black jet and silver marquisite beads. These spectacular T-straps feature the straight, higher heel catalogs refer to as "The New Spike Heel;" they fasten at the sides with small pearl buttons. Stamped on inner sole: "*Genee, from Welton's, Syracuse, N.Y.; made by J & T Cousins Co., New York*". (Cousins, a prestigious New York shoe store, was often featured in *Vogue* and *Harper's Bazar*.) $400-$500

Closeup view of the vamp's intricate beadwork.

29

"Rose Garden" Afternoon Dress

Art - Goût - Beau

For a summer garden party—a "Rose Garden" frock! This charming pochoir depicts a delightful summer frock with a slightly bloused bodice, a modish scarf neckline, and flirty handkerchief hem. *Art Gout Beaute*, ca. 1925-27.

A closeup of the frock's three-dimensional roses!

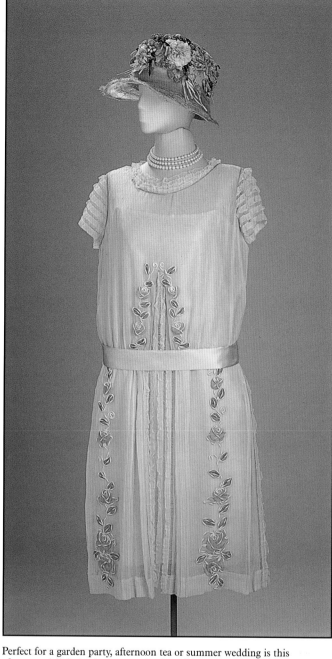

Perfect for a garden party, afternoon tea or summer wedding is this afternoon delight in sheer cotton batiste—it's appliquéd with its own rose garden! Pink organdy roses with green leaves trail over the skirt and bodice, graduating in size from small buds to full blown roses. These roses are formed in a three-dimensional effect; very detailed, they're edged with cream satin stitched embroidery. Rows of picot-edged tulle ruffles adorn the bateau neckline and alternate with fine hemstitching on the skirt at center front, back, and sides; they also form the sleeves and trim the long inverted pleat. The bodice is slightly bloused, and fifteen tiny pintucks at each shoulder add bust emphasis. Pink piping accents the neckline, armscyes, and skirt panels. A pink silk ribbon belt (replacement) emphasizes the low waistline. Note the shorter skirt, which a hasty flapper basted in place. (This delightful dress must have been a favorite—it's been altered at both the waist and hem to the new, shorter silhouette.) A tiny label at the back of the neck reads: (size) "38." $300-$400

The Eighteenth Century Revisited – A Favorite Wedding Theme!

The twenties love affair with the eighteenth century continued—and some *robe de style* gowns have actual hooped panniers! These charming frocks were also known as "Fantasy Gowns"—and this youthful, bouffant look was very popular for weddings. These popular "Fantasy" dresses are pictured in twenties catalogs through 1928.

The Bridal Gown: This breathtaking *robe de style* satin and lace wedding gown is a direct descendent of the gowns of Marie Antoinette's day, right down to the pannier hoops! The dropped waistline is piped in satin, and adorned with a huge velvet and organdy rose with trailing ribbons and leaves. Three wide, scalloped tiers of Chantilly lace grace the skirt, which is sprinkled with prong set rhinestones. Her bonnet headpiece and lace-bordered veil are original to the dress. **The Attendant's Gown:** The attendant's pannier dress is a Garden of Delight—with a coral satin underdress beneath sheer gold georgette, it rivals the beauty of a garden at sunset. Its floral motif is yet another eighteenth century revival; the flowers and buds are formed by georgette appliqués, with silk floss embroidered accents and vines. Prong-set rhinestones are scattered throughout. The scalloped hemline is bordered with two rows of gold metallic lace, which also trims the armholes. The low waist is girdled with a belt of braided metallic ribbons, which ends on the left hem in a bow. Her turban headdress is formed of period materials.

"The Perfect Wedding!" The Whitehouse in El Paso, Texas, had this photo taken of their beautiful window display, ca. 1925-28. The lovely bridal and attendant gowns are displayed on lifelike period mannequins—most likely of wax (see page 129).

For this sweet wedding portrait, the lovely bride has chosen a lace bonnet headpiece; her long illusion veil has a wide lace border. Note her spike-heeled opera pumps—and large rose bouquet! Her handsome groom is attired in a smart double-breasted suit. Studio portrait, ca. 1925-28.

This front view of the satin and lace bridal gown shows the skirt's three scalloped lace tiers and lavish waist bouquet. Note the self-piping at the gown's bateau neckline and lowered waist. The gown is shorter at center front and back. The original (and fragile) long silk illusion veil is bordered with matching Chantilly lace.

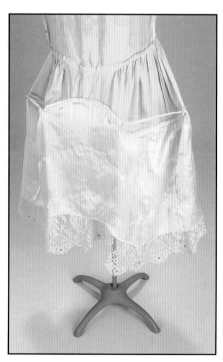

The wired bonnet-style headpiece of matching Chantilly lace, trimmed with pearls and rhinestones. At each side are bouquets of wax orange blossoms and lilies-of-the-valley, and "love-knot" ribbon streamers.

A closeup view of the gown's satin rose bouquet.

An inside view of the gown's pannier hoops! Pannier wedding gown, headpiece, and veil: $800-$1,000

Front view of the attendant's gold pannier gown, with its eighteenth century style ribbon and fabric flowers.

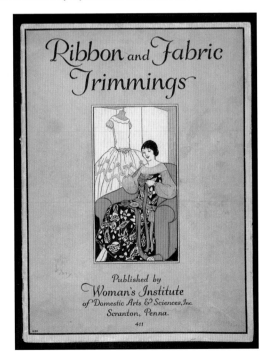

Ribbon and Fabric Trimmings—is an instruction booklet containing "A variety of appropriate dress trimmings that can be made from ribbon and fabric, with directions for their making," published by *Woman's Institute of Domestic Arts & Sciences, Inc., Scranton, Penna"* (copyright, 1925).

This closeup of the skirt's "Garden" shows the spectacular embroidery and appliqué work; note the shaded silk floss rose petals with their three-dimensional pastel georgette centers. The scalloped hem is bordered with two rows of metallic gold lace. It's evident that countless hours of painstaking handwork were lavished on this dress! $800-$1000

Instructions for making a "Flat Ribbon Flower;" Fig. 81 and 82.

The Masquerade Party!

Before television and personal computers became household necessities, costume parties weren't just for Mardi Gras or Halloween—they were as popular as they'd been since the Renaissance!

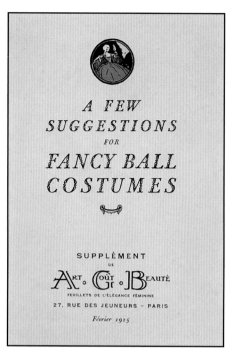

Art Gout Beaute's 1925 magazine cover proposes "A Few Suggestions for Fancy Ball Costumes".

Art Gout Beaute's delightful pochoir plate features Elizabethan Queens, Spanish Infantas, and Court Jesters! Note the wonderful tasseled vanity bag carried by the lady at lower right.

A very similar "clown" and her "bootleg Gangsta" partner pose for the camera ca. 1925. Note his snappy double-breasted suit and fedora.

A delightful clown costume in pink chintz, its "barrel" hips accented with pom-pom tassels that also trim the legs, crown, and front closure. Variations of this pattern appear in several twenties' pattern magazines—the 1926 *Butterick Quarterly* offers "a Pierette Costume for ladies, misses and girls with barrel skirt, tight from knee to hem" for $.45 that requires 3 3/8 yards of fabric. Paul Poiret first showed this popular costume in the teens. $200-$300

Ready for the Masquerade! A bejeweled Gypsy, Charlie Chaplin (holding his trademark Derby), a Pierrot Clown, and a Tyrolean woman pose for the camera, ca. 1925.

What's a party without party HATS?! This *Shure Winner* price list offers a "great variety of crepe paper party hats—for every occasion!", including clowns, Chinese coolies, sailors—even a Fez! From the N. Shure Co., Chicago, ca. 1925.

Authentic twenties Crepe Paper Party Hats!
These charming crepe paper hats are rather fragile, and quite scarce! $20-$40 each.

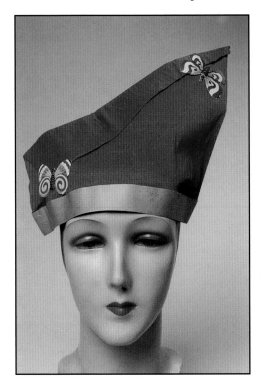

A towering asymmetric red party hat trimmed with butterflies!

A sailor's tam with navy streamers and a red pompom!

A pink tasseled lattice tam, similar to those in Shure's ad, center section, top row!

"The New Ensemble Suit Is All The Rage!"

The versatile coat/dress ensemble that was introduced in the first half of the decade to compliment the tubular chemise frock had become an essential part of a fashionable woman's wardrobe by the second half of the decade... perfectly fulfilling fashion's mandates of Simplicity and Versatility. *Harper's Bazar* claimed to have been the first to announce the head-to-toe ensemble concept or "Costume Complete," declaring it was: "...announced as a mode for the first time in any fashion periodical in June 1923... and since then we've marked its progress and final development, the keying of every detail of the costume to the dress." (August 1924)

And, as *Vogue* advised its readers: "The ensemble costume is the most important in the mode today. The ensemble exercises control over every smallest detail... no single accessory should be purchased until the coat and frock are chosen; then accessories should be given utmost consideration; the time spent in speculation will be repaid by the infallible chic they bring to the costume....". (September 1925)

The ensemble coat is most often seven-eights length, allowing an intriguing peek at the coordinating frock beneath; many featured the new stand-up "Bobby" or "Bobbed Hair" collar.

Jane Regny's smart couture ensemble steps from a background of Art Deco palms and sunny southern skies! In chic earth tones, this ensemble is perfect in every detail - coordinated from head to toe. The low-waisted frock is trimmed with contrasting "fancy" buttons and bands which highlight the natural waist; the skirt portion is accented with ever-so-smart geometric pleating. The ensemble's seven-eights coat is chocolate brown, trimmed to match the frock beneath. To complete this look of "infallible chic", she's accessorized with a two tone tam-cloche and tan scarf with a brown checked border. Imported to one of New York's better stores, this ensemble may have been priced around $80-$90. *Art Gout Beaute*, 1925. *Courtesy of Doris Butler.*

It is interesting to note how quickly catalogs embraced couture's ensemble concept; they enticed customers with such mesmerizing ad copy as:

> *The world is wearing the ensemble suit—so ultra smart, so becoming and so very, very practical. The smart dress is complete in itself when worn without the matching coat; the coat may be worn with other costumes also. Could anything be more desirable? More economical—Two garments for practically the price of one?*

National Style Book, Spring/Summer 1925. Catalog prices for the "ensemble" ranged around $20-40.

National's proclaims: "THE SEASON'S MOST POPULAR STYLE ... A dress—a suit—a separate summer coat—all are yours in this chic Ensemble Suit—Fashion's newest idea!" Their original description boasts:

> *All-wool flannel, soft and finely twilled, is used for the separate knee length coat, and for the lower portion of the dress. The long tunic blouse portion of the dress is made of figured all-silk crepe in a pretty pattern of harmonizing colors... A tailored strap-trimming and pockets of the flannel are set off with fancy buttons. The skirt has two inverted plaits below hip... The coat has the new "bobbed hair" collar, full length front facings of self material and stylish sleeves with turn back cuffs. It is worn open as pictured—there are no fastenings. Colors: tangerine, tan or Saxe blue. (1925)*

It's rare to find a complete ensemble suit today as either the coat or frock has disappeared with the passing years; this original ensemble is a rare example in rayon crepe. It's a three-piece set consisting of a pleated frock skirt, Art Deco print tunic overblouse, and seven-eighs coat. Saluting "infallible chic," we've accessorized with a square-topped velvet cloche in "Reindeer Tan," and a pair of "Maracaibo brown" t-strap pumps.

Three piece ensemble suit, $700-$900; velvet square-topped cloche, $200-$300; suede t-strap pumps, $75-$150 (with light wear).

A back view of the ensemble coat—*Simplicity* at its finest! Note the diagonal seaming trim.

The "Costume Complete" ensemble, ca. 1925-28! The seven-eighs length "French Beige Tan" coat has a smart tuxedo or shawl collar, the bottom bordered with decorative pintucked triangles; the long, straight sleeves have topstitched cuffs. It matches the knife-pleated skirt, providing a perfect contrast to the print tunic.

Closeup of the overblouse's bold geometric print, asymmetric two tone piping, and bakelite buckle, and the skirt's tiny knife pleats.

The two-piece frock—sans coat. Since warm earth tones are extremely chic (especially brown tones), they're given intriguing names: "Beaver" (Tannish brown); "Brioche" (a toast tan); "Chestnut" (medium brown); "Circassian" (light tan); "Chocolate" (a rich deep brown); "Coconut" (light brown); "French Beige Tan" (tan with a rose tint); "Grapenuts" (medium brown); "Havana Brown" (Rich brown); "Maracaibo" (a new rich, deep brown); "Reindeer Tan" (a medium tan); "French Nude" (a dark flesh shade), and "Sun Bronze" (a medium tan with a bronze cast). You'll note that this bold Art Deco print tunic encompasses them all! Original marbleized bakelite circles secure flirty little ties at the bust and hip. The chic v-neck boasts a faux collar that's bordered with two narrow contrasting bands of piping in "Beaver" and "French Beige Tan." This double piping is repeated to accent a tight "girdle" waistband that has asymmetrical detailing at center—at left only, the piping drops diagonally to the bakelite buckle at the bottom.

The frock skirt: the top "slip" portion is sheer cream-colored silk; the skirt *French Beige Tan* to match the coat. The pleated skirt portion is just 12 1/2 inches long.

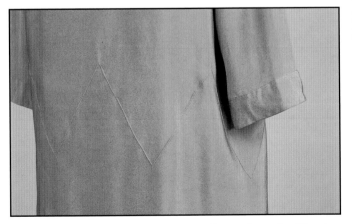

Closeup photo of the coat's pintucked triangular seaming and cuff bands.

Completing our ensemble are these modish *Maracaibo brown* suede t-straps! The vamps are trimmed with bands of silver-edged faux reptile; the sides are also perforated between the bands. The center t-strap is also perforated. The new "spike" heels are 2 1/2" high. They're lined in kid, with insoles stamped *Walk Over - Trademark, Reg. U.S. Patent Off.*

Day Dresses 1925

"Fetching Models Charmingly Express the Spirit of the New Season!" Dresses for day wear exhibited youthful pizzazz, and the new length for day was noticeably shorter—usually a few inches below the knees. Dresses were most often tubular, though the silhouette was varied in subtle ways. Many were cut in one piece with no waist seam; some were cut in two pieces with a waist seam, which was often piped. Styles with a waist seam were sometimes "shirred" at the sides of the waist, to provide "Distinctive style and graceful, slightly flaring lines...". Modish features included sassy ruffles, narrow sash belts, and long, narrow "Chanel" neck ties—or streamers that were often extensions of the collar: "...the collar extends in long Chanel bands which hang down the front"; these bands were "...worn tied about the neck or lying open." V-necks vied with wide bateau necklines for first place. Bodices often featured the beloved vestee inserts; many were "detachable and easily laundered." And, "of course, the sleeves are short in accordance with the youthful mode"—though long sleeves, very short cap sleeves, and sleeveless styles were also worn. Long ribbon ties often fluttered from low waists at sides or back. For sports and day wear, that all-important ease of motion was often provided by the new "inverted" or "kick" pleat, often attributed to Chanel: "...Best of all for this purpose is the simple inverted pleat beloved of Chanel." (*Vogue*, June 15, 1926) Catalogs quickly seized this new development with banners blazing: "Skirt shows the popular Chanel 'kick pleat', which makes a pleasing variation from the perfectly straight silhouette of previous seasons!"(*Bellas Hess*, 1925/26)

Note that day dresses are difficult to find today—unlike evening and wedding gowns, most weren't saved for sentimental reasons.

"Fashion's Prettiest Styles" from the 1925 Spring/Summer *National Style Book*. Note the striped golf frock (top right) that "looks as if it had come direct from one of New York's well known and exclusive sports wear shops;" it features the latest wide hip band or "girdle." At bottom right, the "Quaint and Demure" red slip-on dress features a lace "Bertha" collar, and chic ruffles, "which encircle the skirt and whirl upward at the left side"—both will be very important features through the rest of the decade. Since versatility is more desirable than ever, *National's* advises that the red striped silk frock at left is: "Right for any daytime occasion... suitable when a cotton frock isn't quite dressy enough... though its smart simplicity of style can never let the model give you an overdressed appearance!"

"Mr. Peterson and Mrs." and friends are about to enjoy the forbidden fruit of the vine on a lovely summer's day, ca. 1925. Standing on the running board, Mrs. Peterson wears a delightful summer print tunic dress with short sleeves and long "Chanel" neck ties—while Mr. Peterson, seated on the front bumper, pours wine from a wicker carafe.

Closeup of the sassy ruffles and vivid floral print.

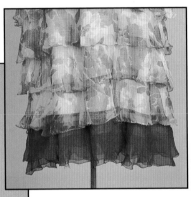

FLAUNT THOSE FLIRTY RUFFLES FANNY!!! Short and oh-so-sassy, this brilliant floral print silk georgette frock is the "Bees Knees"! Six bias cut ruffled tiers form the skirt; the last two are deep purple to match the bows at neck and cuffs. The highest ruffled tier marches up the front of the bodice to form a chic jabot. The bodice has the new "bloused" look, and three inverted pintucks on each shoulder add a suggestion of bust curves. The attached underdress is sheer silk crepe topped with "nude" cotton batiste. It's worn with a creased crown straw cloche with flocked flowers. Frock, $300-$400; cloche, $200-300.

This chic gold silk pongee frock exhibits several of fashion's newest features—it's the new shorter length, and batik printed in a tropical design of Art Deco hibiscus flowers and leaves in pink, magenta, lavender, and navy blue. Its smart turnover collar is accented with long "Chanel" streamers; as *Fashionable Dress* notes: "In summer breezes nothing will flirt so coyly as these fluttering odds and ends..."! The bodice is slightly gathered from a shoulder yoke to provide a bit of bust emphasis, and the "youthful" short sleeves are favorites for summer. "Chanel inverted pleats for easy movement" are placed at each side and at center back. It's shown with a square-topped yellow faille "ribbon" cloche with a pinwheel cockade at right. Batik Frock, $300-$400; cloche, $200-$300.

Closeup of one of the superb batik hibiscus flowers.

Live monkeys, toy monkeys, and monkey jokes abounded as a result the controversial Scopes Monkey Trial of 1925, which took place July 21-25 in Tennessee. The state claimed a young teacher, John T. Scopes, violated state law by teaching Darwin's Theory of Evolution. The highly publicized trial was the Battle of the Titan Lawyers, with William Jennings Bryant for the prosecution, and Clarence Darrow defending Scopes. In 1960, the story of the trial was told in one of the most famous movies of all time—*Inherit the Wind*, which starred Spencer Tracy as Clarence Darrow and Frederick March as William Jennings Bryant, with Dick York as John Scopes.

"Delores and My Pet. Our home in the background", is noted on the back of this adorable snapshot taken ca. 1925. Delores's fetching print frock has the ruffled apron panel *National's* declares is "made so fashionable by one of the most famous Parisian designers..."; "My Pet" wears a tiny bolero jacket!

Scarves

"Chanel" streamers weren't the only things that fluttered from flirty flappers' necks... SCARVES were a Necessary Accessory!

Exquisite scarves to "...complete your new Spring Costume... featuring brilliant large futuristic designs..."! *Bellas Hess* offers these two exquisite printed crepe de chine scarves—one fringed and one picot-edged. (1926)

Clara Bow was obviously not the only one with "IT"! This flapper gal exudes "IT"... with her sensational Art Deco scarf, short skirt, tight cloche—and sassy smile! Snapshot, ca. 1925-30, with original inscription, "IT IS"!

Right:
A marvelous cubist silk crepe de chine scarf in navy, blue, yellow, and pink, bordered in navy with white polka dots; knotted fringed ends. $75-$100

Far right:
A silver grey and magenta silk crepe de chine print scarf, knotted fringed ends. $50-$75

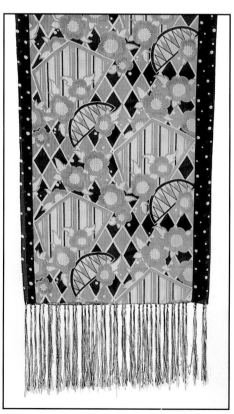

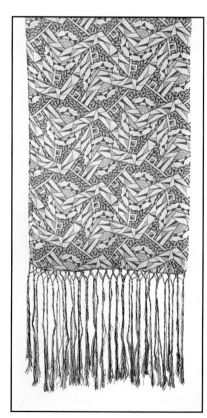

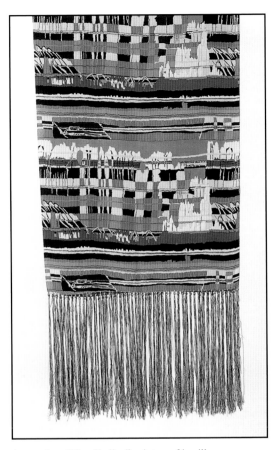

A very deco "City Skyline" print scarf in silk crepe; fringed ends. $75-$100

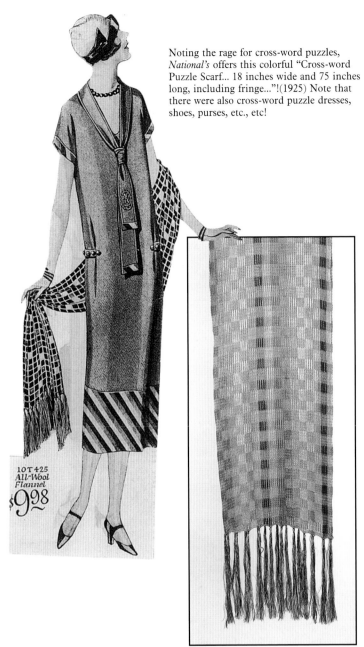

Noting the rage for cross-word puzzles, *National's* offers this colorful "Cross-word Puzzle Scarf... 18 inches wide and 75 inches long, including fringe..."!(1925) Note that there were also cross-word puzzle dresses, shoes, purses, etc., etc!

10 T 425
All-Wool Flannel
$9⁹⁸

A dashing rayon knit Cross Word Puzzle Scarf in shades of orange, turquoise, yellow, and blue, bordered with hand-knotted fringe. $75-$100

From the prestigious *Liberty of London*, a red silk crepe de chine scarf printed in a design of peacock feathers and silvery "Old Man's Money"; hand rolled hem. $150-$300

Closeup, Liberty label.

John Held Jr. Scarves are the Rarest of the Rare!

—"Narrow scarves are smart with all sports things this autumn with their vivid touches of chic and debonair ways of being worn!" (*Vogue* September 1, 1925)

Colorful scarves in bold Art Deco motifs had become flapper favorites by mid-decade. Most were screen printed, though some were hand-painted. Long, rectangular scarves were often finished with "*Deep Hand Knotted Fringe,*" though many had picot or hand-rolled edges.

The "Cynara Silk Tie... one of the new designs by John Held, Jr." Available at Wm. H. Davidow Sons, 550 Seventh Avenue, New York (as advertised in *Vogue*, January 15, 1927)

This pale green crepe de chine scarf was a flapper's pride and glory - with John Held Jr.'s famous *Hellions* cavorting at the borders! The lucky lady who originally owned this scarf did not want her name mentioned, but she did note she'd purchased it in New York City before she left on a European tour... she has fond memories of wearing it to a night club in Paris! She worked for the Department of State during the twenties. Hand rolled borders; excellent condition. By Cynara. $250-$350

Square scarves were also very modish—they were often folded diagonally and worn knotted over one shoulder "*Deauville*" style. Period catalogs not only sold separate scarves, but also offered them with matching dresses—and/or hats!

Showing off their favorite scarves... Three of these lovely gals are wearing chic square scarves; the scarf at right is knotted over one shoulder in the favorite "*Deauville*" style.

Closeup view of "The Kiss".

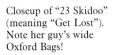

Closeup of "23 Skidoo" (meaning "Get Lost"). Note her guy's wide Oxford Bags!

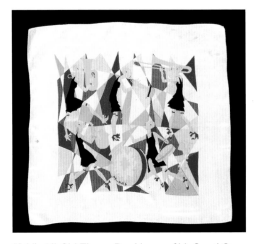

Held's All-Girl Flapper Band is one of his finest! On a background of colorful cubist triangles, a band of five Jazz Babies performs... they're dressed in Held's shortest dresses, garters, and ankle-tie pumps! The trumpet player uses a Derby hat as a mute. Screen-printed Held silk scarf, $200-350.

Short Dresses—and Shorter Hair!

As skirts grew shorter, hairstyles followed suit—and by mid-decade, the short "Shingle" and even shorter "Eton Crop" were becoming very popular. The sleek, geometric lines of these new hairstyles reflected Art Deco's growing influence on the world of fashion.

A marvelous pochoir embellished in gold and silver leaf from *Art Gout Beaute*, depicting three soignee ladies with the new ultra short hairstyles—and short dresses, worn just below the knees. Though these day dresses are straight and low-waisted, you'll note accents at the natural waists—and those modish "Chanel" neck ties. They wear the now mandatory woman-of-the-world expressions as they wave their long cigarette holders! (ca. 1925)

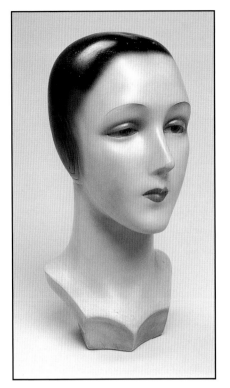

Our soignee Art Deco milliner's mannequin, *Agnes*, is named for the most famous milliner of the second half of the decade—and she does resemble her photographs! Our lady has that look of rather jaded ennui pictured in the era's fashion illustrations. Flappers often slicked these super short Eton cuts with brilliantine—like their men! Agnes is beautifully painted, airbrushed plaster. $600 - $800

"Louise Brooks" in the era's other favorite hairstyle—the "Prince Valiant," a short geometric cut with sassy bangs. Our Louise is an original twenties milliner's head that's celluloid over composition—the painted celluloid was badly deteriorating, and she was beautifully restored by *DecoEyes*—makers of fine milliner's mannequins reproduced from original casts. Original (restored), $500-$700

Showing off her trademark hairdo, the "real" Louise Brooks models "The Louise Brooks Evening Gown" by Sally Milgrim—a lovely frock dripping with the latest ostrich feather plumes. As Milgrim notes, Louise is "now appearing in *A Social Celebrity*." (*House & Garden*, 3/26)

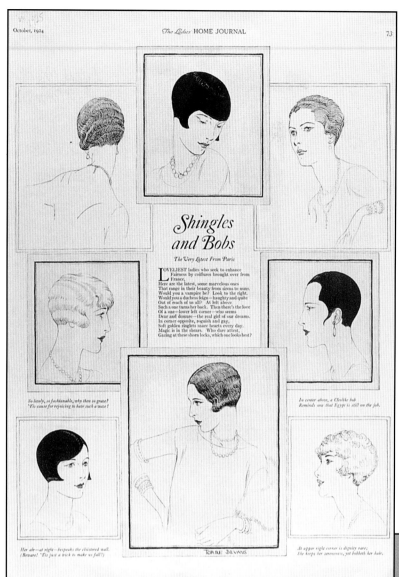

"Shingles and Bobs—The Very Latest from Paris!", a preview of hairstyles that will be trés chic in the second half of the decade—styles "...from sirens to nuns"! Included are two straight "Prince Valiant" cuts (top and bottom left); at center right is a sleek, slicked "vampire" Eton crop (described as a "Cleolike bob reminds one that Egypt is still on the job"); and at bottom right is a short, curly Clara Bow bob that's "rouguish and gay"! *The Ladies Home Journal*, October 1924

The Florence Virginia Beauty Shoppe. This superb photo, taken ca. 1925, pictures two smart beauticians—with Louise Brooks hairstyles! The customer at right has opted for a curly bob—perhaps she's just had a Perm. On top of the glass case at left is a selection of switches. "Dorothy's first job!, 125 W. Main St., Alexandria(Bay?) N.Y." is noted on the reverse.

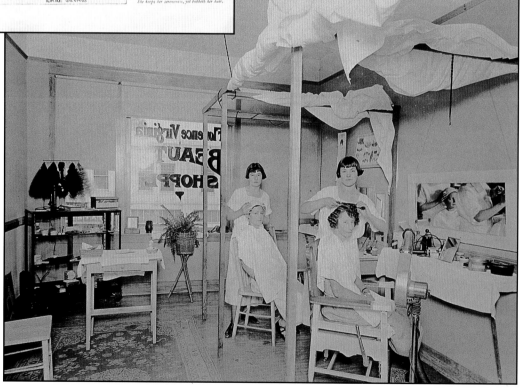

Cloches

The snug fit of the newest cloches made shorter hairstyles a necessity—by mid-decade cloches were so close-fitting that catalogs offered them sized in inches. Crowns were deeper too—as *Vogue's* Edna Woolman Chase later exclaimed, "...to show the forehead would have caused Scandal!"

"How to Find Your Correct Head Size", for a "perfect-fitting *National* Hat... Please measure your head very carefully... and with your order send us the number of inches your head measures." (1926)

As this beautiful flapper illustrates, cloches are not only snug-fitting, but their crowns come to the eyebrows! In this lovely photo postcard, a cutout cloche of real felt fabric lends a realistic air. French hand-tinted photo ca. 1925-29, stamped "*Leo, 940*".

Artist A. Greacen captures the spirit of the era in a wonderful art deco poster depicting "Small Colorful Hats for Sunny Southern Sports". "Spit curls" peek from beneath the brims—and don't you just love those rouged cheeks! This is the original prototype for a counter display for L. Bamberger & Co., in tempura on hardboard, ca. 1925 (Mr. Greacen was a graduate of York's prestigious Pratt Institute).

Another in the series of felt fabric cloche postcards. This beauty's close-fitting red cloche emphasizes her "come hither" glance—and red *Cupidsbow* lips! Her colorful scarf is one of the popular "Cross-word puzzle" scarves. Hand tinted photo postcard ca. 1925, stamped: *Made in France, Oliviery Nanterre*.

Jaunty wool felt hats that are packable, economical—and "CHANGEABLE" are often called "Knockabouts." *National's* pictures "five charming ways to wear this natty hat..." advising "with a few stitches in the crown or a little snip of the scissors to shape the brim you can get the very latest effects." (1927)

In practical "Knockabouts," two fun loving flappers perch on their party car's hood. Though this group of "Vagabonds" is not identified, they certainly capture of spirit of the twenties! Snapshot, ca. 1925.

Gloves

Gloves continued to add a smart finishing touch to ensembles in the second half of the decade. They're jazzed up with the latest cuff treatments—embroidered, perforated, petaled, and even hand-painted!

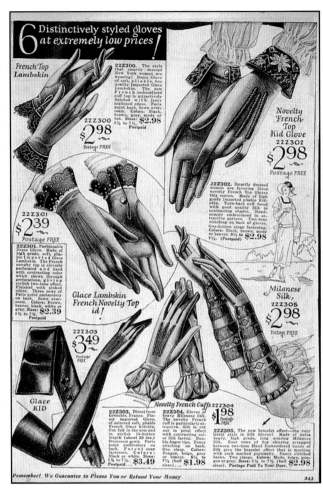

Bellas Hess offers gloves in "The style that smartly dressed New York women are wearing!" At the top right are kid gloves with the extremely popular "turn-back cuffs... handsomely embroidered in an attractive pattern." Pictured at center left are gloves with smart scalloped, perforated cuffs: "Fashionable Dress Gloves... the French novelty top cleverly perforated...". At bottom center is a pair of Milanese silk gloves with "Novelty French Cuffs... cut in petal effect."

For more formal occasions, at bottom left is a pair of 23" long kid gloves "Direct from Grenoble, France." Pictured at bottom right is "The new bracelet effect—the very latest in silk gloves!" with alternating rows of shirring and embroidery. (1925)

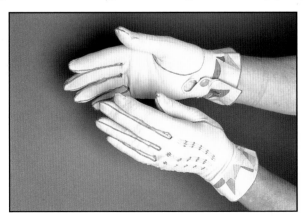

White kid gloves, the cuffs hand-painted in a stunning Cubist design; backs are embroidered and fingers outlined in contrasting stitching. Celluloid snap closures. $75-$100

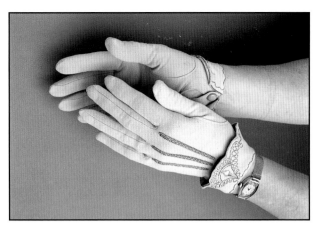

Lilac silk tricot gloves with the latest embroidered "Novelty French Top" cuffs, contrasting stitched backs, and celluloid snap closures. $40-$50.

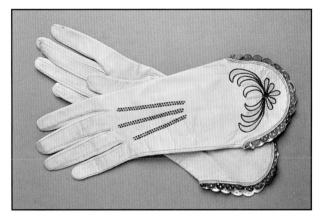

Camel colored kid gloves "handsomely embroidered" in black, and edged in black with scalloped perforations. $50-$75

Closeup view of the perforated scallops and exquisite embroidery.

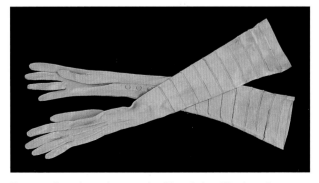

For more formal occasions, a pair of long beige silk tricot gloves, with rows of tiny pintucks extending to the elbows. $50-$75

Umbrellas

Stubby-handled umbrellas were yet another favorite accessory—and umbrellas with handles that featured dogs, parrots, or even monkeys were most desirable!

A darling novelty umbrella—with a Terrier Dog handle! This intricately carved pup has brown glass eyes and a dignified expression. Bakelite top and spoke protectors. (The black rayon cover, edged in brown and black checks, has badly deteriorated.) $55-$75

Purses and Vanity Boxes, 1925-30

The flat envelope bag remained the most popular style of the decade... as *Bellas Hess* advised, they were "just the thing to carry with your new coat or suit." Though they were called "clutch bags" or "underarm envelope bags," many had carrying straps either on top or back. While tooled and embossed leather bags were very popular, those that featured Art Deco cutwork were also very chic!

Butterick also noted that the new, fuller "pouch" bags were becoming very popular for day, and that "pouches of moire or taffeta are smart with afternoon to evening ensembles!" (Pouch bags are gathered at the top, rather than being perfectly flat like the envelope bags.) That perennial favorite, the scenic tapestry bag, was also a popular choice for afternoon into evening; many featured classical or eighteenth century themes. For formal evenings, *Butterick* recommended: "...envelopes with rhinestones, silver or steel beads; or gold or silver kid to match the slippers.... Beaded bags mounted on frames are also smart."

Now that makeup was more important than ever, no-nonsense vanity boxes were a necessity—and, for dancing or cocktails, small celluloid wrist vanities were favored; they often had a tiny tube of lipstick hidden in their tassels.

Bellas Hess offers a fine selection of bags and vanities—including flat envelopes with tooled flaps. They typically include: "a framed change purse, mirror, bill compartments, and a back or outside handkerchief compartment."

At center, a flapper shows off the vanity box pictured below, complete with fitted compartments: "powder and rouge compacts, eyebrow pencil and lipstick holders; powder puff bag; change purse, mirror and space for handkerchief, etc... Name or initial stamped FREE."

At lower right is a "Stunning Bag of rich Imported Tapestry," depicting a romantic eighteenth century couple; it features a "handsome gold plated jeweled frame, chain handle, change purse and fitted mirror." These charming scenic bags were offered in both machine-made tapestry and the more expensive handmade petit point (close examination will show the petit point's stitches to be finer and more distinctive). A beaded bag for evening is shown at bottom left: "Every smartly gowned woman needs one of these exquisite Imported Beaded Bags to complete her costume"; it's a reticule "made in the popular pouch effect with drawstring fastening... iridescent beads with steel loops and tassels of fine beads." (Spring/Summer 1925)

Chic envelope bags are "...frequently trimmed with zigzags, triangles and odd shaped pieces, which give the new modern note of geometrical decoration...." (*Butterick Quarterly* 1926) This witty envelope bag boasts a two-tone flap with a cutwork Art Deco sailboat (smooth caramel-colored leather is placed under dark brown grained leather cutwork). Brass snap closure, beige moire lining with two pocket compartments; partial tag reads: "Nu-Mode, Reg..." $125-$200

A beautiful petit point bag with a neoclassical scene of ladies in Grecian gowns and chubby cherubs! It's bordered with a floral motif and piped in silk. Etched gold-plated frame; one snap clasp is set with a sapphire, the other an amethyst. Gold silk moire lining with pockets on each side. Petit point, $250-350; Tapestry, $55-$100

Vanity Box (closed). Similar to the vanity box in the center of the *Bellas Hess* ad, this black grained simulated leather vanity box was well loved and well used; its lacquered finish has its share of scuffs. Brass tab/slide closure with lock and key.

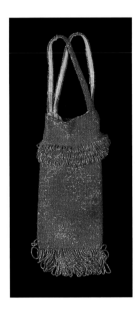

This jazzy red beaded reticule style bag belonged to a very lively flapper—my mother's aunt, Florence "Honey" Vedder! When mother was little, she was allowed to take the bus downtown to visit Aunt Honey, who worked at the Lighting Company. Mother said Honey was never hard to find; she was usually in the middle of a throng of admirers—joking and flirting! $200-$300

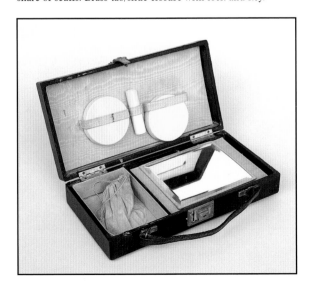

Vanity Box open, showing the "French Ivory" (celluloid) accessories, compacts, and lipstick holder. It's lined in "nude" rayon moire, with an attached moire "powder puff bag" on the left. The beveled mirror in the lower right compartment is edged with moire; it's attached to a pull-up partition, beneath which is a hidden compartment with a moire change purse on a gold chain—and a few old "Bobby" pins (named, of course, for Bobbed hairdos). Dimensions are 5" x 10". $50-$75 (with some scuffs)

As *Vogue* advises, "The every hour act of powdering and lipsticking is performed with such concentration and indifference to spectators as can only flow from a sense of deep importance of the act..." This saucy young flapper unabashedly holds up her vanity box to check her makeup. She's very chic in her short, low-waisted frock with pleated skirt—and note that Louise Brooks hair style and those cutout Mary Jane pumps! Dated on reverse: "May 1, 1927."

Enameled, Armor, and Dresden Art Deco Bags

During the second half of the decade, an Art Deco enameled mesh bag was a MUST! By 1924, Whiting & Davis had begun advertising colored mesh bags in Art Deco patterns in addition to their silver and gold tone bags, and they quickly became the rage. Their owners carried them to afternoon and evening events—selected, of course, to compliment an entire ensemble.

There are two different types of enameled mesh bags: a flat enamel "armor mesh" and a fine "baby ring" mesh known as "Dresden." Printed by a silk screening method, the flat enamels have more definitive lines while the Dresdens, composed of thousands of tiny rings, have the soft look of Impressionist paintings.

Two major firms manufactured these stunning bags: Whiting & Davis, of Plainville, Massachusetts, and Mandalian Mfg. Company of North Attleboro, Massachusetts (founded ca. 1920). Whiting & Davis, the largest firm, had been founded in 1876 by William Wade and Edward P. Davis; Charles Whiting, who had worked there as a boy, joined the firm in 1880, and in 1907 became sole owner. Whiting & Davis advertised extensively. Mandalian bags were produced on a smaller scale and seldom advertised. Around 1940, Mandalian was taken over by Whiting & Davis. These charming bags remained popular through the thirties. Today, they are prized by collectors as examples of fine Deco artwork. Note that recently, Whiting & Davis began reproducing some of their Art Deco bags.

Bottoms were cut straight across or v-shaped (some "stepped"); favorite borders or "skirts" included ring mesh fringe and vandyked armor. They often featured beaded drops, either alone or combined with mesh fringe; though both firms used drops, it was a Mandalian specialty. Frames included embossed or openwork silver and gold tone (some set with semi-precious stones), mosaic frames, and frames with enamel work that complimented the design of the bag. Whiting & Davis even made bags for little girls, advising "... don't forget little Whiting & Davis mesh bags delight the hearts of Tiny Maidens"!

Whiting & Davis 1927 catalog pages with original prices: Whiting & Davis offers the following assortment of bags in the 1927 *The Blue Book Store* catalog—a wholesale catalog sent to fine jewelers and gift shops.

This page features Flat Enamel Mesh Bags, some with silk linings, pockets, and mirrors; most are offered in a choice of sizes. Originally $5.25-$19.50. Frames include the 24k "finish," or a less expensive silver plate. A "mosaic" frame bag is pictured at the top left.

Closeup of bag's satin lining.

This page features fine Dresden or "Baby Soldered Mesh" Bags. You'll note these Dresden bags are much more expensive than the flat enamels, with original prices ranging from $16.50-$33.00. Pictured at the right are silver-plated bags with spectacular enameled frames.

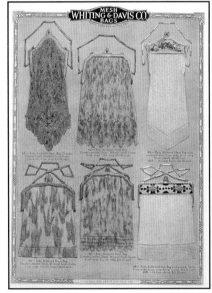

A superb example of a Whiting & Davis Dresden mesh bag, patterned in a lovely, soft design reminiscent of a Monet watercolor! Its spectacular frame combines black onyx with marquisites; the wide bottom border is scalloped fringed mesh. This is a medium sized bag, measuring 9 inches by 5 inches; it's fully lined, with its original mirror. $400-$500

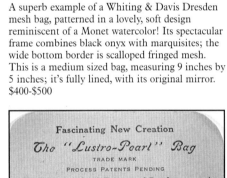

A portion of the original Mandalian box, describing their patent pending, chip-proof "Fascinating New Creation – The 'Lustro-Pearl' bag!... The acme of perfection."

On this page are Whiting & Davis Vanity and Envelope Bags—these mesh specialty bags are highly prized by today's collectors! Pictured here are their delightful vanity bags, tasseled cigarette cases, and at the center top, an Art Deco *Princess Mary* envelope-flap bag. Vanities typically contained rouge, powder, mirror, and compartments for cigarettes. Originally priced at $9.00-$36.

Mandalian's fine flat enamel "Lustro-Pearl" mesh bag. This bag features a bold Art Deco floral pattern; its distinctive stepped bottom is finished with Mandalian's favorite teardrops. $400-$500 (with box)

The Mandalian logo, stamped inside frame.

Lingerie... "Intimate Apparel!"

As frocks grew briefer, the "Intimate Apparel" beneath followed suit... and there were many lovely options to choose from. Lingerie was often trimmed with pintucks, pleats, and laces, including "Val" (Valenciennes), Blonde lace, "Filet pattern lace," and "Handsomely embroidered ecru net." Pert and pretty boudoir caps enjoyed popularity throughout the decade.

LINGERIE

✦ ✦ ✦

Créations Martial et Armand
Parure en Supercrêpe A. G. B.

"LINGERIE"! This wonderful pochoir depicts "Creations Martial et Armand" in "Supercrepe." Clad in a beautiful quilted and embroidered robe, a lady of fashion indicates the evening's selection to her maid—a pleated nightgown with matching boudoir jacket, both pintucked, pleated, and trimmed with lavish lace. On the stool beside her rests a sheer Teddy, its straight-cut top adorned with lace medallions. The backdrop is a superb lacquer screen with bold Art Deco flowers. *Art Gout Beaute*, October 1926. *Courtesy of Mrs. Doris Butler.*

Lingerie that's every bit as lovely as *Art Gout Beaute's* selection...

Nighties and Robes

Closeup of the robe's "deco-tized" Renaissance pattern.

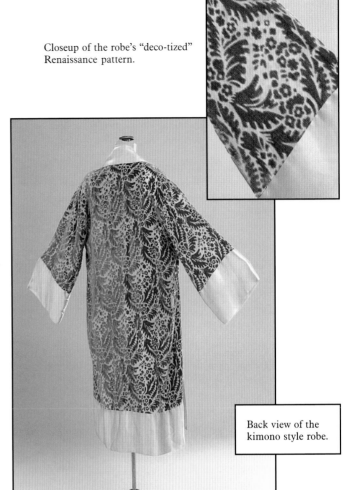

Back view of the kimono style robe.

This sensuous satin nightie or "nightrobe" has a peekaboo bodice and border of lavish lace. The magnificent robe beside it is sheer blue velvet transparent velvet or "burnout" with wide borders of blue satin. Then: In 1925, you could purchase a "nightrobe of trousseau crepe" for $10.75 at B. Altman's. Now: Collectors may pay $200-$300. A similar kimono style robe or negligee was priced at $19.75 at B. Altman's—Now: $400-$500

Right:
Front view of the satin nightie, showing the ribbon trim, pintucked bodice, and asymmetrical hem, which dips lower in back.

The satin and lace nightie is part of a wedding trousseau; it matches the "Dance Set" bra and panties worn beneath the robe, (also see page 59). These items may have been old store stock as they don't appear to have been worn.

Far right:
A beautiful (and rather daring) blush-pink satin nightie trimmed in ecru Blonde lace, that leaves *One Shoulder Bare* but for a wide satin strap with ribbon rose bouquet. It was originally worn by "Mrs. Davis"! $200-$300

B. Altman's lingerie display window includes fabulous feather-trimmed robes, frilly boudoir jackets, nighties—and a flapper's favorite companion, a boudoir doll! Stamped on reverse: B. Altman's, NYC 1926 (by Permaflector Lighting Company for their portfolio)

Right:
"IT GIRL" Clara Bow flaunts a frilly lace lounging robe trimmed in marabou—and worn over a sheer, beribboned lace teddy! Marabou tipped satin mules complete her ensemble. Photo postcard ca. 1925 with Paramount Pictures symbol at lower right, stamped Ross Verlag.

Far right:
A robe to rival Clara's! This vibrant pink negligee of vertically ribbed silk chenille has matching ostrich feather trim around the neckline and wide kimono cuffs. Surplice (wrap) style front closure with self-ties on the left; lined in sheer white silk with supporting inner-ties. Then: In 1925, at B. Altman's, "a negligee of miraline trimmed with self color marabou" is $18.75; while a similar robe with "fluffy curled ostrich" from Bellas Hess is $7.98. Now: $500-$700

Clara Bow

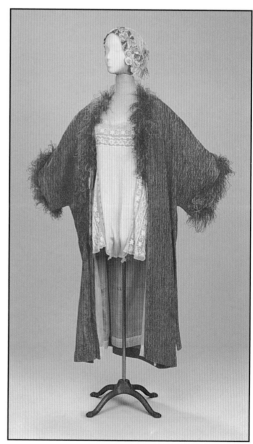

Pajamas

Pajamas were more popular then ever during the second half of the decade!

As this delightful pair of silk crepe pajamas with peekaboo lace indicates, by mid-decade even pajamas are more daring! These stunning pajamas feature a naughty but nice lace bodice with a demure ribbon rose at center; fine pleating adds a couture touch. The ribbon waist tie is original. The pants have sensuous "harem" lace-trimmed cuffs with bows at the sides and an elastic waistband. These pajamas are old store stock. $300-$500

Closeup photo of the lace bodice, ribbon rose, and tiny pleating.

A charming reminder of their eighteenth century ancestors, twenties ribbon bouquets were considered *tres chic* on lovely lingerie! They could be purchased in ready-made packages as well made from directions in instruction booklets (perhaps too time-consuming for many busy flappers).

Marvelous Mules

A pair of sensuous satin mules ofen complimented flappers' luxurious lingerie.

Perfect to trim luscious lingerie is this "Handmade - 100% Silk" ribbon bouquet appliqués from *Simply Stitches*! $25-$45.

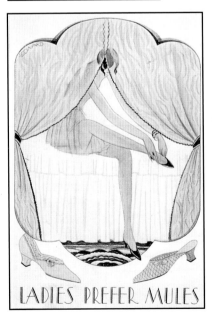

"Ladies Prefer Mules" to compliment their lovely lingerie. As Daniel Green's Comfy Slippers ad advises: "Just now there is great vogue for the smart mule... To rise from soothing slumber, and slip your feet into the quilted caress of one of these exquisite creations of Daniel Green is to start the day with the utmost promise of a comfortable mind and a comfortable body". Illustration by Leonard for Daniel Green of Dolgeville, New York (Ad, *Vogue*, 1/27)

Just perfect for lounging around the boudoir—a to-die-for pair of satin mules tipped with huge marabou poufs that almost hide the blue ribbon bouquets nestled in their centers! Two inch, slightly curved "Baby Louis" heels. $300-$400

This romantic negligee is the most delectable color... just between pink and peach. It's rayon satin, and the long flowing Medieval sleeves of sheer silk georgette. Both the sleeves and collar are trimmed with a wide band of ecru Val lace. Surplice style front, with snap closure at left trimmed with a big bouquet of ribbon rosebuds. $300-$400

Tantalizing Teddies

Les Emplois du " SUPER CREPE " A.G.B. en Lingerie

Sheerer, Shorter, Sexier...! In this wonderful pochoir, a slip-clad jazz baby admires a radiant rainbow of the latest teddies, step-in panties, and slips—all trimmed in a pretty profusion of lace, pintucks, ruffles, and embroidery. Two of the slips dip down and are cut to accentuate the bust, while one is cut straight across. Note our gal's "Prince Valiant" hair, long cigarette holder, and stylish mules! *Art Gote Beaute*, ca. 1925-28. *Courtesy of Doris Butler*

By the second half of the decade, the rather sedate one piece "envelope chemise" had shortened into the sassy, sexy "Teddy!" Busts were cut straight across, and drawstrings adjusted to size; lace or ribbon straps were basted to proper fit. Teddies "slip on" over the head; many have snap or button crotches, and their slashed sides were not only sensuous but convenient when visiting the "Ladies Room."

The exuberant steps of the Charleston require freedom of movement—so savvy *National Style Book* presents "THE CHARLESTON TEDDY," noting: "This smart and dainty Charleston 'Teddy Step-in' is very popular with up-to-date girls... made of tub silk (silk and cotton) and has all-around bandeau style yoke of wide fancy pattern fine lace. Val lace finishes the lower edge and slashed sides which give the convenience of open drawers... ribbon shoulder straps." (1927)

Closeup of the exquisite Val lace, pintucked medallion, and ribbon bouquet.

This sweet but sensuous yellow Teddy is whisper-thin silk georgette, trimmed with pintucks, pleats, and ecru Val lace—with a tiny ribbon rose center. It's cut straight across the front, and the drawstring ribbon that adjusts the width is visible at right. The self-fabric straps are basted to fit. Note the scalloped bottom and sassy "slashed sides"! Snap bottom closure. $100-$200

Here, the top border is floral lace, embroidered in pink and blue; beneath are bands of Val insertion lace. Bands of re-embroidered lace lilies alternate with Val insertion to form the spectacular bottom slashes, which are also edged with ruffled silk tulle; they're a full six inches wide on each side. Snap closure at bottom. $150-$250

Cigarette smoking is a favorite vice of twenties' "Bright Young Things"... and long cigarette holders are a MUST! This jade green bakelite holder is a full seven inches long, with rhinestones surrounding a turquoise bead in the center. It features a push-up mechanism to eject the cigarette butt. The original box is stamped: Artguild Deluxe, "Handcrafted Cigarette Holders, Imported from Vienna, Austria." $150-$250.

This Risqué French Garconne poses in her boudoir in a sheer, lace trimmed Teddy... her long cigarette holder emphasizes her "Come Hither" look! Stamped *P.C. Paris, 1372.*

Bloomers/Brassieres

Bloomers with bandeau brassieres and bloomer/brassiere combinations were also popular lingerie options...

Closeup of the bandeau's hand-painted nymph!

This delightful bandeau brassiere and bloomers set features vignettes of hand-painted nymphs against a background of peacock feathers—their long hair cascading *a la* Lady Godiva! In transparent silk crepe georgette trimmed with lace and ribbon bouquets; elastic waistband, bloomer cuffs, and bandeau top. This stunning set is from a trousseau. $400-$500

Fashionable Dress offers three lingerie patterns that a gal could run up on her new electric Singer. Descriptions: 501, "Beadeau and bloomers inset with medallions of cream lace; for evening, if desired, flesh colored net without straps may be substituted" (YOWSA!); 508, "a simple camasole [sic] and step-in slightly fulled at top and waist... cut with amply full drawers"; 512, "a slip of Lingette...skirt fullness is let in at the hip (side gathers) in approved manner, and a deep hem is another desirable detail." (June 1926)

Bottom right:
The latest Teddy-Bloomers—perfect to wear beneath tailored or sporty ensembles! As *Bellas Hess* advises: "Every woman who appreciates dainty underthings will want to try this new style which combines vest and bloomers in a one-piece garment. It has all the roominess of ordinary bloomers with no elastic at the waistband, thus doing away with all bulkiness. Slashed sides, legs have elastic run knees and one leg has practical side openings to provide the convenience of open drawers. Glove silk, $2.39; rayon, $1.25".
Our store stock Teddy-Bloomers combine a silk tricot bodice with sheer tricot bloomers.
Concealed hook and eye closure at bodice left; the bloomer portion has elastic cuffs and slashed sides with self-covered snap fastenings. $100-$150

Camiknickers to Teddy Bloomers

One-piece brassiere/bloomer combinations were "granddaughters" of the old Edwardian camiknickers...

One-piece Edwardian camiknickers—"Twenticized!" They've been given a new name too—"TEDDY BLOOMERS"—as modeled by the lady on *Kayser's* "Italian" Silk Underwear box. She's modestly draped in a transparent silk shawl, which matches her green satin mules. Box, $50-$75

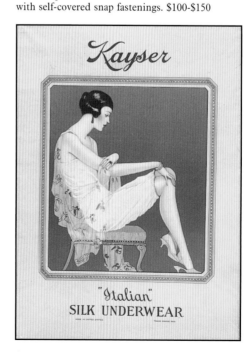

Daring Dance Sets

By mid-decade, though straight bandeau brassieres were still very popular, brassieres with hints of shaping were beginning to appear... made to enhance fashion's new emphasis on feminine curves. These new brassieres merely suggested a bustline—they either dipped between the breasts or were shirred at center to provide a bit more support—and *Viola* the modern bra emerged! Period catalogs called this new bra "The Uplift Bandeau: The very newest cut with slightly shirred center... which gives the natural form". They were often paired with matching step-in panties—and advertised as "DANCE SETS"!

Step-in Panties have wide legs and elastic waists. Bandeaux or brassieres either slip-on or hook and eye at back—and some were beginning to gently shape the bust with "uplift."

Note that though the bandeau-brassieres and the new "uplift" brassieres were very popular with stylish young women, catalogs continued to show both undershirt vests and waist-length camisole tops during the second half of the decade.

Bellas Hess announces: "A BIG HIT!! The New 2-Piece Dance Set," exclaiming: "The new two piece Dansette Set... consists of a snug fitting uplift bandeau and dainty full cut step-ins of beautiful quality, lustrous all silk crepe de chine. Step-ins are trimmed with embroidered and plain net and fine Val lace bandeau is trimmed in embroidered net and plain net around edge. The front of the bandeau and tops of the slit legs of the step-ins are finished with ribbon rosebuds and two tone satin ribbon forms should straps of bandeau, which hooks in back." Note the chic "Hosette" knee-length hose with "Attractively Striped Cuffs," described as: "Our popular new Hosette knit of clear quality silk plaited over lustrous rayon with smooth fitting double cuff top with interwoven three color stripes!" (1926)

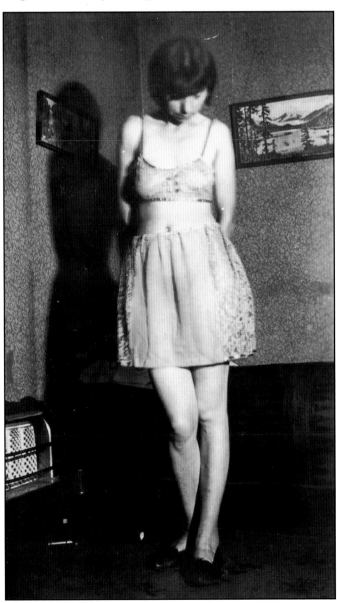

Shy yet sensuous! This lovely lady poses in a dance set much like ours. Snapshot ca. 1925.

This luscious "Dance Set" is part of a trousseau ensemble (see matching nightie, pg. 53. The satin and lace "uplift" bandeau brassiere is seamed for a bit more bust emphasis; it dips slightly in the center for a suggestion of separation. It has a back fastening with three hooks and eyes. The matching step-in panties are slashed at the sides and cut with a yoke front waist with elastic in back. Both bandeau and panties are trimmed with tiny ribbon rose bouquets. Note that today these panties are often called "Tap Pants"! Dance Set, $300-$400

Hosiery

The short new dresses showcased a new erogenous zone... *LEGS*! Hidden for centuries, legs were now dizzily, dazzlingly VISIBLE—and covered, more or less, with stockings in a wide variety of colors and textures. Sheer "Dress Stockings" that came in every color of the rainbow were worn for more formal day, afternoon, and evening events—while for sport, the imagination ran rampant with bold patterns and weaves in heavier hose of wool, cotton, silk, and rayon—and their blends.

Dress Stockings

As *National's* noted, they were formed to "cling to the ankle, enhancing the charm of one's appearance" (stockings were seamed up the back to achieve this shapeliness). And, as *Butterick Quarterly* advised: "Evening stockings are so fine one has to see the seam in back to make sure the leg is not bare; they match the color of the skin exactly and have a single clock at the side." Colored stockings matching colored satin slippers were also shown. (1926)

National's advised that stockings "Can be worn full length—or rolled"; they came in such intriguing colors as French Nude (flesh tan), Dawn (deep peach), Airedale (soft light brown), Atmosphere (pale flesh), Jack Rabbit Grey, Fog Grey, and Banana (pale yellow). (1925)

Artist Tenngren's famous Blue Moon Fairy sits beneath a rainbow of "Color-Smart" dress stockings from: "Blue Moon, America's Most Beautiful Silk Stockings... in thirty-two new tints and hues of alluring loveliness..."! (Ad for Blue Moon, Largman, Gray Co., 1929)

Seamed silk dress stockings in French Nude, Nile green, Dawn, red, and navy blue—with Fine Feathers Hosiery box from Smith Hosiery Mills of Chattanooga, Tennessee. Colored stockings, $30-$50 per pair; Box, $25-$40

Sport Stockings

Of course, stockings for sports wear were as different from dress hose as Night from Day... as *Vogue* advised: "Golf stockings must be wool or lisle; a silk stocking on the course is as unthinkable as a woolen stocking on the nightclub floor." (6/26)

Bellas Hess offers this fine selection of "Popular Fancies" sport stockings—including colorful stripes, novelty plaids and checks, jacquards, argyles, ribs, and "fancy pineapple stitched" hose. They're available in wool, silk/wool blends, "thread silk," rayon, and cotton lisle. Sport hose is also seamed and "Shaped in the knitting from toe to top". Note the ribbon garters (center top) are even shown with sport hose; they're described as "The Rage in New York!" Men's hose is pictured at the bottom center. (1925/26 Fall/Winter)

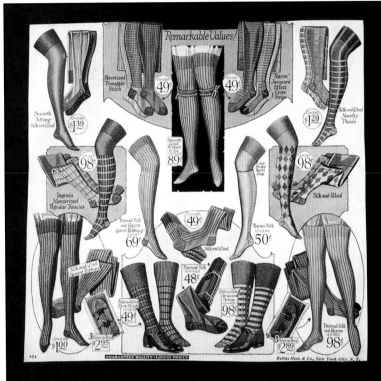

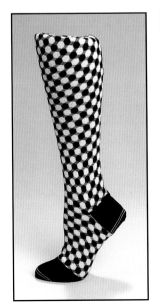

Far left:
Pizzazz Plus! Cotton lisle sport hose in a checkerboard pattern; black cotton reinforced heel and toe. $45-$75

Left:
Dynamic plaid sport hose labeled "Randolph CUTIES 'Sports'" in rayon/cotton lisle; they're never worn store stock. $45-$75

Garters

As many flappers opted to go without corsets or even girdles, stockings were often rolled down over plain elastic garters! These sexy Rolled Stockings caused such a sensation that they were immortalized in song—and featured on the silver screen.

"Roll 'Em Girls" this hit tune advises! This bevy of beauties from the Bobby Heath Revue shows off their gams—and rolled stockings—on the cover of this 1925 sheet music by Joe Morris Music Co., Broadway. Partial lyrics:

> Listen girls...when you bobbed your hair
> You were criticized a lot, but still you didn't care
> When you shortened your dresses, you gave us some shocks,
> But we never thought that soon you'd be wearing socks!
> (Chorus) Roll 'em girls, Roll 'em...
> Roll em down and show your pretty knees...
> Roll 'em high or low just as you please
> Don't let people tell you that it's shocking,
> Paint your sweeties picture on your stocking!
> Laugh at Ma, Laugh at Pa, give them all the ha! ha!
> Roll 'em girlies, Roll 'em, Roll your own!

This evocative publicity photo promotes Paramount's 1927 silent film *Rolled Stockings*... Star Louise Brooks shows the favorite length for rolled stockings—just below the knee!

There's nothing like a little '*WHOPEE!*' these two flappers cry as they hike their skirts to show off—Rolled Stockings! Snapshot, ca. 1925.

To roll stockings, of course, one must have garters. These no-nonsense garters are just right for rolling, in green rayon cased elastic (shown with a Flapper face boudoir mirror). Garters, $15-$20; Mirror, $35-$45

Though stockings were most often rolled to below the knee, they were also rolled thigh high—as this lovely gal illustrates! Risqué photo postcard, ca. 1925, *P.C. Paris, #2891.*

Decorative Garters... Meant to Attract Attention!

Talk about attention grabbers! These gorgeous garters are beaded in a dramatic Deco design of butterflies and flowers; at each end is a hand-painted button—*Flapper Awake* on one side, and *Flapper Asleep* on the other! DYNAMITE! $200-$300

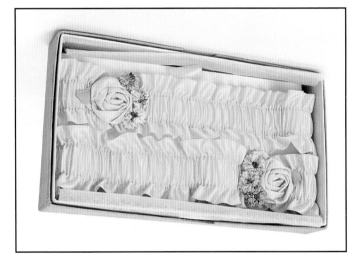

These lavish satin garters are bit more demure... perhaps they peeped from beneath a young lady's *robe de style*! In yellow satin with exquisite ribbon rose bouquets. Never worn, original box. $50-$75.

The ultimate! Mischievous turban-topped flapper faces on lilac satin—these garters are the ultimate in convenience as one has a little pocket complete with a puff for rouging the knees! Even *Vogue* magazine takes note of this latest craze, observing that decorative garters and rouged knees are "Most Becoming"! $200-$300

Closeup of the rouge puff—with a bit of twenties' rouge still on it!

In a clinch like this, it's no wonder this gal's sassy satin garter shows! Snapshot, ca. 1925.

Decorative garters could be purchased separately or in boxed gift sets that included a hanky and/or shoe trees—many catalogs advertised them as perfect Christmas Stocking Stuffers.

Catalogs also offered hose with "built-in" garters, touting: "The newest idea—Women's Hosettes (knee length stockings)... finished with turn-down cuffs just below the knee"! Hosettes were available in both plain cuffs and "attractively striped cuffs." (See illustration, pg. 59)

Girdles, Garter Belts, and Corsets

Of course, in 1925 many women continued to wear girdles, garter belts, and even corsets that had attached "hose supporters" to hold up stockings. *Butterick Quarterly* offered advice on selecting foundation garments:

> *Corsets and garter today shade from well-boned coutils to "take the large figure firmly in hand" to absolute zero for the young girl and for the slender, almost fleshless figure. The younger woman who can keep slim and firm with golf, tennis, and dancing either wears no corset at all or a tiny girdle of satin or glove silk, and an equally ephemeral bust-supporter of lace or net.* (1926)

Throughout the decade, catalogs continued to offer a variety of girdles, longline combinations, garter belts—and for the "stout woman"—a selection of torturous laced, hooked, and boned corsets.

As this French photo postcard illustrates, stockings are also secured with "hose supporters"—garters attached to a girdle, corset or brief garter belt, which this charming gal wears under her teddy! Stamped *P.C. Paris, 1757,* ca. 1925.

Cleopatra, of course, is not forgotten—for gentle support, *National's* advocates: "The New Cleopatra Girdle... For girls or slender women who want the grace of uncorseted lines, yet require comfortable figure support... designed to confine the hips and give flat lines in the back—to give the silhouette demanded by the fashionable straight-line dresses." Note the long elastic hose supporters. (1924/25 Fall/Winter)

"Hardly anyone—nowadays wears a corset all the time"! This wisp of a garter belt, the Girdlon, was patented in 1925 "...to hold your stockings up". (Ad, *Vogue* 6/1927)

Women with ample but unfortunately unfashionable curves were coaxed into corsets with more or less tactful admonitions: "Fleshy hips and abdomen are straightened into modish lines by this expertly designed corset... If your figure is too large in the abdomen and hips you can correct it with this splendid National Guaranteed Reducing Corset designed to reduce the hips and abdomen gradually about four inches without discomfort..."; and, "A corset which controls the flesh over hips and abdomen and gives the smooth flat lines so much desired; elastic inserts at top of front provide comfortable expansion and permit deep breathing..."

An ample lady might also opt for a "No Diet, No Exercise, Rubber Reducing Corset," designed to reduce superfluous flesh via perspiration!

Above:

The Rubber Reducing Corset: "A boon to the woman with large abdomen, hips and bust...! The Rubber Reducing Corset induces perspiration, and is the safest and quickest way by which you can reduce your hips, thighs and abdomen—no special exercises and NO DIETING are necessary... Made of steam cured Para Rubber covered with Tricot weave jersey." *National's* notes an undergarment should be worn under the Rubber Reducing Corset.

Chapter Two
1926 Women's Fashions

Timeline

March 16: An experimental rocket launched by physicist Robert H. Goddard reaches an altitude of 40 feet; Goddard states it's now possible to fly to the moon!

May 18: Sister Aimee Semple McPherson, a popular radio evangelist, is thought to have drowned after she disappears from a California beach. When she reappears a few weeks later, she says she'd been kidnapped—though several witnesses had seen her at various hotels with the temple's radio operator, Kenneth Ormiston, causing many think the pair had been on a romantic tryst.

August 6: American Gertrude Ederle is hailed as the first woman to swim the English Channel. In a brief swim suit, with her body thoroughly greased, she speed through the rough waters in record time—14 hours, 31 minutes—beating the prior men's record by more than two hours!

August 6: The first public exhibit of a Vitaphone, an invention for reproducing sound synchronized with film, debuts at the Manhattan Opera House in New York. Will H. Hays, the "First Man to Address Public Through New Device," introduces this new sound process, predicting that it will be the beginning of a "New era of pictures and music"! The opening night audience views Warner's *Don Juan*, starring John Barrymore—a silent film with Vitaphone recorded musical accompaniment. On October 27, 1926, *Variety* banners: "VITAPHONE THRILLS L.A.... Critical audience of celebrities and general public thrills at introduction of new instrument—Vitaphone called Great Invention".

August 23: Screen idol Rudolph Valentino dies unexpectedly of peritonitis/appendicitis in New York City. Paramour Pola Negri had rushed to his bedside with a nurse and public relations man in tow—and at his funeral she swoons dramatically. Among his ardent fans, the terrible news creates mass hysteria—30,000 women rush to the funeral home, and from New York to Los Angeles, huge crowds gather as his funeral train passes by. A few desperate women even commit suicide on hearing of his death. Rudy's last film was *Son of Sheik*, with Vilma Banky.

October 31: Master magician Harry Houdini dies on Halloween night... while in Montreal, several students asked Houdini if he could take any punch to the stomach by a strong man, and before Houdini could tighten his stomach muscles, one of them punched him hard, three times.

Houdini seemed to recover, and refused to see a doctor; several days later he died of peritonitis.

November 27: NBC begins broadcasting with twenty-four stations.

December 30: *Chicago*, a play by Maurine Watkins, debuts at the Music Box Theatre in New York.

On the Silent Screen

By 1926 there were over 14,000 movie theaters in America. "IT Girl" Clara Bow received some 20,000 fan letters a week! Swedish beauty Greta Garbo was sensational in MGM's *Torrent*, her first American film; it was quickly followed by *Temptress*. Chaplin charmed in *The Circus*. Ronald Coleman thrilled in *Beau Geste*. Paramount's pert vamp Louise Brooks starred in *Love 'Em and Leave 'Em* and *The Show Off*. Paramount released *The Great Gatsby*, based on F. Scott Fitzgerald's blockbuster novel. MGM's blockbuster, *Ben Hur*, starred Ramon Novarro and Francis X. Bushman—it cost an unprecedented $4,000,000. Warner Bros' new star Myrna Loy appeared in *Why Girls Go Back Home*. Gloria Swanson played a society girl in *The Untamed Lady*—wearing a bathing suit to an evening party, she boasted that no man could tame her. Of course, she eventually met a man who stole her heart, and though she "*laid him low*," at his hospital bed she capitulated by falling into his "*one good arm*." In the film, as *Fashionable Dress* commented, "*she wears some very smart gowns*"! Using a new process called "Technicolor," United Artist's sensational *The Black Pirate* starred (who else?) Doug Fairbanks—it was described as "a continuous delight to the eyes". At the premiere was "...perhaps the most brilliant gathering that ever attended the premiere of a motion picture in New York," including Doug and Mary, and "everyone else in the amusement and social life of the metropolis." Fox introduced the popular *Movietone Newsreels*.

Favorite New Recordings

Hit records included "Some of These Days" by Sophie Tucker with the Ted Lewis Jazz Band; "When the Red Red Robin Comes Bob Bob Bobbin' Along" by Paul Whiteman; "I'm Sitting on Top of the World" by Al Jolson; "Bye Bye Blackbird" by Gene Austin; and "Gimmie a Little Kiss Will Ya' Huh?" by Whispering Jack Smith.

In Literature

Winnie-the Pooh stories, introduced by British author A.A. Milne, were written for his son—Christopher Robin!

The Sun Also Rises, Ernest Hemingway's new novel, was published to great acclaim—he was noted as one of the Lost Generation's best writers.

In Fashion 1926 –
Shorter Styles Diversify!

Diversity was fashion's watchword in 1926 as couture advanced new, more figure-hugging fashions utilizing "...complicated cuts disguised as simplicity". As Baron de Meyer advised: "although styles are hardly altered, one might reasonably state the 1926 fashions are more beautiful, more luxuriously Simple, and what seems even more important, more Youthful than ever before... for clothes nowadays are only really successful, up-to-date and smart when expressing the undefinable buoyancy which characterizes modern youth". (*Harper's* October 1926)

Couture Trends

There was a more pronounced focus on the upper body in 1926, due in part to the popular blouson look; bodices were "bloused" all around or in back only. Boleros and bolero effects also accented the upper body—at Jenny, "boleros are numerous, very short, they float away". The beloved vestee remained; many frocks now featured long v-necks, open to the low waist, with square-topped vestee inserts. The new "asymmetric" neckline was seen along with the v-neck and the bateau. Sleeves also diversified! As *Harper's* Marjorie Howard observed: "The new kimono and leg of mutton are significant, but long, plain sleeves are most seen. Many have a tendency to widen at the wrist, others at the elbow." Tappe noted that Martial et Armand's designer, Madame Vallet, had designed a frock with "huge bat sleeves that button all the way from neck to tight cuffs"; several houses featured "batwing" sleeves this year. The "Chinese Lantern" sleeve was chic; it puffed from elbow to wrist where it was cuffed in a tight band.

Waistlines diversified. As Howard noted, "The waist may be emphasized today from the very top of the hip or well below it; under the bust; up one side and down the other; pulled up in front (or back); girdled; left alone—or even suppressed altogether...". The "moulded hip" effect seen on the Egyptian and Indo-Chinese fashions of 1923 returned with a vengeance—both the swathed "Gipsy Girdle" and its kissing cousin, the inset waist/hip yoke, were popular waist treatments; both focused attention on the natural waist and hips. Howard observed, "full short skirts and gipsy-girdles are shown on nearly anything and everything you can imagine". Since shorter skirts and tight yoke or girdle effects required an "arrow-slim" figure, commentator Rosita Forbes remarked: "Bones are fashionable and legs popular as complexes!... The wasp waist of a century ago is nothing to the torture that a Venus would-be Victrix endures today on a 700 calorie a day diet... women have demanded all sorts of freedoms, moral, social and economic, but "caloric" should have been included". (*Vogue* June 1926)

Frocks' skirts also diversified—"Skirts can touch the floor in one model and barely reach the knee in another; they can be snug as rubber bands or spread into a half circle; they can have even hems or trail in back, front or one (or both) sides!" (*Butterick Quarterly*, Spring 1926). While frocks' skirts continued to shorten, many had a "dip" at some point—as

Marjorie Howard pointed out: "uneven hemlines have invaded every phase of the mode; even tailored frocks (may) have a long end somewhere..." Tiered skirts remained in the mode, and tunic effects retained their popularity (the tunic had been a fashion factor since Paul Poiret's 1908 revolution).

For evening, Howard noted that there were three main types of gowns: "slim and richly surfaced; chiffon and fluttery with uneven hemlines, or long and full robes de style ...all, however, exhibit Diversity". Chanel featured "untrimmed chiffon evening gowns" in her collection, "not quite so simple as they look, when you examine them you will find subtle foldings and stitchings, and tricky combinations unsuspected in the apparently simple effect". Howard noted that many Chanel evening gowns were "...heavy with exquisite embroideries and glitter with jewels, beads, spangles—especially the new Rodier fringes called 'perlic' of which Chanel has made a feature". Describing a Doeuillet evening frock with "a bolero effect at the natural waistline", and "a high pointed line that accents the loose natural waistline, and a corresponding center point in the skirt's front," she exclaimed: "With Diversity like that, how in the name of Eve, the first dressmaker, can you get much that is new?"

For afternoon and evening, couture provided not only diversity, but novelty—Worth put satin knee breeches under satin skirts as did Cheruit—and Poiret created a much talked about draped satin afternoon frock that revealed a "culotte on one leg only." Howard commented: "I can't see much object in having trousers under afternoon or evening dresses... it isn't as if we did the 'Maxixe' anymore"! (The Maxixe was very popular ca. 1910-1920.)

"Paris decrees: Ostrich is Ruler of Fashion"! Ostrich feathers encircle evening gowns, edge tunics, fall in long streamers from waistlines; they form enormous collars on capes, trim shawls, and float from necks as boas—and, of course, "one finds them in those huge fans which are leisurely waved by their proud owners". Ostrich is prominently featured in the collections of Worth, Patou, Lelong, Drecoll, Premet, Martial et Armand, and Jenny (where Baron De Mayer finds "...pink ostrich feather scarves and pink fringed shawls designed by Madame VanDonegen, the great painter's wife.") (*Harper's* October 1926)

Baron DeMeyer Selects Couture Dream Gowns

At Vionnet, DeMeyer admired a white evening gown of net, with spider webs embroidered in rhinestones ended in silver thread fringes; also an evening gown in yellow over pink was embroidered all over with wisps of yellow ostrich feathers and rhinestones. The Baron remarked that "Madeleine Vionnet is a name with a strong vibration which, incessantly repeated, gains in strength from year to year. Vionnet is so successful ...because of her sartorial genius and her architectural brain... she designs her models as an architect builds a church." Chanel's collection was "...the expression of an elegant woman's taste. All models are wearable, devoid of eccentricity. They are a combination of plaits, tucks, panels and ties which result in trim, neat and excellently cut Chanel Gowns." He favored her black beaded tube with knotted fringes forming a short cape which fell over the bare back; also Chanel's chiffon evening gowns "...composed of panels, bolero effects, tails and side draperies, in bright violet, bright blue, lavender and black." At Patou, he noted a chiffon evening frock with blouson vestee bodice and short godet-flared skirt, trimmed with vertical ostrich bands (available at Arnold Constable). Cheruit presented net ball gowns composed of ruchings and flowers, with tight satin bodices and full skirts..., clouds of net enveloped fruit and butterflies, lengths of satin trailed on the ground; ostrich feathers were shown in fluffy profusion and silk fringes graced many Cheruit gowns.

Many couturiers selected enticing names for their creations, and at Lanvin, De Meyer was enchanted by "No No Nanette"—a gown in soft Lanvin blue taffeta with a rounded short shoulder cape, pink ties, and silver embroideries; he also noted "Karenine," one of her famous "period gowns"—a full black belted tunic, embroidered in silver disks over a green skirt with full, slashed gigot sleeves. At Lelong, he was taken with "Indiscret"—black satin pajamas with a short, loose silver coat, embroidered in green and orange; and "Leopard," a gown with leopard spots embroidered in diamonds! (*Harper's*, October 1926)

Worth offered a flame red, very short, slim evening frock with rounded neckline and three-tiered skirt with the longer cascading draped side panel, topped with ostrich "puffs."

"The Coat is the Foundation of the Smart Woman's Wardrobe!" *Vogue's Pattern Book* Declares!

For evening: "...coats are sometimes more spectacular than the dresses beneath; of course, both must coordinate," *Harper's* Marjorie Howard advised, and "Coats outnumber capes; many feature large full sleeves or full in upper portion, narrow below. Many are gold; there's splendid fur trimmings". At Molyneux, she admired an evening coat "...in white chiffon velvet over rose, entirely embroidered in a magnificent pattern of silvery leaves, with collar of chinchilla."

For day, *Vogue Pattern Book* advised:

> ...rugged tweeds are recommended for travel, motoring and country wear. A bit more formal coat is needed for town - perhaps a straight silhouette with long, narrow shawl collar and elbow length cape. Large cape sleeves are also smart. For sports, a printed linen coat is suggested, worn with a sleeveless white jersey sweater and green jersey skirt with inverted pleats... The most popular coat length is 7/8, which allows a few inches of the dress to show. (1927).

Howard also observed: "Most of the new French coats are straight; though many flare or are full..." Stopping at Bernard et Cie, she noted: "I found their collection particularly strong in coats, all of which have the new importance across the shoulders, either in a yoke, in shirring or in some sort of fullness. Wide sleeves added to this fullness lend importance to the upper part of the body...". And, the rage for the ubiquitous fox neckpiece had not abated—*Vogue* declared: "The smart world wears a fox scarf..."; they were seen everywhere—even at the beach!

Shops and Catalogs Interpret the Mode for the "Average Woman"

For day, conservative catalogs were showing skirts just a bit shorter than in 1925—about one to two inches below the knee. The ensemble concept remained strong; two different fabrics and/or colors were modish, and jackets were 7/8 or "fingertip" length, though some were hip length. *Fashionable Dress* noted that it was "Surely a tied up season again—never were there so many ties—fore and aft, right and left, up and down...in summer breezes, nothing will flirt so coyly as these fluttering odds and ends". In addition to ties at the neck, there were long ties that knotted "between the shoulders in the middle of the back and

fall to the hem;" side ties that "gather up all available fullness at one hip or both hips, then stand out in pert little loops and ends." Wrists ties were a new note, and, "frequently refusing to tie, they remain narrow and merely snap together, leaving two long ends to float where they will." Large, ruffley jabots continued to "float smartly from collars;" Jenny had created a frock with jabots that fell from neck to hem and below to end in points. Chanel's beloved shirrings (smocking) were everywhere, "almost any place they will fit they are employed"—including shoulders, waistlines, and hiplines; skirts were shirred to bodices, and godets and panels were often shirred at the tops; sleeves too were often shirred at shoulders and/or cuffs! And "Hips achieve fresh importance;" they were accented with couture's chic girdle or yoke effects, diagonal inserts, cascade draperies, and hip bouquets—and by the new, short, flaring peplums.

Fashionable Dress visited Auteuil to observe the new coats: "The opening of the races at Auteuil proclaims a subtle change in coats... there's a battle royal between the Dolman's and Flared styles, the two most popular. Dolmans are large with dropped shoulder treatments—the yoke often drops the shoulder." Coat dresses were "well marked in Paris," also cape coats or caped sleeves. *Bellas Hess* offered both straight and flared coats, most had surplice wrap fronts closed with a large celluloid button, though some had no fastenings at all (their coat prices ranged from $12.98-$32.75). Inexpensive "faux" furs were more popular then ever—the irrepressible *Chicago Mail Order* catalog boasted: "Since those primitive days when her mate himself slew some beast of the wilds to provide fur wraps for his lady fair, many a woman has cherished them as unfulfilled dreams because of their prohibitive cost... now Science has given us this substitute—almost indistinguishable from a Real Pelt!" *Chicago* stated their Napalam and Karakin "closely resemble the expensive Caracul fur", and their plush Kunipelt Fur Fabric "dazzles with its magnificence"!

Note that existing twenties frocks have sometimes been altered by thrifty flappers. *Butterick Quarterly* offers advice on how to add this year's new features to last year's frocks:

> The fashion of combining fabrics or colors makes it possible to amplify last year's tube frocks, since the new material need not match the old... Last year's frock may be cut to blouse length and worn with a pleated skirt... new inverted pleats may be inserted into an old straight frock at front and/or back. For afternoon, circular frills or panels of georgette give new motion and animation to a straight afternoon frock... Shirred godets running from the hip will add new flare to a straight frock; they may be of a contrasting shade... Last season's tube can be recut on the lines of a princess body and a flaring circular flounce added. A new long Chinese Lantern sleeve will bring a dress up to date; sheer material added may match the dress, contrasting lace of embroidered fabric will also be smart. Last year's print will be difficult to match, but solid contrasting color will give it a new look.

Coats for Evening

For evening, coats were often more spectacular than the gowns beneath—both, of course, had to coordinate. For evening, there was a selection of coats and capes for every occasion—including opera coats, cinema coats, and theatre coats. *Harper's* Howard commented that, "Many are gold; there's splendid fur trimmings". Coats were often shirred under the collar to "produce the essential fullness."

JEAN PATOU

This fabulous pochoir by Leon Benigni appeared in the June 1926 issue of *Art Gout Beaute* ... illustrated are "Theatre Coats" by Jean Patou. Note the fullness achieved by the fine diagonal pintucking—also a favorite feature of Madeleine Vionnet.

Beaded Oriental Evening Coat

Orientalism at its Most Opulent is evident in this breathtaking evening coat, beaded and embroidered in Japanese motifs on silk panné velvet! The spectacular beadwork consists of thousands of hand-applied mercury glass beads, red and silver glass bugle beads, and prong set rubies. Silver Koi with ruby eyes swim through sea grasses of silver soutache braid and flat silver leaf—and coral reefs formed of rubies and silver soutache. At the center back and front, a circular medallion worked in red and silver bugle beads is surrounded by scrolling curves. The large convertible collar and wide cuffs are chinchilla; shirring under the collar provides "essential fullness." Sleeves are straight and embellished with a band of embroidery to just below the elbow where they flare, gathered from a piped seam. There is no label present, but family members claim their grandmother wore this coat at Court when she was presented to Queen Mary. It is lined in peach satin, banded with silver lamé. Worn with a coral velvet cloche with a tucked crown, encircled with bands of silver lamé ribbon.

A full back view of this incredible evening coat, showing the beaded Oriental motif, huge chinchilla collar, and cuffs. Coat, $15,000-$20,000. Cloche, $300-$400

A full front view of the coat; you'll note the pattern of the beadwork is the same in front and back.

A closeup of one of the koi, with its mercury glass bead body outlined in silver soutache!

A closeup of the back of the coat showing the ruby sea grasses, coral reefs, and center medallion.

Dressed for an evening on the town in a lovely embroidered evening coat, this elegant lady and her escort are about to depart for a night on the town. Note the short length of her magnificent fox-trimmed coat—and her high spike heels! (Hupmobile Ad, *Harper's Bazar*, 10/26)

Egyptian Lamé Coat

Though beaded coats are very chic, many prefer luminescent lamé. (continued on opposite page)

A wonderful coat illustration for Max Furs (*Fourrures Max*) of Paris by Jean Dupas, one of the most famous Art Deco artists—the stylized gazelles are Art Deco favorites. Note the luxurious fur trim banding the collar, surplice front, cuffs, and hem. (*Vogue*, 1/15/27)

This closeup shows the shading and fine detailing of the wings' feathers!

A back view of the coat's exquisite "Wings!"

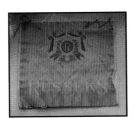

The Russeks label.

Fifth Avenue Glamour—Egyptian Style! This beautiful evening coat features huge overlapping Egyptian wings of gold and black lamé, alternating with light pink shading to deep rose and gold lamé—it's designed to shimmer seductively under the evening lights! The full sleeves are piped at the wide armscyes and gathered to white fox cuffs. Shirring under the collar provides proper fullness. Tucked in the right cuff was a sweet memento—a fine linen hanky left by its flapper so many years ago! Ecru silk crepe lining sporting the label: *RUSSEKS* (located at Fifth Avenue at 36th, Russeks' motto was "America's Most Beautiful Store"). Coat, $1200-$1600. *Courtesy of Karen Augusta.* It's shown with a lamé evening cloche trimmed with pink bugle beads and sequins, $300-$400.

Red Fringed Dance Frock

Beneath her luxurious lamé coat, our flapper wears a delightful dance frock of cherry red crepe georgette—its asymmetric fringe designed to swing and sway to the steps of the Charleston. As the 1926 *Butterick Quarterly* observed: "There is a distinct movement toward styles that outline or mold the body"—and this is evident in this frock's new bloused bodice and tight "girdle" effect at the hips. Naturally, the new girdle effects required a slim figure, prompting fashion commentator Rosita Howard's comments: "The wasp waist of a century ago is nothing to the torture that the Venus would be Victix endures today... Bones are fashionable—and legs as popular as complexes"! (*Vogue*, June 1926)

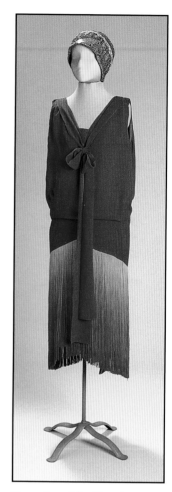

This stunning dress embraces many of couture's latest features—it's a three-piece ensemble which includes a satin underslip, a straight tubular underdress, and a long fringed overdress. The overdress features the new bloused bodice that gives a "bolero" effect, which lends fullness while focusing attention on the natural waist. The tight "girdle" smartly moulds the hips. Sassy asymmetric fringe, ombreed to shade from light pink to deep red, is placed to point up in the center and down on the sides; this treatment is mirrored at the uneven hemline. Though this fringed overdress may look simple, it has a complicated construction; back and front are cut in one piece and seamed at the shoulders (there are no side seams). The blouson effect is achieved via a shorter, attached inner lining, and at each side three tiny pleats accent the low waist. Pleating at the shoulders lends additional fullness to the bodice. Long picot-edged Chanel streamers are attached at the shoulders; they tie in a bow at center front, trailing to the hem. The back of the overdress plunges to the hips where it meets in a daring derriere bow; shirring at either side of the bow emphasizes hip curves. The georgette underdress has plunging, piped v-necklines in front and back; in front, two top-stitched shoulder pleats add fullness, and in back small waist pleats provide subtle shaping. Beneath, a tubular satin slip features a straight-cut georgette top, which is meant to show beneath the v-neck of the overdress. Both underdress and slip have snaps to secure at the shoulders. $600-$800

Front view of the fringed dress, showing the bloused bodice and the extremely chic "Chanel" streamers! Note the svelte lines of the new "girdle," emphasized by the placement of the fringe!

Ostrich Fans and the Red Fringed Beaded Bag

Harper's Bazar noted this year's penchant for feathers, proclaiming "Ostrich is Ruler of Fashion!"—ostrich trim is featured on many couture dresses and coats, and "...one finds them in those huge fans which are leisurely waved by their proud owners"! (October 1926)

A perfect compliment to our red fringed frock—a red fringed evening bag! This diamond-shaped beaded bag is 16 inches long; the fringe alone measures 8 inches. Gold-plated embossed frame; red moire lining edged with ribbon leaf trim. $350-$500

For sheer drama, our gal carries an enormous red ostrich fan—a full 25 inches long! Its four huge plumes are mounted on faux tortoise or "tortine" sticks. $300-$400

Coats for Day & Sports Wear

Coats for casual day and sports wear were not items that were simply worn for warmth—they were very stylish and carefully selected to compliment the look of one's whole ensemble. Various fashion magazines kept "smart" women abreast of the latest trends in coats.

"THE COAT IS THE FOUNDATION OF THE SMART WOMAN'S WARDROBE!" *Vogue* proclaimed, advocating "rugged tweed coats for travel, motoring and country—and a bit more formal style for town wear... perhaps a straight silhouette with long, narrow shawl collar, and elbow length cape...". For sports wear, "a printed linen, worn with a sleeveless white jersey sweater and green jersey skirt with inverted pleats" was suggested. (June 1927)

Harper's Marjorie Howard observed: "Most of the new French coats are straight; though many flare or are full... Sports coats are perfectly straight and extremely simple." *Harper's* also noted the importance of capes and cape effects: "Paris goes right on stressing cape coats and cape sleeves..."; they also noted that (separate) "Capes are worn as well as coats." (October 1926)

Stewart & Company's prestigious New York store at Fifth Avenue & 37th presented: "...coats created in Paris, REPRODUCED by Stewart's..."—a flared-front style with fur trim all around was priced at $149.50, and a slender, short coat with fur trimmed collar, cuffs, and hem was $185. (Ad, *Harper's* October 1926) The 1926 *Bellas Hess* Spring/Summer catalog offered more economical but similar styles; their prices ranged from $12.98-$29.98.

Fashionable Dress magazine advised their readers: "The opening of the races at Auteuil proclaims a subtle change in coats. The two most popular are Dolmans and Flared types, there's a battle royal between the two. Dolmans are large, with dropped shoulder treatments; the yoke plays the game of the drop shoulder often".

Clad in warm fur-trimmed coats, three flapper gals meet at the mailbox... The gal at left, posting the letter, wears the new "flare" style, while the other two have opted for the straight silhouette. Though their coats look warm, they've neglected to wear their galoshes! Snapshot, 1926.

This sylph-slim gal shows off a chic cape coat—worn with the latest "ripple brim" cloche!

Bicycling at the Beach—in a very smart straight coat, trimmed with a fur collar and cuffs. Note her Mary Jane pumps! Snapshot, ca. 1926-29.

FETCH! Dorothy Longfellow, a descendent of poet Henry Wadsworth Longfellow, plays ball with "Lady Jane and companion!" She's wearing a fetching fur trimmed coat, and, of course, Mary Jane pumps.

"Too Many Parties and Too Many Pals" this pretty flapper laments as she appeals to the Judge—she's clad in a delectable *short* fur-trimmed coat! However, the stern old judge advises the jury:
Don't let her beauty sway you, don't mind her ready tears
Don't let her youth mislead you, she's wise beyond her years
She isn't like her Mother, and yet she might have been
...*If it hadn't been for petting parties, cigarettes and gin!*
(Leo Feist, 1925)

Anniversary Sale! A wonderful window display photo of the latest fur and fur-trimmed coats at Hecht Brothers & Co. of Baltimore, Maryland. It was taken in 1926 for Permaflector Lighting Company's portfolio.

Off for a ride on a chilly winter day! Both Mother and daughter are dressed in luxurious fur coats to ward off winter's chill—mom's double-breasted style resembles the coat at left in Hecht's window display! Snapshot, ca. 1926.

Note how closely the coats in Hecht Brothers' window follow the latest French fashions! In this fascinating pochoir from *Art Gout Beaute*, two Parisian ladies inspect the new automobiles at the *Renault* showroom. At left, the grey ensemble's coat, with fur collar, cuffs, and hem perfectly compliments the matching dress beneath; she's selected a "mannish" fedora-style cloche. The smart red coat at right boasts wide flared sleeves and a wide belt accents its low waist; it's worn with a puffy, creased crown "Gigalo."

The smart Bellas Hess catalog, claiming "THE MOST FORTUNATE NEW YORK MISS COULD POSSESS NO SMARTER COATS THAN THESE!" Bellas Hess offered styles with the couture's latest features at prices the average woman could afford.

Original descriptions include: **Top left (435):** Handsome tweed sports coat is a straight line model with big patch pockets and Bobby collar. The cape coat at **bottom left (436):** a sporty looking cape coat all wool fancy tweed check; the slightly circular cape is bordered with suede velour cut in scalloped points...Bobby collar. **To its right, (437)** is the latest flared coat: "for correct street wear... all wool Poiret with full length underarm panels cut in odd points over the hips and joined to a circular insert flare at bottom." **At top center (438)** is a blue button-trimmed flared coat: "wool suede velour features the popular set-in panel at the sides that is cut to give a smart flare to the Coat, side panels are adorned with rows of harmonizing silk stitching, fine self cording and rows of matching buttons..." **Pictured at top right (439)** is the alternative "Tuxedo" collar: "A Stunning Tuxedo Shawl Collar of novelty silk metallic cloth edged with soft summer squirrel fur; close fitting sleeves adorned with row of metal buttons and loops almost to the elbow. The coat is cut to fasten over to the side (surplice) and the long row of metal buttons and tailored loops which forms the closing at the left side is repeated at the seam on the right side". **At bottom right (440),** versatility triumphs with a DETACHABLE cape coat: "Two Coats for the Price of One... A chic little French Coat of beautiful Poiret Sheen... delightful full flare cape is cut in scallops and piped around the bottom with matching color silk braid. The cuffs on the sleeves are also piped with silk braid and are cut in a tab which buttons over the sides of cape which is readily detachable and coat when worn without cape is a beautiful straight line model, thereby giving you really TWO COATS!"

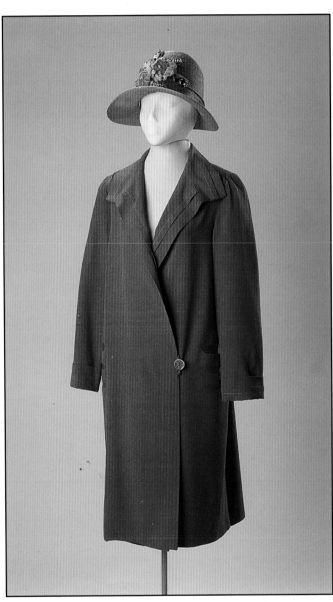

For Spring and Summer 1926, *Bellas Hess* pictures a variety of the latest coats—some smart and straight, others exhibiting the flirty new Flair. Note the surplice wrap closings, fastened with a single button, and the stand-up "New Bobby Collars" (the convertible "Bobby" collar was all the rage in the second half of the decade; *National's* refered to it as "The New Bobbed Hair Collar"). Other popular collars included the turnover "Johnny" collar, similar to the Bobby; the "Tuxedo" shawl collar, and the sporty "mannish notched collar." Two of the newest cape coats were offered, as *Fashionable Dress* advised: "Call it Cape or Cape collar, it is admittedly chic...!"

The straight tubular silhouette is well represented in this delightful Spring coat of cherry red silk faille. Its new "Bobby" collar is trimmed with a decorative pleat that's topstitched in white. The revers (lapels) are similarly pleated, as are the narrow cuffs. The faille fabric is cut horizontally rather than vertically, providing more depth of color. Shirring at the back of the neck and top of the shoulders provides ease of motion. Three decorative topstitched pockets at each side add a nice couture touch; the top pocket is functional, the two beneath are faux. Surplice closure with a single carved bakelite button and self-fabric loop. It's fully lined in matching red silk pongee. THEN: At a Fifth Avenue shop, $25-$50; catalog price, $15-$30. NOW: $300-$400

"Paris goes right on stressing cape coats!" *Fashionable Dress* proclaims. This fetching flapper heeded their advice—she's just returned from a shopping spree wearing a chic caped coat, with a scalloped border, similar to the one *Bellas Hess* pictures at the lower left. Note her fabulous Art Deco pumps! Snapshot, ca. 1926.

The Bon Marché label.

Right:
This chic cape coat has a smart military air! It's fine wool gabardine, with a waist-length attached cape that draws attention to the natural waistline; it's decorated at each side with a row of six carved bakelite buttons. Twelve rows of tiny pintucks support the convertible Bobby collar; the edge is trimmed with soft brown "Summer Squirrel." The cape features topstitched raglan seams; the straight, narrow sleeves beneath are cuffed. Surplice closure with a large carved bakelite button and self-fabric loop. A smaller matching button at the convertible collar enables it to be worn "close about the neck as well as open". Both the coat and attached cape are lined in mocha-colored crepe; inner ties also secure. There is a small inner pocket on each side of the front opening. (The lining, while intact, is beginning to split, as is usual for linings of this era.) Label: *Bon Marché*. It's worn with a petaled flocked velvet cloche from Lane Bryant. Coat, $400-$500; Cloche, $200-$300

Far right:
This side view shows the cape back, and fabulous button trim.

Travel

Post war "Wanderlust" induces many people to travel in the twenties—and whether one's contemplating a trip to Europe or an American destination, smart, versatile clothing is a must!

Seven Smart Flappers Tour Rome's Seven Hills! They're posing in front of the Pantheon at the Piazza Della Rotonda, built by Marcus Agrippa in 27-25 B.C.—wearing a variety of chic Spring coats in solids, stripes, and plaids! Note the popular surplice closures. The gals accessorize with smart, snug cloches; their shoes include oxfords, Mary Janes, and classic Colonial pumps (third from right). Snapshot dated 1926.

Couture Day Coat

An Art Deco Masterpiece! This haute couture coat from Bernard & Cie, 33 Avenue de l'Opera, Paris, is a fine example of the full style coat. It features fantastic deco embroidery on a coarsely woven mocha wool, worked in burnt orange wool and fine gold soutache braid. Bands of burnt orange spirals alternate with gold soutache on the collar and cuffs—and delineate the low waist in front. Two roomy pockets are formed via openings in this waistband trim. It's smartly shirred for fullness below the wide standup "Directoire" collar. The dramatic Dolman sleeves are cut in one with the coat's front; in back, they're connected via a topstitched raglan seam. It has a front closure with a single carved bakelite button, and is fully lined in orange pongee.

This front view of the coat shows the Art Deco circles and embroidered trim accenting the low waist, collar, and cuffs. It's worn with a matching cloche in a scalloped design, the scallops outlined in gold soutache braid; tiny horsehair brim. Coat $5000 - $8000; cloche $300-$500

Sightseeing at the *Place du Concorde*, Paris! Two supremely chic ladies model haute couture ensembles; both the coat and cape are the popular 7/8 length, allowing the bottoms of the dresses to show. At left, the tailored coat in a vibrant rose print is worn over a red dress with lace vestee. At right is a cocoa brown dress with a matching full cape that's lavishly embroidered on the high collar and hem. Pochoir plate, *Art Gout Beaute*, ca. 1926-27.

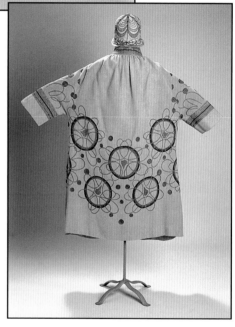

Back view of the coat—note the different trim placement and the shirring beneath the collar.

Closeup of one of the finely worked Art Deco circles.

Bernard & Cie label.

Bernard & Cie's card, *Harper's Bazar* October 1926.

This coat was originally worn by Helen Edwards Smith, who selected her wardrobe from the smartest Parisian couturiers. Her husband, Elwyn Lawrence Smith, was president of Smith-Corona Typewriter's European Branch.

In the October 1926 issue of *Harper's Bazar*, commentator Marjorie Howard reported on her visit to Bernard & Cie:

> I found the collection particularly strong in coats, all of which have the new importance across the shoulders, either in a yoke, in shirring or in some sort of fullness. Wide sleeves added to this fullness lend importance to the upper part of the body at the expense of the lower in a new way.

Howard goes on to note that this season Bernard et Cie is showing "sport suits with LONG, MANLY TROUSERS!"

Travel by Train

In Europe, the famous Train Bleu carries the *beau monde* to the glamorous Rivera, and "at Biarritz, LeTouquet and Deauville, Fashion Triumphs with clothes in informal careless perfection..." as *Vogue's* Rosita Forbes proclaimed in June 1926!

The train's arrival was an "event":

> The arrival of the Train Bleu is the scene of a reunion of the "elegantes" on the station platform... The train stops at Cannes station; many smart women are on the platform waiting for other smart women who are getting out of the Train Bleu... All of the coats that these women wear have that incomparable sports feeling... The valises and bags of all sizes which the ladies' maids are distributing among the porters have a sleek, trim, handsome appearance, such as one only sees in

these trains "de luxe." There is no jostling and hustling in this group. We leave the station with dignity, as we would pass from one drawing room to another....

It is as indispensable to spend a certain time on the Rivera as it is to show oneself on Monday night at the opera... The pace of life along the coast has been in accord with the rhythm of progress: instead of one casino, there are many now between Saint-Raphael and Monte Carlo; instead of a smart carriage and horses, there are now Rolls Royces or Hispanos, but it is still the same kind of existence; with tennis, golf, walking, baccara, dancing... The Dolly Sisters are the delight of the evening gatherings in the gaming room; they play high, winning or losing enormous sums, both seated at the same table... there is always a crowd to watch them.

...and so it goes until the Rivera season is over, and the smart women again take the Train Bleu and are scattered over other cities and countries... (*Vogue*, May 1927)

Art - Goût - Beauté

ALL ABOARD—The Train Bleu is about to depart for the Rivera! For the trip, the lady at left has selected a tailored ensemble consisting of a three-quarter length broadtail coat and a tubular green dress, bordered with matching broadtail. A close-fitting square topped cloche and large handled bag complete her ensemble. Her friend has opted for the flared silhouette with a suit that's a delicious shade of cafe au lait, a jacket with contrasting lapels and cuffs; her bright pink blouse is bow-tied with fluttering streamers. She wears a matching snug fitting cloche, and carries a bold plaid coat and an envelope clutch purse. (Pochoir plate, *Art Gout Beaute*, ca. 1926-28)

For American travelers, *Vogue* noted: "For crossing the continent by train, an ensemble suit is recommended for traveling that one will be able to wear when arriving in Chicago the next morning..." (June 1926)

Right:
Destination—Grand Central Station, New York! This coordinated ensemble consists of a seven-eights length wool knit coat, worn over a tailored pink faille dress. The coat is bordered at hem and sleeves with an Art Deco version of New York's famous skyline; it's trimmed all around in charcoal grey. Topping this delightful ensemble is the "Newest Ripple Brim" cloche. Knit Coat, $500-$800

Far right:
Front view, showing the coat's "mannish" notched collar.

Closeup of the fascinating deco skyline.

The "Newest Ripple Brim—An Unusually Becoming Style" as offered by the 1927 *National Style Book*, who declared it was "...a new idea in brim shape... becoming to the older face as well as to the youthful one". These ravishing ripple brims were very popular in the second half of the decade. THEN: Note that while *National's* Ripple Brim is $1.98, "English Felts" with ripple brims at Best & Co. on Fifth Avenue are $15.

This sporty wool felt ripple brim is the perfect compliment to a slim tailored ensemble. Its ripple brim is smartly slashed in front, allowing three felt tabs with square marquisite buckles to extend over the crown ribbon. The satin crown ribbon ends in a bow at center back. It's in "Pandora Rose... a new soft Ashes of Roses shade"! Rayon plaid lining in rose, brown, and grey. $200-$300

Sports Dresses & Separates—Perfect for Travel!

Sporty Day Dresses and Chic Separates are Fetching, Form-fitting—and *PACKABLE*! Socialites wear casual frocks and sporty knit separates by couturiers like Chanel and Patou—and their fashions quickly pave the way for innumerable "replicas" and "adaptations."

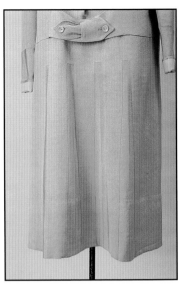

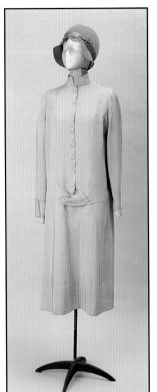

Closeup photo of the skirt's intriguing godets.

At the *Grand Hotel*, Venice! Three *soignee* sisters prepare to tour Venice by Gondola—clad in a colorful array of sporty styles with long, low-waisted bodices and short skirts. At left, the green frock's skirt portion combines side knife pleats with an inverted pleat at center; the bodice has a deep "v" vestee effect. The stunning pink two-piece sweater and skirt ensemble at center features a long-sleeved knit top with a Peter Pan collar and embroidered faux vestee; the matching skirt is knife pleated all around. At right, the bold red and black two-piece ensemble adds a vivid splash of color with both horizontal and vertical stripes—a favorite twenties treatment. (The striped poles at right are to moor the gondolas.) Pochoir plate, *Art Gout Beaute*, ca. 1926-28.

An impeccably tailored day dress in a wide-ribbed knit faille. Though this straight frock achieves fashion's "Simplicity," its construction is quite complicated, with the ribbed fabric cut both horizontally and vertically. On the skirt portion, its couture look is "achieved by tapering inset godets:" in front, the horizontally-cut fabric is complimented by four vertically cut and top-stitched godets—when in motion, these godets catch the eye as the light hits them. The shirtwaist style bodice has a vertically cut vestee effect, which fastens with eight hard plastic buttons; the horizontally cut sides extend to the center of the low waist to form a loop-through belt. The long narrow sleeves are horizontal to below the elbow, then vertical to the narrow cuffs, which are faced with blush pink crepe de chine. The stand-up Mandarin collar is faced with matching crepe de chine. The bodice back is cut horizontally, with a narrow inset top-stitched vertical "v" shaped band at the shoulders which continues down center back to the hem. THEN: On Fifth Avenue, approximately $30-$50; catalog "interpretation" about $15. NOW: $400-$500

LOST! This exasperated gal is trying to find out exactly where she is... she's been reading her road map, evidently to no avail! She's smartly dressed—even for such an activity as camping—in a tailored sports dress and cloche hat! Snapshot, ca. 1926.

Camping was a craze during the twenties as millions took to the roads "Searching for Adventure!" Tents that attached to the old Model T were very popular. *National's* offered a car tent that was: "Roomy, Compact and Durable! This Ideal tourist tent can be used with divided front opened and snapped to extension flap, which is stretched over top of car as illustrated... $20.95" (The equivalent of approximately $200 today.)

Interchangeable sweaters, blouses, jackets and skirts are the ultimate in versatility, ideal for sports and travel! As *Vogue* noted: "Striped sweaters worn with pleated skirts that match or contrast are a costume that is so popular it's almost a uniform of chic!" (January 1927). Catalogs promoted separates with words that mirrored the modern spirit—including "Swagger," "Trig," and "Peppy!" Sadly, these outrageously popular separates are very difficult to find today, even in poor condition.

Couture's chic knit sweaters are quickly captured by the catalogs— "Brilliant Rayon" sweaters are offered for as little as $1.98! The 1926 Bellas Hess catalog offers:

> *The new Sweater that takes the place of Sweater and Blouse for dressy sports wear. It is a short kimono sleeve style knit in a stunning pattern of two harmonizing tones of lustrous Rayon (Fibre silk). The sleeves are finished with matching color Rayon braid and Rayon tie bow fastens the neat pointed white linen collar. Attractive interknit border around hips. Tan and tangerine.*

Two "Peppy" blouses by *National Style Book.* At left is the new "Novelty Vest" blouse with "mannish notched collar and two welt vest pockets... for wear with your sport suits or riding habit, skirts or knickers...". Double-breasted and pintucked, it's "delightfully cool and comfortable" cotton broadcloth. At right is a waistband "Hip Blouse with embroidered Peter Pan collar... the cotton figures tie adds smartness". As *National's* advised, banded "hip" blouses "May be worn as an overblouse or in tuck-in fashion". (1927)

Skirts

Skirts were available with both attached bodice tops (frock skirts) and separately. And, as *Vogue* advised: "Pleats appear on almost all sports dresses this season—being narrow or wide or a mixture of both."

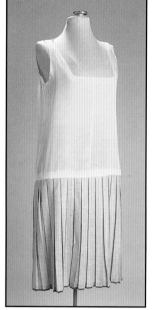

An absolute necessity—the overwhelmingly popular pleated skirt! This example is a beige wool flannel skirt attached to a "bodice top;" it's bordered at the hem with a narrow band of burnt orange. Sometimes called a "frock skirt," it was worn with an overblouse. $75-$150

Separate skirts... "There's nothing smarter nor more practical for general spring and summer wear that a separate plaited skirt!" *National's* offered this "knife plaited and extremely smart skirt... for sports and general wear". (1927)

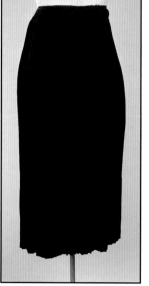

This separate knife-pleated twenties' skirt in black silk crepe is extremely rare—in over twenty years, I've only seen a handful of these beloved pleated skirts! It has an inner grosgrain waistband with snap closure at left. $250-$300

National's mannish "New Swagger Outfit" pictures yet another popular pleat option—pleats are topstitched to a few inches below the waist, then left open to the hem. *National's* noted this outfit was "...a tuck-in shirt blouse and all wool flannel skirt to be worn 3 inches below natural waistline."(1927)

1926 Day Dresses

Day Frocks for 1926 were noticeably shorter, and the ruffled "Jabot" was all the rage!

Chic Day Frocks from the 1926 *National Style Book* include both tailored straight and flared models—with features "seen in so many of New York's handsomest gowns!" Note the new feminine emphasis provided by the flared skirts and "softly shirred shoulders." On the more tailored models, ease of motion is provided via "Chanel" inverted kick pleats, by box pleats, knife pleats, and various combinations thereof. The "Smart New Jabot Dress" at center right appeared around mid-decade, and by 1926 it had become the rage! The vestee remained a favorite, and the popular stand-up "Bobby" collar was seen on dresses as well as coats. And note that lustrous satin was not just for evening—it was very popular for day wear!

Original descriptions, left to right:
The tailored red dress (102):

> ... Every woman who dresses smartly will want one of the new tailored dresses... Soft fluffy coney fur in shades of brown trims the collar and welts of simulated pockets. Buttons add a smart touch to pocket welts, sleeves and dress front. Vestee of harmonizing color crepe and kick plaits at center and side plaits at sides of skirt are smart. Buckle trimmed belt of self material completes the tailored look of this one piece dress.

The black satin frock (103):

> Rich, colorful embroidery, box plaited skirt front and puff sleeves, all new fashion features... all silk Canton Crepe means the dress is one you can wear for many, many occasions; the style is most appropriate for dressy wear. Long scarf collar tying softly in front, gives a becoming line, and the puff sleeves show a bright colored embroidery to match the panel font. A pretty buckle completes the self belt.

New Jabot Dress (104):

> A georgette Crepe Jabot Collar is Smart! Here's a handsome and very pretty dress that every woman will enjoy wearing... of rich looking velveteen with popular front flare given by a circular front skirt section. georgette crepe in harmonizing color is used for the graceful jabot collar, the vestee and the cuffs. Front of the bodice is shirred at the shoulders, giving the fullness most figures need. In beltless style finished with a fancy jeweled metal buckle at the low waistline in front; back is in plain one-piece style.

Satin Charmeuse Frock for *"Stout Women"*(105):

> A wonderful combination of style and money-saving value for you of the larger figure! The trim, slenderizing lines of this coat style dress are ideal for large figures and the all-silk satin charmeuse material used makes it an appropriate selection for dressy wear... Featuring a full length front panel of harmonizing color silk crepe; the front section of the skirt is cut with a graceful circular flare... back is in one-piece style with a narrow sash belt. Vestee closing. (Fall/Winter 1926-27)

Closeup of the satin frock's circular tunic skirt, showing the row of covered buttons and striped trim.

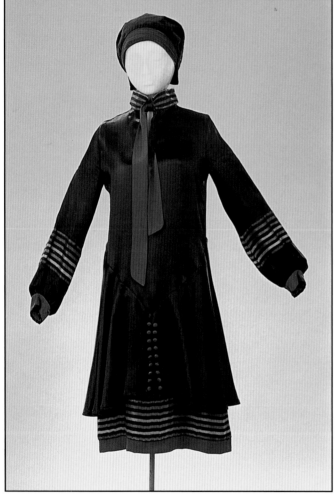

Exquisite black satin pumps with a very Deco look! They're piped in white all around, the piping curving from the keyhole opening across the vamp to the sole. They feature the latest three-inch spike heels and new rounded toes. Wide two-button straps fasten at the sides. They're stamped on insole: "Smart Style, Narrow Heel, Combination Last". $150-$250

Satin for Cycling! Dressed in smart satin day dresses, these two flappers show their glamorous gams as they rev up the Harley. The gal in back holds up her hanky to wave *YOO-HOO!*

Pola Negri Hanky! Decorative "Flirtation" hankies are the Cat's Meow! This sheer crepe hanky is hand-painted with a likeness of our gal's favorite Vamp. $50-$75

"Satin is attaining a striking prominence... Satin crepes are favorites for evening; satin dresses are shown for day and afternoon wear as well..." as *Vogue* observes (January 1927). This exuberant satin tunic dress combines many of fashion's newest features—flare, puffed "Chinese Lantern" sleeves, and "Chanel" streamers! The circular flared tunic skirt is piped all around; it extends from the natural waistline at the sides to form a deep "v" at center, where it's split to the hem. Along each side of this split is a row of nine covered buttons in "Pencil Blue" (the new shade of Royal Blue). The black satin underskirt is trimmed with a wide band of multi-colored stripes and bordered in Pencil Blue. On the bodice portion, a matching striped standup collar extends to long streamers—black satin on one side and pencil blue crepe on the reverse (these streamers were either tied in a bow or left to "flutter"). The "graceful puff sleeves" have a wide striped band at the elbows and are gathered to narrow cuffs of pencil blue crepe; the v neck is piped in black satin. It's a slip-on frock, there are no closures. It's shown with black satin pumps and a new "tam effect" cloche, as worn by the lady at right in *National's* illustration (also see page 87). Tunic dress, $300-$400

Jazzy Jabots are Everywhere!

The new "Graceful Jabot Collar Dress"—in a shade of pink so vivid it rivals Schiaparelli's "Shocking"! This flared silk crepe de chine frock features huge, scalloped jabots that float to the dropped waist; the skirt portion repeats the look with two scalloped panels that flutter to the short, scalloped hem. The skirt is circular, bias-cut for that flirty flair. On the inside, it is weighted at both side seams and back waistline to maintain the proper silhouette. "Chanel" shirring at the shoulders emphasizes the bust. The narrow Mandarin collar extends in criss-cross ties that pull through self-loops; this effect is repeated on the sleeves' narrow cuffs. $300-$400.

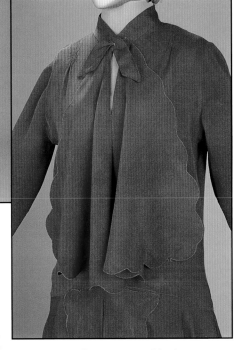

On July 29, 1926, this beautiful gal posed to show off fashion's latest favorite—a frock with the largest, floppiest Jabot imaginable! She wears smart T-strap pumps and a brimmed cloche that she's tilted at a jaunty angle (they were usually worn straight). Written on the reverse is simply *"HOME!"*... which says it all.

Closeup photo of the enormous Jabot!

This stunning Whiting and Davis bag would have complimented either of these two fine frocks! It's flat enamel "armor" mesh, with colorful birds and flowers on a black background. The frame is blue and black enamel; it has a chain link handle. The bottom is vandyked, with ring mesh fringe (missing a few strands). $300-$500

Fine haute couture footwear with a Baltic flavor—a fabulous Deco design that's hand-painted on kid in shades of red, magenta, blue, green, gold, and black. The laced edges are similar to those seen on the Nouveau tooled handbags. These shoes are fashioned with no center back seam; they're piped in brown leather where the spike heels are connected to the shoes. Pearl button fastenings at the sides. On the bottom of soles, which are quite worn, is a partially legible stamp: Made in France Cousu - Main(?). $600-$800

(A similar hand painted, laced-edged pair of shoes is in the Victoria and Albert museum collection—pictured in their book, *Shoes*, by Pratt & Woolley, they're described as: "Leather T-bar shoe decorated with painted motifs, Monaco, ca. 1925; By A. RAMBALDI")

Full view of this exquisite pair of couture shoes!

Dressy Afternoon Frocks and Hats

Abroad or at home, for luncheon and other dressy afternoon occasions, elegant frocks were seen with extravagant hats.

Two creations by Martial et Armand

DÉNICHEUSE. — *Blue serge afternoon dress, trimmed with taffeta ruches to match.*

IMPRUDENTE. — *Nut-brown crepe georgine afternoon dress, trimmed with silver braid.*

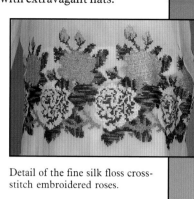

Detail of the fine silk floss cross-stitch embroidered roses.

Art Gout Beaute's lovely pochoir pictures two afternoon frocks by Martial et Armand. The smart blue serge frock at left features a tiered skirt with flaring "taffeta ruches"; it's worn with a matching square topped cloche. At right is a beautiful crepe georgine with the newest wide "girdle"; its smart pleated skirt is complimented by pleated bell sleeves and a pleated jabot tie. Completing her ensemble is a devastating capeline with pleated trim, and she carries the ever-popular fox scarf. (October 1926)

This lovely silk georgette afternoon frock flaunts its tight new girdle with a band of exquisite cross-stitched roses! Narrower bands of roses trim the fashionable puffed sleeves that gather to narrow cuffs. The narrow collar extends to form long "Chanel" streamers, which are also tipped at the ends with cross-stitched roses. Smart scalloped piping joins the low waist to the short skirt. The skirt portion's narrow knife pleats alternate with bias cut flares to draw attention to that new erogenous zone—the LEGS! Then: Deja Inc. of 550 7th Avenue offered similar summer frocks "copied from Jenny, Patou, Lanvin, and Molyneux" for $39.50; Macy's shows "cool, sheer crepes—smartest for afternoon, dinner or dance" between $27.75 - $44.75. (As advertised in *Vogue*, June 1926) Now: $400-$500

This magnificent white felt capeline echoes the splendor of the hat at right in *Art Gout Beaute's* pochoir! The brim is 14 inches wide at the sides, narrowing at center back. Both brim and crown are adorned with wide faille ribbon that's pleated to form Art Deco triangles, ending on the right in a fringed border. A Deco marbleized celluloid hatpin provides the perfect accent. $350-$500

Worn with our embroidered afternoon dress is a lovely velvet cloche, adorned with a garden of Art Deco flowers! The stylized mum at center is formed of silk floss loops with fringed anthers; on either side rows of ruched faille ribbon forms columns of blue delphiniums and lavish leaves. On either side, whimsical grapes, hand-painted on felt, add a dash of panache. The crown is black velvet, with a contrasting underbrim of royal blue velvet; this 12-inch brim narrows to disappear at center back. $350-$500

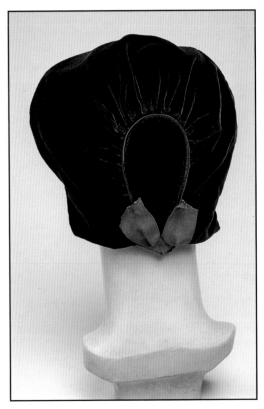

By the second half of the decade, flattering turban/tam cloches have become very popular. *National's* version, "New in Every Detail," is described as an "ultra chic Turban with fashionably draped tam crown. It is one of our newest and most attractive hats with that Parisian air that appeals to the smart woman". While *National's* "Very New and Chic" tam effect turban is $4.29, at a smart Fifth Avenue shop one might expect to pay between $18-$20! (1927)

Afternoon dresses—and modish hats! In October 1926, these three flapper gals posed for the camera, dressed in the very latest styles. Left to right: a smart satin dress with wide lapels and vestee front; center, a tunic effect frock with neckband streamers—left untied to "flutter." The gal at right wears a dress with the ultra chic embroidered girdle waist similar to ours; note her flirty flared skirt and fox neck scarf. Two of the gals (center and right) have accessorized with a new draped "turban/tam" cloche!

Back view, showing the calash bonnet effect!

This "ultra chic" draped Turban/Tam in royal blue velvet features a face-flattering band of pintucked satin around the front. The back, in keeping with the flappers' penchant for Marie Antoinette styles, is formed like an eighteenth century calash bonnet! Lined in rayon; no label present. $200-$300

Beach Wear

Whether one was planning to travel to the exclusive beaches of the Rivera—or join the throngs at New York's Coney Island—Beach Wear was selected with utmost consideration!

In the second half of the decade, beach fashions bared with ever briefer styles; many featured plunging fronts—and backs! Though haute couture continued to show dress style "bathing" suits, many couturiers were also showing clingy wool knit "swim" suits—Jean Patou in particular worked with inventors to create knits that would not stretch after prolonged dips in salty ocean waters. Of course, fashions worn on the Rivera set swimsuit styles... and as *Vogue* noted, Palm Beach, "with gay cabanas dotting the shores," was the "Lido of America"! They advised readers that at Palm Beach, women were wearing "knit bathing costumes in brightly colored stripes with the low cut that most of the suits at the Lido adopted."

"Bathing" Suits! *Art Gout Beaute's* delightful Deco pochoir features the latest in haute couture beach fashions with *Creations de Jeanne Lanvin*, dress style bathing ensembles for Fun in the Sun! (*Art Gout Beaute*, August 1925)

Créations de Jeanne Lanvin

The ultimate in Swim Suit Chic! This fabulous red knit swimsuit features a "mannish" vest style bodice outlined in white soutache; it fastens with five tan bakelite buttons, and is topped by a smart black turnover collar. It's a one-piece, with "trunks attached at waist" (note that the bottom portion, though very short, still retains a vestigial modesty skirt). Label: *Bentzknit Ribstitch, All Wool, copyright 1920 by Pacific Knitting Mills, Los Angeles, Cal.* $200-$300

The average beach-bound flapper, however, favored the clingy California-style knit "swim" suit—like these two offered by *Bellas Hess* in their Spring/Summer 1926 catalog!

"Step into My Parlour said the Spider to the Fly!" *Bellas Hess* describes their dramatic spider web swimsuit:

A distinctive and delightfully original new Bathing Suit with spider web ornamentation. Knit in close ribbed elastic stitch of high grade worsted yarns. One piece model with trunks attached at the waist; one-button shoulder fastening. A lustrous black Rayon Silk spider is embroidered center of front clinging to a strand of his web which is formed as pictured by applied soutache braid. Colors: Phantom red, peacock blue or purple, all with black trim.

Her cap is described as: "A fancy diving cap of pure gum rubber with contrasting rosette and band"; her bathing slippers, "Comfy new Radio Pure Gum Rubber Bathing Shoes, the ideal swimming and beach shoes".

At right is a Fair Isle knit suit:

All-wool worsted suit with all over rayon embroidered pattern—The Rage at Palm Beach! ...Shapely colorful Bathing Suit with contrasting color All Over lustrous Rayon (fibre silk) embroidery in attractive design. Suit is knit in close elastic stitch of high grade All Wool Worsted with trunks attached at waist and one button shoulder fastening. In phantom red with black, purple with gold (shown) or Kelley Green with white.

Her cap is: "The newest thing in Aviation Style Caps, pure gum rubber with a chin strap. Her oxford-style bathing slippers are "durable duck bathing slippers with white bindings".

Note that these two Bathing Beauties wear stockings rolled to just below their knees, though many women are entirely omitting swim stockings now.

Note that today's collectors can expect these wool suits to have some moth nibbles—and many have shrunk, stretched, and/or faded during long days at the beach—but they're still endearing reminders of their era!

Five Flirty Flappers set off for Coney Island(?!) dressed in dashing knit swimsuits! Note that the gate on the running board was used to hold luggage as well as flappers! Snapshot, ca. 1926-29.

"NO DOUBT, IT'S CONEY ISLAND!" While social-ites frequent Palm Beach, New York's famous Coney Island provides plenty of fun for everyone.

New York's Coney Island – "Who Wouldn't?!"

By the twenties, Coney Island had become a Mecca for Millions! It was as American an icon as the Statue of Liberty—with over one million sun worshipers flocking to its beaches on sunny summer Sundays. When the subway extension to Coney Island opened in 1920, Coney became accessible to the poor as well as the well-to-do; a nickel fare brought throngs to this place "to play and get away"! In 1923, a new municipal bath house opened, and even with some 12,000 fifty cent lock-ers, lines could be blocks long—so many beach goers wore bath-ing suits under their clothes, while others simply changed un-der beach blankets—if there was enough space for a blanket!

Coney was not only the world's largest beach resort, it was also the King of America's Amusement Parks, the home of the such magical places as Luna Park and Steeplechase. Thrill seek-ers lined up for rides on its famous roller coasters—Luna's Mile Sky Chaser with its eighty foot drop; Steeplechase's The Limit; and the Bowery's Thunderbolt. On June 26, 1927, Coney's most famous roller coaster, the screaming Cyclone, opened. Designed in a figure eight, it had a daredevil drop of eighty-five feet! Tamer rides included Steeplechase's famous mechanical horse rides, the gigantic 130' diameter "Wonder Wheel" (Ferris Wheel), and the ever-popular carousels. In the "Tunnel of Love," Sheiks and Shebas could "neck and pet." Rides gener-ally cost between a nickel and a quarter.

The midway was a phantasmagoria. There were games of skill and chance, including pitching games (knock over six bottles, and win your honey a kewpie!), put a nickel in slot for nine balls of *Skeeball* bowling, shoot a row of ducks for a gaudy chalkware prize! You could oogle Hoochie Coochie dancers, visit penny arcades, fortune tellers, and palmists! If it rained, everyone with fifty cents to spare headed for the Fun House, Steeplechase's Pavilion of Fun! The Bowery, a four block long alley running from Steeplechase to Feltman's Arcade, was the heart of Coney Island.

In 1924 Coney's first beauty contest was held during Democratic National Convention. There were forty-eight con-testants—one from each state. It was such a success that by 1925 the beauty pageant had become an annual event.

Food was cheap and delicious. Coney Island is the birth-place of the All-American Hotdog—a German frankfurter on a roll invented in 1867 by Charles Feltman (some critics claimed Feltman used "dog" meat, thus the name *HOTDOG*). In 1915, Nathan Handwerker got a job at Feltman's, saving his salary to open a lunch stand that offered *RED HOTS* for a nickel, along with root beer, Coke, and potato chips. By the twenties, Nathan's had become Coney's favorite hotdog stand—and even with some fifty employees serving customers, lines were often fif-teen deep, with overflow spilling into Surf Ave. and blocking traffic—and Nathan's is still popular today!

Coney Island had been sighted by Henry Hudson, sail-ing in the *Half Moon*, in September of 1609. By 1829, Shell Road was constructed, with a bridge connecting Coney Is-land to the mainland; the Coney Island House hotel was con-structed, and Coney quickly became a playground for the well-to-do. In 1865, Peter Tilyou built the Surf House Hotel and Restaurant—and, never one to miss an opportunity, rented "fancy flannel bathing suits" to bathers. There are several theories as to how Coney Island got its name—the favorite being that the name derived from the early Dutch settlers' word for "Rabbit," *Konjn Koh*, which referred to a large popu-lation of reputedly vicious rabbits that inhabited the island.

The thrilling lights of Coney Island's Luna Park! This exciting photo postcard pictures The Lagoon and Chute The Chutes by Night; left to right are the Human Dynamo, Chute the Chutes, Terrace and Ballroom.

"No Doubt, its Coney Is. 1926"

"No Doubt, it's Coney Is. 1926" – Bathers enjoy the sun, sand, and picnics on the beach.

Cool off with an enchanting advertising fan! This sensuous bathing beauty wears a colorful beach turban. The fan is entitled *Dream Girl*, by artist Rolf Armstrong. Many stores gave away these paper fans, as noted on the reverse. This one is: Courtesy of W.C. Hanks, Plumbing and Heating, Telephone 13-W, Salem, New York. $45-$75

"Who Wouldn't?" is noted on the reverse of this snapshot of a sultry flapper and her handsome beau! Coney Island, 1926.

Posing on the roller coaster tracks—dressed to the nines! Snapshot, ca. 1926.

Children's swimwear is similar to adult's. Here, sweet little Mary Ann Ainsworth shows off her new knit swimsuit with an owl appliqué. Noted on the reverse: "July 1926, Beach Bluff, Ma." *Courtesy of Janet Andrews.*

Coney Island's first beauty contest was held during the Democratic National Convention in 1924; by 1925 it had become an annual event! This lovely participant is dressed for the swimsuit competition—note her clingy knit suit and fetching bamboo parasol (unfortunately, her state's banner isn't legible). Snapshot, ca. 1926.

Beach Coats, Carryalls, and Beach Slippers

Beach coats that often doubled as boudoir robes were popular coverups. Flappers tucked their suits, beach slippers, and robes into fetching carryalls.

17 X 777
Printed
Serpentine
Crepe
$1.98 *yd*

17 X 778
Printed
Rayon
$3.98 *yd*

National Bellas Hess offers two similar robes in printed rayon at just $1.98! (1928)

Right:
Art Deco fireworks explode on this vibrant rayon print robe, which is bordered all around in contrasting Nile green. It's shown with a gum rubber bathing cap and a Japanese rice paper parasol! Beach/boudoir robe $75-$150; early rubber bathing cap $25-$45; bamboo parasol $55-$75.

Far right:
Rear view of "Fireworks" robe.

This enterprising beauty wears a similar beach coat over her suit as she poses in front of her Coca-Cola/Peanut stand, At Wilmington (CA) 1927.

A super beach carry-all, decorated with an "attractive colored design" – a thoroughly modern pirate lass, wearing a striped beach ensemble with a pair of *flapping flapper galoshes!* She puffs away on her cigarette as she watches the seagulls fly overhead. Her beach umbrella is at left while at right stately Palms provide a bit of shade. This black leatherette carry-all was evidently a favorite. It has lost its original suitcase handle, which at some point was replaced with an orange braid cord. Stamped inside the white waterproof lining: The Carry-all Utility bag, S. Knapp & Co., Inc., Kansas City-St. Louis. $50-$75

Pictured beside the carry-all are orange rubber bathing slippers with stylish low-heeled T-straps, embossed with diving beauties frolicking in the waves! $50-$75

"Ideal for Bathing Suits!" is *National's* black leatherette carry-all case, with "white enameled waterproof cloth lining." At 10 inches high, 11 inches wide, and 4 1/2 inches deep, it's just the right size for a bathing suit, slippers, a small purse, and a Kodak camera! Fronts are "decorated in attractive colored assorted designs". (1926)

One might wonder how many guys faked "drowning" to get such a beautiful lifeguard to come to the rescue. She wears a similar pair of beach slippers! Snapshot, ca. 1926.

Men's Day and Sports Wear Fashions,
& Children's Fashions,
1925-1930

Men's Fashions

Chapters One and Four of our companion book, *Roaring '20s Fashion: Jazz*, covered the history of men's clothes leading up to men's fashions of the twenties—including the influence of the decade's male fashion icon, the Prince of Wales. In this book, covering the second half of the decade, you'll note that men's fashions had changed dramatically, due in large part to his influence. They were becoming much more like men's fashions of today, with roomier jackets and wider pants. We will see men's clothes continue to grow ever more casual, as sports clothes come to the fore.

Charles Lindbergh—
Hero of the Decade!

Charles A. Lindbergh's historic transatlantic flight is one of the most important events of the twentieth century. At 7:52 a.m. on May 20, 1927, Lindbergh, a civilian airmail pilot, took off from Roosevelt Field in Long Island in his single engine plane, *The Spirit of St. Louis*. He was one of many pilots hoping to win a prize that had been offered by hotel magnate Raymond Orteig in 1919, $25,000 to the first person to fly non-stop from New York to Paris. Flying both non-stop and solo, Lindbergh flew some 3500 miles, fighting fog, sleet, and fatigue, with only a compass and airspeed indicator to guide him.

Millions listened breathlessly to radio reports, then passed word on "town crier" style to everyone they saw; in cities and towns, stores set up banners and maps with pins to mark his progress. Every sighting brought rejoicing; he was spotted over Nova Scotia and then Newfoundland... but then came agonizing hours with no word at all, until at last he was seen near the coast of Ireland (at one point, he saw fishing boats and flew low to try to get the fishermen to point to Ireland!). He circled the Eiffel Tower before approaching the lights of LeBourget Field, and touched down on May 21, at 10:22 p.m., amazed to see 100,000 jubilant Frenchmen screaming *VIVE!* His incredible flight had taken thirty-three hours and thirty minutes.

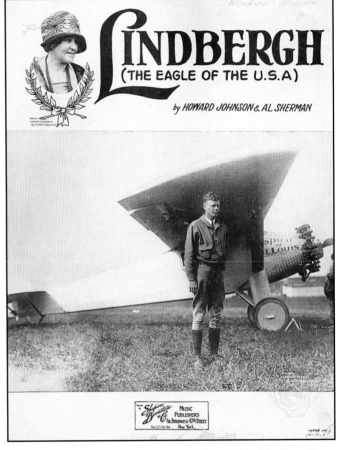

Sheet music, 1927, "Lindbergh (The Eagle of the U.S.A.)," by Howard Johnson and Al Sherman. The cover features Underwood & Underwood's famous photo of Lucky Lindy beside the plane that was almost a part of him, the *Spirit of St. Louis*. At upper left, Lindbergh's mother, Evangeline, looks on anxiously (that photo was taken at a press interview a few days before his historic flight). Partial Lyrics:

In the cold gray dawn, when the stars were gone
In a mighty aeroplane, Flew a boy in search of fame
Far across the bounding main,
Like a bird on high out to do or die...
Many million hearts beat for him,
And the whole world said a prayer for
Lindbergh – Oh! What a Wonder Boy is he
Lindbergh, his name will live in History,
Over the ocean he flew all alone,
Gambling with Fate, and with dangers unknown
Others may make that trip across the sea Upon some future day
But take your hats off to Plucky Charlie Lindbergh
The Eagle of the U.S.A.!

"Charlie Lindbergh" models an early leather aviator's cap labeled Slote & Klein. $75-$125 (Our Charlie is a male hatter's mannequin, reproduced from an original period mold by DecoEyes!

On his return to America, jubilant crowds welcomed Lindy wherever he went. New York City had its biggest tickertape ever... and every boy longed to be like a hero like Lindy.

This daring young "Lindy" prepares for takeoff in a splendid model plane named *THE SPIRIT OF CHILDHOOD*. He's wearing an aviator's helmet just like his hero's. Snapshot, ca. 1927.

By September, a new dance had been introduced – The Lindy Hop. Harlem's famous Savoy Ballroom claimed that it was first performed there by George "Shorty" Snowden, who when asked what the dance was called, replied, "It's the Lindy Hop – We're Flyin' Like Lindy"! The Lindy Hop, with its breakaway steps, is considered the first Swing dance.

Though Lindy was young and handsome, he was not a fashion plate on the order of the Prince of Wales— after his amazing flight, however, his dashing aviator's breeches were adopted by both men and women.

This photo postcard of Lindbergh and his mother, Evangeline, taken a few days before his flight, offers a fine view of Lindy's famous breeches. Evangeline, though a lady who believed that a public show of emotion was unseemly, appears distraught as she clutches her purse. Note her marvelous fur-trimmed coat, and rather flamboyant flowered cloche!

You'll be as dashing as Lucky Lindy in *National's* "Durable Whipcord Breeches in cotton twill whipcord," with "leg patches of soft suede leather and double seat of self-material to insure long wear... buttoned below knees, full cut; well tailored. They're worn with oxfords and leather puttees. (1927).

In addition to whipcord ("a strongly twilled cotton fabric that stands the hardest kind of wear"), breeches came in "tough, heavy duck;" moleskin (a very strong cotton with firmly woven outer surface and soft fleecing inside); water-repellant corduroy ("nothing wears like a good corduroy!"); and wool melton Army surplus: "U.S. Army all wool Melton, tailored to meet U.S. Army standards, points of strain securely bartacked to prevent ripping." Breeches either laced or buttoned from the knees and were reinforced with "double seats and leg patches."

And breeches weren't just for aviators... they'd earned their bold reputation during WWI, and during the twenties were especially popular with former Doughboys. As *National Style Book* advised, they're worn by "campers, surveyors, mechanics, in fact every out-of-doors man will find plenty of use for these breeches!"

Riding

Of course, breeches are also mandatory attire for riding, as this Brooks Brothers ad illustrates...

Breeches for "The Horseman"! *Brooks Brothers* carries "Complete and Correct Equipment for Hunting, etc." The uninitiated may send for their helpful pamphlet, *Hunting Hints for the Novice*!(Ad, *Country Life*, 10/27)

Knickers or "Plus-fours"

Though a pair Lindbergh breeches were a must, knickers remained favorites for sport and casual wear, though they were now much baggier—by the second half of the decade, they were PLUS-FOURS! As early as the 1923 National Open, scouts for the prestigious *Men's Wear* magazine reported that the snappiest professional golfers were wearing knickers that hung a full four inches below their knees (another fad started by the Prince of Wales), and by mid-decade, these "Plus-Fours" had become the rage. Even more extreme models were worn too – in 1925, *Men's Wear* scouts at the smartest resorts reported spotting Ivy Leaguers in "Plus-Sixes" and even "Plus-Eights"!

There was quite a controversy as to whether plus-fours should be center creased; most are shown creased, although *Men's Wear* advised: "the absence of the crease gives the correct informal, nonchalant, country sport effect". Favorite fabrics include wool tweeds, flannels, and "cassimere"; and, "When real warm weather comes, linen knickers, plain white or checked, are both popular and practical... they launder to perfection, for they're Real Linen – every thread!" Palm Beach cloth knickers were also hot weather favorites.

Button-down shirts and sweaters were often paired with plus-fours; ties were sometimes omitted. Sweaters include V or round "cricket" necks, sleeveless sweater vests, and cardigans. Patterned jacquards (Fair Isles) and argyles were most desirable, and these jazzy sweaters were often offered with matching golf socks. By mid-decade, many stores have departments for golf clothes and accessories, and they're prominently featured in period catalogs.

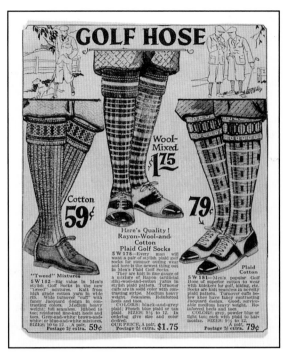

The 1927 *National Style Book's* illustration of the latest golf hose and shoes. Left to right: "New tweed mixture cotton golf socks with wide Jacquard (Fair Isle style) turnover cuffs," worn with classic leather oxfords; "Stylish plaid golf socks" in a rayon-wool-cotton blend that "Every man will want for summer outing wear" (worn with snappy two tone saddle oxfords); and "Plaid cotton golf hose with Jacquard or Fair Isle style turnover cuffs," worn with smart two-tone golf oxfords with wing tip vamps.

Step through time and onto the links of 1927. Four snazzy golfers pose at the Country Club in baggy plus fours, sweaters, and snappy golf socks (note those jazzy argyle socks on the golfer at far right – "what every man will want!"). The man second from right wears a smart Fair Isle sweater with a round neck and open shirt. Note their golf shoes—the two men at right wear snappy two-tone saddle oxfords. By mid-decade, many golf shoes now have spikes (visible on the golfer at far left). Photo by Cazarnick Commercial Photographers, 5005 Euclid Ave., Cleveland, Tel: Randolph 7852

For the golf enthusiast – a "Glossary of Golf Terms," appearing in *Life Magazine's* April 26, 1928, issue:

GOLF WIDOW: A woman whose husband has succumbed to the deadly bite of the golf bug and gone in for

GOLF: a health-building game for which virile men get up at 4 a.m. and render themselves unfit for a day at the office by too much application to the

PUTTER: Variant of "putter," to trifle or idle away the time after the manner of a confirmed golfer or a

CADDY: A youth incapable of finding a golf ball until its owner has left the vicinity of the

GOLF LINKS: The links which chain the slaves of the

GOLF HABIT: The peculiar dress worn by golf addicts, knee trousers being used to indicate the tendency toward returning childishness; sometimes affected by the

STARTER: An embryo politician accustoming himself to the reception of bribes, especially at the

NINETEENTH HOLE: The hole where you never miss a putt, particularly if it's coming from some other party's

LOCKER: A repository for beverages much stronger than

TEE: The thing you always knock out from under the ball if somebody stops to watch your stroke.

By Asia Kagowan

Swagger plus-four knickers in a checked wool flannel, with buckles to adjust the cuffs, and, of course, a button fly. These knickers are old store stock from Eagle Trousers, New York, as their original store label attests. They were originally priced at $4.95; Now, $150-$200. (They're worn with a period striped shirt and red tie, and a bit later Pringle Argyll sweater.)

Bellas Hess offered this trig "Sweater and Hose Set," with "Wool Overplaid Cassimere Golf Knickers!" It was described as: "Sport outdoor set for the man who golfs or hikes or just enjoys outdoor comfort. Set consists of sweater and golf hose to match. Knit of fine high grade all worsted yarns with striped Jacquard (Fair Isle type) design interknit with contrasting colored yarns. Cricket neck, cuffs, hip bands, and hose tops have attractive striped finish. You could not select a better looking Sport Outfit than this one and you are getting a wonderful value besides"! (Note that at fine men's shops, authentic Fair Isle sweaters might sell for between $35-$50.)

The "Swagger Golf Knickers" are: "...golf knickers cut on swagger lines that will give you wonderful service for the money. Cut extra full from excellent quality all-wool cassimere, the kind that can stand a lot of knockabout sport wear and yet always show up smartly in a well dressed crowd!" Looking on is Warner Bros.' canine star, Rin-Tin-Tin, who in 1927 starred in *A Dog of the Regiment*.

Closeup the blue checked flannel fabric and buckle fastening.

Sweater and Hose Set All Worsted 15K373 $6.75

All Wool Overplaid Cassimere Golf Knickers 49K690 $4.25

As this wonderful vintage photo indicates, plus-fours weren't just worn for golf, but for all types of casual wear. This jaunty gent proudly parades them on the sidewalks of New York. Snapshot, 1927.

Style Changes 1925-1930

Men's clothing as well as women's exhibited style changes during the second half of the decade... clothing grew ever more modern as men's fashions made the transition from "Snug" to "Snappy"! The emphasis was on comfort. Colors were more vivid and patterns bolder.

"Oxford Bags" Trousers

During the second half of the decade, men of all ages adopted the full cut trousers that replaced the rather short, tight-fitting trousers worn in the early twenties. This trend towards full trousers was evident in period catalogs as early as 1924—and by 1925 it exploded with the arrival of the famed "English Oxford Bags." Wanamaker's New York store introduced Oxford bags to America with an electrifying ad, announcing:

> *The trousers that have created such a furore in England. Originated by the students at Oxford, they are worn in many places by young men of fashion 20-25 inches wide at foot... almost as wide at the knee. Fashioned after the English style with high-cut waistline and pleats in front... May be worn with braces but equipped with belt loops and side straps and buckles as a concession to the American habit.*

Soon even rather conservative period catalogs showed trousers ranging from 17" - 20" around the cuffs. They enticed the young (and young at heart) with such descriptive words as "Swagger," "Spiffy," and "Collegiate," offering: "...just the type of trousers that the swagger college youth like!" Of course, most ads mentioned the all-important "English" cut and/or "English Style; well made, high grade all wool cassimere trousers cut on extreme English lines with 20" bottoms. These trousers are of the exclusive style that is seen in Fifth Avenue shops!" (*Bellas Hess*, 1925-26)

The vast majority of trousers in catalogs of the second half of the decade had unpleated waists, though by 1928 a few pleated "collegiate" models were seen, described as "All the rage-smartly pleated pants...!" *Chicago Mail Order* pictured a snappy double breasted suit, with "...trousers have that added swagger which comes of Piccadilly Pleats at the waistline...!" Most trousers were shown cuffed, but uncuffed

6 K 5672—Waist 28 to 36 ins.; Inseam 28 to 34 inches. All the rage—smartly pleated pants of shape-retaining, dressy, neat looking All Wool Cassimere, in herringbone weave. Have belt loops, suspender buttons, wide legs, cuffed bottoms. COLORS — Blue-gray mixture, or Light Brown mixture. Please state size, color. $3.95 Send post. for 1 ¹²/₁₆ lbs.

"All the Rage!"... baggy trousers with "SMART NEW PLEATS!" Though the vast majority of twenties trousers are unpleated, the original Oxford Bags advertised by Wanamaker's in 1925 had pleated waists; evidently it took a while for pleated versions to become popular enough for conservative catalogs. (*Chicago Mail Order* 28-9)

trousers were also available, though they were generally pictured on mature men.

It is also important to note that though plus-four knickers were King of the Course, as early as 1925 men's fashion scouts had noted a new trend—long lightweight flannel trousers, "plain or with stripes," were popping up on the golf links at the smartest summer resorts.

I Scream-You Scream – We All Scream for ICE CREAM! These great graphics illustrate the screaming popularity of both the Ice Cream Cone *and* wide Oxford Bag Trousers!
The chorus, "Brightly", goes:
> *I scream, you scream, We all scream for Ice Cream*
> *RAH! RAH! RAH!*
> *Tuesdays, Mondays We all scream for Sundaes*
> *SISS! BOOM! BAH!*
> *Boo-la Boo-la - Sas-pa-ROO-la!*
> *If you've got Choc-o-LET*
> *We'll take Va-NOO-la!*

By Howard Johnson, Billy Moll and Robert King (coincidentally, in 1925 a different Howard Johnson was starting a new business – with 28 Original Flavors of ICE CREAM!)

97

Sports Coats and Flannel Slacks

Classic sports coats and flannel slacks were more popular than ever in the second half of the decade.

Three pairs of *unpleated* "Bags" from *National Bellas Hess*, with snappy ad copy:
41X629, Genuine mohair – ideal for summer! There's nothing so practical, cool and comfortable for summer wear as these striped Genuine mohair trousers. The crisp woven fabric sheds the dust and does not wrinkle... you can look trim and dapper on the most trying 'dog days' (note the golf bag!) 41X698: Striped trousers that "...need no introduction to you for they are well tailored of the Genuine Palm Beach Cloth known the world over – a crisp, cool, close-woven wool worsted and cotton fabric. Pictured at right (41X701) are the most popular sports trousers of the decade – Baggy White Flannels: "For Dress Wear with Dark Coat!... Follow the swagger dressy style for summer by getting our famous high grade All-Wool White Flannel Trousers!" (1928)

This elegant gent wears the twenties' favorite sports "uniform" – white flannels and navy double-breasted jacket, with snappy Spectator or "Co-respondent" oxfords. The lady at left wears the woman's version of this stylish oxford, and both gals wear scarves tied over one shoulder, Deauville style. (Camels ad, R.J. Reynolds Tobacco Co. 1929).

This classic men's combo is still popular today—it's been a favorite since the birth of trousers in Beau Brummel's day! By the mid-twenties, catalogs are offering separate sports coat/trouser combinations; they also offer suits with an additional pair of light flannels at "a small extra charge." Note that although men's fashion commentators report that "sharp dressed men" have several separate sports coats in their wardrobes, many men simply continue to wear their dark suit coats with light flannels.

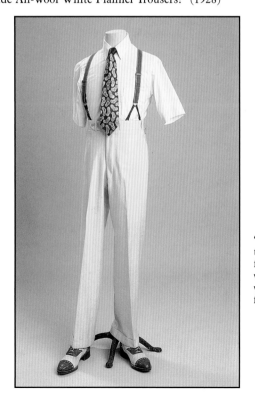

"Every young chap wants a pair of white flannel trousers!"—and this pair of "swagger, dressy style white flannel trousers" is cuffed to a full 23"! Unpleated 30" waist, with both belt loops and buttons inside for those who prefer suspenders. Popular two-button waistband; four-button fly closure. $100-$200

No wonder this popular combo was all the rage! Our full cut white flannels are paired with a sharp double-breasted navy pinstriped suit coat (see next image). The snazzy spectator oxfords are a perfect compliment.

"This is the correct costume for summer dress or sports occasions!" *Bellas Hess* offers this natty combo, priced separately, noting that the "High Grade Navy Blue All Wool Flannel Coat" is a "shapely double-breasted model, beautifully hand tailored... just the coat for dress or sport wear with flannel trousers"! The contrasting trousers are "splendidly tailored English cut, wide all wool flannel trousers for dress or sport wear... in this soft shade of grey they look very smart when worn with coat, with wide 19" cuffs." (1926)

Note that though double-breasted sports coats were considered the smartest, single-breasted sport jackets were also worn. Navy blue was favored, but many men opted for camel gabardine – or various shades of grey, green, and brown. In 1928, *Men's Wear* observed: "The standard dark blue that has so long been associated with jackets for wear with white flannels is overshadowed by brighter hues." Ivy League trend setters were wearing brightly colored jackets with their flannels – even "Robin's Egg Blue." While flannel fabrics were favored, gabardines, tweeds, worsteds, and sharkskins were also worn.

Eddie, dressed to swagger in a dark sports coat, baggy white flannels, snap-brim fedora, and co-respondent shoes, steps on the running board of *Our Chevie*. Snapshot, ca. 1927-30.

Perforated and pinked – these are a fine example of "Co-respondent" Spectator Oxfords. Two-tone oxfords have stepped from a shoe made exclusively for sports to a true fashion statement. Favorite combinations include brown and white, black and white, and red and white. This pair is old store stock. Custom made in China, they're labeled "*Leung Yau*". $200-$300

Blazers

Nautical blazers were yet another favorite with sharp dressed men. They had created quite a stir at England's fashionable Henley Regatta in 1924, as *Men's Wear* noted. The blazer was considered a bit jazzier type of sports coat—it is a classic that was originally adapted by English civilians from Victorian sailors' jackets. The traditional Blazer is navy blue with brass buttons—some collegiate blazers featured club insignia.

Suits

By the second half of the decade, suits were cut with fuller, looser lines—the "Stylish English Lines" introduced by the Prince of Wales. Due to his influence, many stores and catalogs during second half of decade emphasized English tailoring:

> *What young man doesn't desire to be known as the best dresser in his set?... This is one of those natty looking suits that the smartly dressed man is so proud to wear. It's a real beauty, cut on shapely PRINCE OF WALES lines... with single breasted English Cut sack coat, blunt bottom vest and Extra Wide Prince of Wales Trousers!* (*Bellas Hess* 1926).

Suit jackets now boasted "broad shoulders, deep chest, moderately defined waist and snug hips". Both single and double-breasted styles were worn, though the double-breasted was considered the smartest - as *National's* proclaimed in 1925: "The double breasted suit has come into its own this year and you can see... how smartly the younger fellows can wear this English Style". Lapels were wider on both styles (generally, between three and four inches). They're typically described: "Coat has the new wide Semi-peeked Lapels that help to give the broad-shouldered look... lapels are rolled to the second button..." Some suit jackets had a "plain back with no vent"; others had a "short, straight vent in back". Vests are pictured with both single- and double-breasted suits.

Suits were often offered in combinations: with two pairs of trousers, with trousers and knickers, or with an additional pair of flannel trousers. *National Style Book*, for example, offered a "Navy blue serge suit with light grey wool flannels, $5.75 extra."

Closeup of Sambro's label, with its jazzy jockey logo.

Suit's full cut trousers were generally between 17-22 inches around the bottom – and though the majority of trousers were shown cuffed, suits were advertised with "bottoms straight or cuffed as desired."

The craze for the flannel suit is yet another trend attributed to the Prince of Wales—on a 1923 visit to America, he made an indelible impact in a double-breasted gray flannel suit with white stripes, lapels that were 3 3/4" wide, and a broad tie with a double "Windsor" knot. Snappy Glenurquhart or "Glen plaids" also became popular after the Prince of Wales introduced them. Favorite suit fabrics included wool tweeds, worsteds, serges, cheviots, lightweight mohairs, and "cassimeres" – and "For the Dog Days of Summer" – linens, cottons, and of course the famous Palm Beach cloth.

The Two Piece Double Breasted Suit

"Here's the double breasted suit that New York's Well Dressed Men are demanding... you'll notice the correct style touches that all the younger fellows want this season!" This impeccably tailored navy blue double-breasted pinstripe suit is from Sambro Clothier of Louisville, Kentucky. It boasts broad shoulders, 3 3/4 inch lapels, two flap pockets, a welt breast pocket, and inside breast pocket. The back is not vented. The full cut trousers have 21" cuffs; the waist is unpleated. $300-$500

The two favorite suit styles of the second half of the decade are illustrated by *Bellas Hess:*

The Double-breasted Suit (50K825):

Every smartly dressed young man these days must have a double breasted suit in order to feel that he's keeping up to the minute in appearance... this remarkable example is a splendidly hand tailored model of high grade diagonal weave all wool cheviot in the most desirable shades of grey or navy blue. English cut vest... the shapely wide cut English Trousers may be ordered with or without cuffed bottoms.

The Single-breasted Suit (50K826):

A popular Broadway tailor turned out this natty business suit and sold it for $80! We of copied it in every detail... with our immense buying power it cost us far less than it would have cost the Broadway tailor. Available with or without cuff bottoms. Shapely two-button coat; nicely fitted regular cut vest. (1926)

A delightful example of sartorial splendor! This elegant trio performs under the palms – the vocalist attired in a snappy double-breasted suit, the pianist in a double-breasted jacket and white flannels. Snapshot, ca. 1925-30.

Hats

By mid-decade, the *SNAP BRIM FEDORA* has become *THE* hat of the sharp dressed man!

The Broadway... "Genuine 'class' in a snap-brimmed hat... in Bud Grey or Aloe Tan!" (*Chicago Mail Order*, 1929)

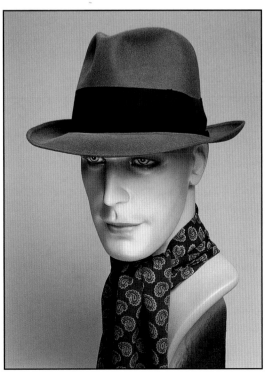

"Borsalino – The World's Finest" – A classic grey felt snap brim fedora with a wide grosgrain ribbon band and button/safety cord. Snap brims from this prestigious Italian firm command the highest prices. $150-$250

The Borsalino label. Note that the white satin lining is not protected with plastic at this time.

The Single-breasted Three Piece Suit

Just as dashing as the gent in the *Bellas Hess* ad, this natty Ivy Leaguer poses in a sharp pinstriped, three piece vested suit. Snapshot, 1929.

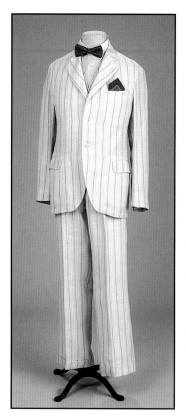

The *ULTIMATE* summer suit! Impeccable tailoring marks this fine three-piece single-breasted suit with fitted vest. The fabric is superb – the finest Irish linen with woven vertical stripes, both a nubby-textured white stripe and a flat medium blue stripe. The "shapely two-button coat" features two flap pockets and a welt pocket; the sleeve cuffs have two pearl buttons. The back is seamed down the center and is not vented. All seams are finely topstitched. The trousers have stylish 21" wide cuffs and all the requisite pockets, including a watch pocket; the waistband has belt loops and suspender buttons. The fly fastens with five bakelite buttons. It's worn with a blue pinstriped shirt with detachable collar, and we've added a contemporary red paisley bow tie (L.L. Bean) and silk pocket handkerchief for a splash of color! Suit, $500-$600

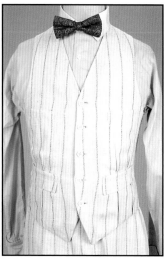

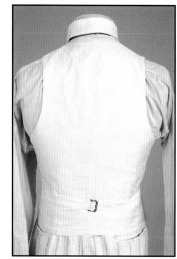

Far left:
A closeup of the jacket, which is unlined to allow a cool summer breeze to pass through.

Center:
So very *SWAGGER* – The Vest! This pointed vest is cleverly fitted via pleats at the flapped waistline pockets; it also has two welt chest pockets. Front closure with five pearl buttons.

Left:
While the vest front is lined in polished cotton, the back of the vest is plain white polished cotton. It's adjustable at the waistline via buckled tabs.

The inside pocket label: *Exclusive Linen Importations, Belfast Crash, Rd. U.S. Pat. Off.* Note the fine linen pinstriped fabric.

An additional label, at the back of the collar, warns: "This suit <u>MUST NOT</u> be washed in BOILING WATER"(it was washable in tepid water).

The perfect compliment to our fine Irish Linen Suit – a Panama Snap-Brim with a texture so fine it resembles linen! It's stamped on the sweatband: Supernatural, Reg. U.S. Pat. Off., Ecuadorian Panama Hat Co. New York, Genuine Panama, and The Willard Shop, Stoneleigh Court, Washington, D.C. It features the typical central crown ridge; its original black grosgrain crown band is one inch high. $150-$200

Vests

Vests made a fashion statement of their own during the second half of the decade, imparting that all-important *SWAGGER!* The new "asymmetric" vests are the *Bees Knees!*

Chicago Mail Order offers the natty cheviot suit at right (B), which comes with a new reversible asymmetric vest. Known for their provocative ad copy, *Chicago* boasts:

See that "sizzling hot" vest. Ain't nobody in town going to have anything jazz-er. Wear it with the light side out when you want to look your 'snappiest' – turn the dark side out for less dressy occasions.

This suit is fashioned of "a swagger Navy blue wool cheviot in a faint herringbone weave... the Nobby trousers, PLEATED to give a peg-top effect, have 20-inch cuffed bottoms." (1929)

Note that the vest with the single breasted suit at left (A), is cut straight across rather than pointed; both vests have asymmetric closures and very wide lapels. The ad copy trumpets: "A Big Style Hit in New York – The Double-breasted VEST!... There is nothing smarter than the double-breasted vest!"

Exuding sex appeal, heartthrob Rudolph Valentino poses ca. 1926 in a very smart white vest, cut with the popular asymmetric front; it's banded diagonally and trimmed with a diamond pin.

Men's Shoes

"There's nothing like a pair of new shoes to 'perk' a man up, and these lively brogues... are certain to sweeten up your wardrobe as well as your viewpoint!" (1927 *Chicago Mail Order*)

As this illustration from the 1927 *National Style Book* shows, square-toed shoes were "Nobby" during the second half of the decade.

A LEADER IN STYLE, QUALITY AND LOW PRICE

Feature Value $3.48

Calf-Finished Leather Goodyear Welt
630 W 3627—Tan.   630 W 3629—Black.
One of the best shoe values in years! Men's Genuine GOODYEAR WELT Lace Oxford of sturdy Calf-finished Leather on a new square toe last. Notice the smart new stitching on tip, vamp and quarter—and the soft boxed toe. Well made. Grain leather innersole; guaranteed counter; leather quarter lining. Attached rubber heel. Good quality leather sole attached by the genuine Goodyear welt process.
SIZES: 5 to 12; widths D and E.
EACH PAIR. $3.48
Postage each pair 12¢ extra.

These spectacular custom made Italian suede and calf leather oxfords are the snappiest square toes around! With spiffy "saw" edges and plenty of perforations, they're sure to perk up even the unperkiest man! They're stamped on the sole Enith, Made in Italy, and on the insole: Volare Exclusive, Paulo Leoni(?). Original rayon laces (missing brass tips). Expensive then (perhaps around $40-$50) – and now, $300-$400.

Men's Shirts

Shirts were bolder too in the second half of the decade – in vivid colors, stripes, plaids, and patterns. The detached collar was beginning to wane as more men opted for shirts with attached collars – either plain turnovers or button-downs.

National's shirts for 1927 – "Styled in the New York Manner." Bold stripes and brighter colors are shown, with both separate and attached collars. Note the four-in-hand ties shown are worn rather short!

Ties

Ties kept pace with the latest trends and also made more of a statement—they were more colorful, bigger, and bolder! Four-in-hands were wider as were sporty bow ties. While many men still preferred "tie your own" bow ties, pre-tied styles were gaining ground.

A nice selection of the wider four-in-hand ties in art deco prints and jazzy stripes.

Spur Tie's "Smart Bow Ties"! Their copy boasts:
Nature-made beauty: Mt. Rainier, seen in the distance. Man-made beauty: Spur Tie, seen everywhere. ... expert feminine fingers fashion and shape each Spur Tie in the making. At Haberdashery counters everywhere! (*Saturday Evening Post*, October 1, 1927)

Bow ties: at left, a tie your own in a magnificent Deco tropical print; at right, a wide pre-tied "Tux" tie in black silk faille. Tropical print, $45-$55; black bow tie, $35-45.

Men's Underwear, 1925-30

During the second half of the decade, both one-piece combination "union suits" and separate undershirts and drawers continued to be worn. RAYON tricot knit union suits were new; they dried in a minute—a 1928 *Men's Wear* article stated that a man wearing a rayon union suit could "stand under the shower in it, soap it well and wash it then and there while on his body... then rinse and hang it up and it would be dry before he'd had time to dry himself!" The forerunners of modern men's shorts or briefs appeared as "Running pants"—and sleeveless "athletic" undershirts were also very popular.

"Shaving"

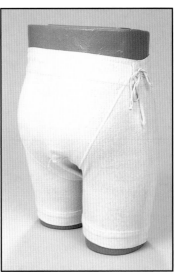

"Shaving," ca. 1927! This man is wearing an athletic knit undershirt—these sleeveless undershirts are still popular today, now called "Beaters." Note the old-fashioned shaving brush over the sink—our guy's using a straight razor!

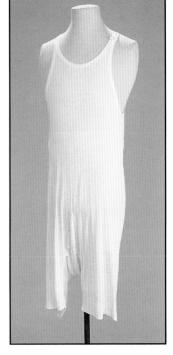

A new Athletic One-piece Union Suit in quick-drying (and very sensuous) rayon tricot knit. It fastens at the left shoulder with a mother of pearl button. Label: *The Globe, Tailor Made, Size 42.* $45-$75

The Sultan of Swat endorses "Babe Ruth All America Athletic Underwear"! Babe Ruth, the idol of millions, was one of the first sports stars to promote products. The Bambino made headlines on October 1, 1927, as the *New York Times* headlined, "Home Run Record Falls as Ruth Hits 60th". Babe had topped his own home run record! In 1919, the Boston Red Sox had sold Babe to the Yankees, beginning the famous "Curse of the Bambino," which endured for eighty-six years – until the Red Sox beat the Yankees in the 2004 World Series.

The two most popular underwear choices from the 1928 *National Bellas Hess* catalog: A one-piece "Fine and Cool Athletic Union Suit" and the new two-piece Athletic separates – a sleeveless undershirt and "Running Pants" briefs. The "Decidedly New and Different" athletic undershirt is: "The latest idea in a 'classy' athletic style undershirt of brilliant, silky Rayon..."; it's offered in white, flesh-pink or blue. The briefs are: "Men's Track, Athletic or Running Pants of genuine English broadcloth... Adjustable laced tabs at waistline". They were available in white, blue or tan.

The latest in comfort – "Athletic" running shorts! These clingy, stretchy cotton jersey knit shorts are forerunners of today's briefs or "jockey" shorts. They have a flat-seamed front fly placket, and a cotton broadcloth waistband that adjusts via gusset inserts with ties on each side. There is no label present, just a size tag, "38." These shorts are never worn old store stock. $45-$75

In back, diagonal seaming contours the buttocks.

Men's Pajamas, 1925-30

Men's pajamas also made more of a fashion statement in the second half of the decade, as period advertisements claimed, they're not merely for sleeping now, but "For Lounging."

Label: *ZARA, B.D. Galata Saray, Istanbul.*

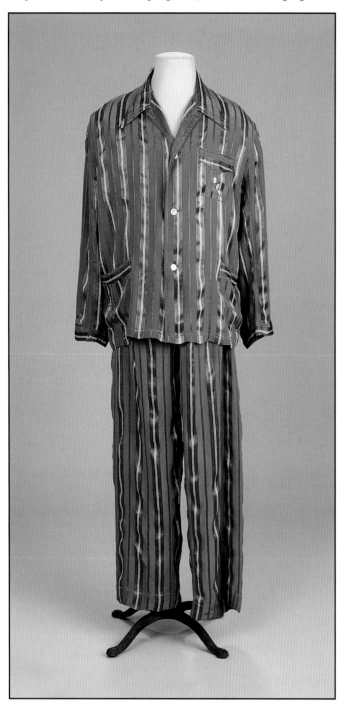

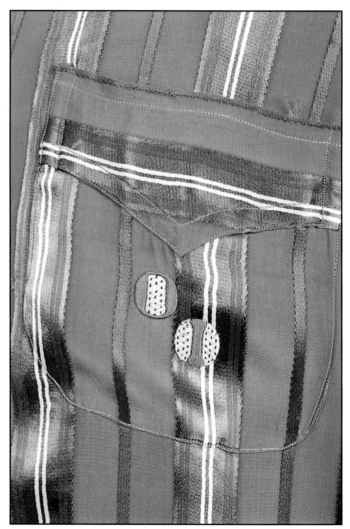

Sexy as a Sheik's – "Oriental" Lounging Pajamas! These exotic lounging pajamas from Zara of Istanbul are just the ticket for a seductive scene on the *Orient Express*. They're a rich rayon satin that's as plush as a Pasha's, with woven stripes in bold blue, red, and white. The top is smartly styled with a spread collar and front closure with four pearl buttons. There are plenty of pockets—two patch pockets and a chest "cigarette" pocket with an embroidered logo: O - I. The pants have a two pearl-button fly and a self-fabric drawstring (though note that period catalogs also show pajamas with elastic waistbands at this time). $150-$200

Closeup of chest pocket with logo, "O - I", and the luxurious striped fabric.

Boy's Wear, 1925-30

Older Boys' Styles

Boy's wear, like men's, was roomier and more comfortable in the second half of the decade. For dressy occasions, older boys wore suits with long pants or "Longies"—like Dad's, they were "styled with a mannish cut that all boys like!" They were often offered with matching knickers. Older boys' sizes were generally 8-17. For play, older boys' favorites were shirts, sweaters, and knickers.

Younger Boys' Styles

For summer playwear, boys about three to eight wore rough and tumble "wash" suits that were practical, comfortable, and colorful. You will note the sailor or "middy" suit remains a favorite. Many of these suits came with both long and short pants.

The 1927 *National Style Book* offers a great selection of boys' wear that "Will stand lots of hard wear". Their sharp double-breasted suit (A) is styled just like Dad's...

You'll be proud of your boy when he wears this special "boy-proof suit" with longies and plus-four knicker pants! The smart double-breasted coat is an English model in the season's correct style. Notice the three-button closing with correct wide notch lapels rolled to the second button. The handsome all wool fancy weave cassimere showing a tasteful "Overplaid" is a long wearing fabric found only in the better grade of boys' suits. Sizes 9 to 18 years.

Note that the suit jacket is often belted only in back now.

Wash suits are well represented—note the profusion of snappy plaids and stripes! Fig. D, similar to the green striped wash suit opposite, is described as: "A smart wash suit with plaid pattern waist (shirt); buttoned-on straight pants of solid color; sport collar and cuffs are solid collar. Novelty buckled sport belt. Sizes 3-8." And, as you'll note, there's several versions of the perennially popular sailor suit, in styles with both long and short pants.

Though oxfords and one-strap shoes are popular, boys generally wear high top shoes as Moms think they strengthen the ankles. My uncle Leon reports that when he was a boy, the high tops that all the boys wanted had a knife pocket—he remembers how disappointed he was when his mother said he couldn't have a pair (she told him they'd make him look like a little Cossack).

Jack Tar label, and closeup of the linen fabric.

School's out for summer – and "Joe" is wearing a smart striped linen wash suit that's perfect for play! It's about a size 6, and bears the popular "Jack Tar" label. It features a separate self belt, breast welt pocket, and roomy pants pockets (the fly is not buttoned, but a simple placket opening) $50-$75

National Bellas Hess offers "This big husky Scout Boot that ALL THE BOYS ARE WILD ABOUT! ... with a specially built pocket in the side of every pair, containing a good solid steel 2-inch blade knife" perfect for a rousing game of "Mumbly-Peg"! (1928)

Little brother "Jimmy" models a spiffy salmon color "dressy wash suit" in cotton gabardine. The shirt features a contrasting blue linen collar and front inset plackets topped with decorative pockets. It has a front closure with small pearl buttons. The short, straight pants button to the top; the buttons are hidden by the separate self belt. Hidden fly placket. Label: *Joseph Horne Co., Pittsburgh.* $50-$75

These two future Ivy Leaguers, dressed in snappy double-breasted "Plus-Four" knicker suits similar to *National's* "A" (top center), pose with their bicycles, ca. 1927.

Dressed in comfortable wash suits, and looking like they just stepped out of a *Spanky and Our Gang* movie, these three youngsters show off their jazzy new auto! Glass negative print, ca. 1925.

Girl's Wear, 1925-30

Older Girls' Styles

Older girl's wore styles that echoed their moms – frocks that were short and smart, but a bit more modest as befitting a young lady. As *Vogue* advised:

> *A frock designed for a young teen girl should incorporate such grownup features as the bolero, tiers and scallops, but should be modified to make it suitable for the young miss. She should wear more modest and unassuming styles than women. The junior miss may have a robe de style, but in a modified version... Exposure to chic now will extend into adulthood.* (1927)

The 1927 *National Style Book* pictures "New York's Smartest Styles, Sizes 7-14 Years"! Note the features' Moms also favor; flares, vestees, boleros, "Chanel" streamers, and, of course, dropped waists, some shirred, some with triangular points or scallops.

A summer frock for a girl of about twelve, in a charming voile print of sprigged blue flowers. Its dropped waistline is formed of rows of smart "shirring"; the contrasting white organdy collar and cuffs are piped in the same blue print. Fashionable fluttering streamers float from the collar's bright blue grosgrain bow. This dress is home sewn from fabric like that offered by *National's* in the following advertisement. $75-$125

"2 YARDS MAKE A DRESS"! Dainty sprigged prints in batiste and voile offered by *National Style Book* in 1927.

Kewpies were the "children" of Rose O'Neill – artist, author, suffragist, and leader of Greenwich Village society. After her Kewpie illustrations debuted in the December 1909 issue of *Ladies Home Journal*, these little imps soon won a place in everyone's heart. In 1913, Rose patented the Kewpie Doll, and by the twenties every little girl had at least one.

Closeup of the sheer piped collar and sweet sprigged print!

This charming young "mommy" has her hands full with her three lively Kewpie babies! Many young girls learned to sew by making clothes for dollies – with Mom or Grandma lending a hand!

Kewpie shows off her chic printed voile frock, which features a shirred neckline, dropped waist, and a skirt replete with picot-edged ruffled tiers. It may have been made by some little mama for her favorite Kewpie with skill and love—and some help from Mom! Beneath she wears a rayon tricot step-in. Dress, $20-$30. Kewpie – *Priceless!* (She's 12" tall, composition with "starfish" fingers, and flirty side-glancing eyes).

Little Girls' Styles

For little girls, sizes 2 to 6, "Costumes for playtime hours are simple and cool," as *Vogue Pattern Book* (June/July 27) advised. Though many tots' dresses simply fell straight from the shoulders or a gathered yoke, some featured the chic dropped waists that mom wore. The beloved bloomer dresses remained very popular.

What girl wouldn't long for these snazzy black patent Mary Janes with art deco stitching and overlays?! $45-$55.

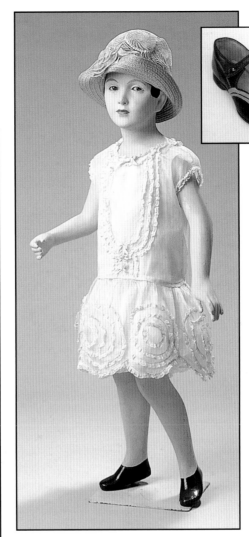

Harriet models her favorite "grown up" frock, with a modish low waist just like big sister's! The bodice is trimmed with three rows of lace for a chic vestee effect; three cream satin bows trim the neck and waist. The low waistline is self-piped and the short cap sleeves are banded with piping and also lace trimmed. The fashionable flared skirt is adorned with lace cockades and the hem is fashionably scalloped. Back pearl button fastening. Harriet's accessories include a child's cloche with a turned up straw brim and lace crown, trimmed with a grosgrain ribbon pinwheel on the right. Frock, $100-$150; Cloche, $100-$200

National's offers a wonderful variety of frocks in sizes 2-6, and coats in sizes 2-9. Many adorable bloomer dresses are shown, and there are several styles with dropped waists. Pictured at the top right (E) is a dropped waist frock that's similar to ours – it's described as a: "Girls' handmade summer Frock of sheer cotton voile embellished with colored hand-embroidery and hand-drawn (shirred) threads; ribbon sash and rosettes... in green, light blue or pink; sizes 2 to 6." Coats are also styled like big sister's, with standup "Bobby" collars. Note the jazzy "Tomato Red Slicker" at the lower right, and the two little girls' cloches at bottom.

Right:
This proud young momma holds her dolly tight – though it's almost as big as she is! Her coat is a style similar those in *National's* ad, with its luxurious fur collar and cuffs. Snapshot, ca. 1927.

Far right:
"Nancy," Arranbee's composition doll, is modeling a favorite style for little girls. Similar to many of National's frocks, it's waistless—softly gathered under the collar, it simply falls straight to the hem. Self ruffles down the sides add a "flapperish" touch; the big Peter Pan collar is edged with self ruffles and a satin bow. Nancy completes her original ensemble with a matching green ruffled cloche and Mary Jane pumps with rayon socks! A matching dress and cloche for a "real" little girl might be priced between $75-$100 today.

Chapter Four

1927 Women's Fashions

Timeline

January 7: First transatlantic telephone service, New York City to London.

The Harlem Globetrotters play their first game.

May 21: Charles "Lucky Lindy" Lindbergh touches down in the Spirit of St. Louis at Paris' *Le Bourget* airport after his historic solo transatlantic flight. He flew from Long Island to France in 33 1/3 grueling hours – braving fatigue, fog, and icing. He returns to a hero's welcome with the largest tickertape parade in New York City's history.

May 23: Philo Farnsworth transmits experimental television images at Bell Telephone in New York before 600 members of the American Institute of Electrical Engineers and the Institute of Radio Engineers.

August 23: Sacco and Vanzetti are executed in Massachusetts.

September 17: Sultan of Swat Babe Ruth hits his 60th home run off pitcher Tom Zachary of the Washington Senators; the Yanks sweep the World Series this year, winning four straight games!

November 13: At midnight, President Calvin Coolidge presides at the opening of the Holland Tunnel, which runs under the Hudson River, connecting New York and New Jersey. Named for the chief engineer, Clifford M. Holland, this amazing feat of engineering was constructed between 1920 and 1927. The first non-official vehicle to pass is a truck headed for Bloomingdales! In the first day, over 50,000 vehicles are counted; they pay a toll of $.50 cents for the eight-minute trip.

December 2: Henry Ford introduces the new Model A, which replaces the beloved Model T.

December 4: Jazz great Duke Ellington performs his "Black and Tan Fantasy" before huge crowds at Harlem's famed Cotton Club.

On the Silent Screen

The year 1927 was a banner year for films. On May 11, the American Academy of Motion Picture Arts and Sciences was formed—the first Academy Awards were for films of 1927 and 1928. It was a difficult choice between several films that are considered classics today.

Clara Bow starred with Richard Arlen and Gary Cooper in Paramount's *Wings*, a film about WWI aviators that won a Best Production award. Clara also starred in a film version of "IT." The first Academy Award for best actress went to relative newcomer Janet Gaynor for three films: *Seventh Heaven,* *Street Angel,* and *Sunrise.* Directed by F.W. Murnau, Fox's *Sunrise* is considered one of the finest silent films of all time; Miss Gaynor played the wronged wife, George O'Brien her errant husband, and Margaret Livingston the man-eating vamp. Emil Jannings won Best Actor for his performances in *The Way of All Flesh* and *The Last Command.* Greta Garbo and John Gilbert set temperatures rising in the erotic *Flesh and the Devil,* and Joan Crawford was a dancer for money in *The Taxi Dancer.* Cecil B. DeMille's classic *King of Kings* was released to great acclaim; fan Will Rogers remarked, "*There will never be a greater picture because there is no greater subject*".

"Talkies"

In October 1927, Warner Bros.'s first hit part-"Talkie", *The Jazz Singer,* debuted in Vitaphone. Starring Al Jolson, it created a sensation—it's silent up to the part where Al suddenly talks, saying: "**Wait, You Ain't Heard Nothin' Yet!**" to his mother before crooning "Blue Skies!" Warner's crowed: "At last, Pictures that Talk like Living People! ... You see and hear them act, talk, sing and play—like human beings in the flesh!" (On July 15, 1928, Warner's released *Lights of New York,* the first ALL-talking picture.)

Favorite New Recordings

Top recordings included "Lucky Lindy" by Nat Shilkret; "Stardust" by Hoagy Carmichael; "The Black Water Blues" by Bessie Smith; "50 Million Frenchmen Can't Be Wrong" by Sophie Tucker (with Miff Mole and his Little Molers); "The Sweetheart of Sigma Chi" by Ted Lewis Jazz Band; "The Varsity Drag" by Ruth Etting; and "My Blue Heaven" by Gene Austin.

In Literature

New in 1927, *The Weary Blues* by black poet Langston Hughes; *The Bridge of San Luis Rey* by Thornton Wilder; *To the Lighthouse* by Virginia Woolf; and *Something About Eve* by James Cobell.

In Fashion 1927—

Shorter and "Simpler" Still!

Vogue advised that for day, "The skirt comes to just a trifle below the knees"—while for afternoon and evening, the uneven hem was most modish! And, as *Vogue* observed, "**Sim-**

plicity has become so fundamental and permanent a part of the mode that the coming season can no longer bring sweeping changes. Women's clothes are now practical garments suited to the modern woman's life, not merely a frivolous means of increasing her charms and amusing her fancy."

Couture Trends

Nowhere was "Simplicity" more evident than in Sports fashions—and as Jean Patou declares, "**Every day one notices the influence of Sport upon clothes...**". Couture was devoting more time than ever before to sports wear; over half of the daytime showings were reserved for sports fashions that were described as "...clothes in informal, careless perfection... clothes of unconscious sophistication." Commentators advised that the new sports clothes were so smart they were now "Seen in Town."

"Ingenuity of Cut" was evident at all the famous couture houses—as "the use of diagonal lines, curved lines, and straight lines in tucks, seams and pleats" vary the mandatory simplicity. Vionnet personified "Ingenuity of cut"; she pioneered the famed bias cut which provided "the curved and diagonal line that leads the way to the new silhouette." In several of her most exquisite creations, Vionnet further emphasized her diagonal or curved lines with row upon row of incredible pintucking. Vogue highlighted Vionnet's ensemble suit in "reptile printed beige for frock and lining...", and noted her "particularly striking" almost backless bathing suit in black and green jersey, "designed with her famous geometric cut". Vogue also lauded Vionnet beach pajamas in three tones of burgundy crepe de chine, with wide "Oxford bag trousers" (imported to Lord & Taylor).

Chanel was famed for her ensembles with printed frocks that match their coordinating coat's lining; Vogue exclaimed over a Chanel beige/green print frock with a street length coat lined to match: "...this is one of Chanel's youthful, becoming and versatile models, suitable for every moment of the New York day." (January 1927) Commentators raved that nothing could be "Simpler" than Chanel's *Country Tweeds*"! Her supple Jersey frocks continued to be daytime favorites (they were introduced in the mid-teens). Her faux jewelry was more popular than ever. Stripes – horizontal, vertical, diagonal or chevron, were stronger than ever in 1927; Chanel and Patou were foremost among the couturiers showing stunningly "simple" striped sweater sets. Paired with pleated skirts that matched or contrasted, they became so popular Vogue exclaimed they were "almost a uniform of chic"! As Vogue noted, "Pleats appear on almost all sports dresses this season"; they were narrow or wide or a combination of both—and Chanel's inverted "kick" pleats "offer smart, slim lines and freedom of movement" on both sports and day wear fashions. Jenny showed "fluid frocks of silk or light wool... simple in appearance but of complicated form... (with) cutouts, fine lines, diminutive pleated and superimposed panels and transversal bands." New at Jenny was the use of lamé for morning and sports frocks (woolen fabric woven with metal threads).

The diagonal surplice line was more modish than ever—this year it was "in front, back - or both." And even necklines were diagonal, as the new "asymmetric" neckline became fashionable. Vogue noted that "Compose," the use of contrasting fabrics and/or textures in two or more shades of the same color,

"makes costumes of distinction." The rage for the bloused bodice grew stronger, and side ties and "pointed extensions" were even seen for day. Newcomer Elsa Schiaparelli opened "*Pour le Sport*" this year; she conceived the idea for the famous *Trompe l'oeil* bow sweater that skyrocketed her career—by 1928 she would be a force to be reckoned with! English designer Norman Hartnell also opened in Paris that year, showing elegant flowing frocks in satin, lace, and chiffon.

"**UNEVEN GO THE HEMS THAT GRACE THE NIGHT!**", *Vogue Pattern Book* proclaimed, noting that "Long skirt drapery achieves the important **Uneven Hemline**." (October/November 1927). Afternoon and evening skirts often dipped with "pointed extensions" that were "cut in one with the frock" or via triangular-topped gores or panels. These trailing tails dipped from just one side or from both sides. For afternoon and evening events, handkerchief skirts, tiered skirts, and even petal skirts were seen. The enchanting petal skirt, a favorite of the early twenties, was revived by Cheruit. Vogue raved "it transforms the models into flower frocks!" Constructed of many layers of picot-edged tabs, it was so flattering that skirts with "petal-like panels" blossomed in profusion. Scalloped or pointed waists and/or hems continued in the mode. "Soft fullness adds grace to formal gowns" via bloused bodices, shirred fronts, and cape backs. For outer wear, shawls and coats were lavish as "Velvets and lamés wrap the evening mode... coats have fullish tops, narrow bottoms..."; many were surplice wraps. Evening "jackets" were chic too; as Vogue advised, "Even an evening frock may have a jacket"!

"Lipstick Red" was one of couture's favorite colors this year—and Patou offered a lipstick red georgette dinner dress with a back bolero effect that gathered to a large fabric rose at the left hip and a long draped panel that descends from the shoulder to the floor. It was a look that would be widely copied. Evening décolletage, both back and front, was generally "V" or oval shaped—and very low. Lace, fringe, and beads are "much used" for evening. "Picturesque as Always," various versions of Lanvin's *robe de style* remained "youthful" favorites for afternoon and evening.

Yokes were "Important" in 1927 and they were seen on necklines as well as hips. Several houses, including Jenny and Lelong, were showing "Encrusted" (jeweled and/or embroidered) yokes in 1927. Couture's beloved "girdle" effect was more modish than ever—as Vogue noted: "There's a tendency to accent the hips at the low waistline by means of a swathed girdle (often encrusted)." Vogue advised taking one's figure into consideration when selecting a new frock this year, as "the present mode offers many pitfalls with its very deep décolletages, [and] a tendency to swathe the hips at a low point (which may give vulgar line to even a slim figure)..." (January 1927)

Couturiers continued to accent the derriere with large bows or choux that lend a dramatic bustle effect—they may also perch on one hip, often topped by hip brooches or "ornaments." The eighteenth century influence was also seen. Vogue observed that "...very chic are tunic skirt portions that are open to the center of the lowered waist, showing a contrasting underskirt beneath"; tunic effects were seen for both day and evening.

"Perfect for summer afternoons," printed chiffons were ultra chic! Satin and "satin backed crepe" continued to be popular for afternoon, evening, and dressy day wear. For Bridge or Tea, *Vogue Pattern Book* recommended "Semi-afternoon dresses of metallic tissue or 'new' velvets in real or artificial silk, which are incredibly light and fall into the most graceful folds" and "...velvets in fine geometrical prints." (August/September 1927)

Vogue Pattern Book also offered sage advice for selecting a wardrobe:

> *The trouble with most wardrobes is that they just happen... a smart wardrobe is never assembled in such a manner; it is visualized as a whole and accumulated deliberately in accordance with a definite plan, and when it is all assembled, everything slips into place like a picture puzzle.*

Smart Shops and Catalogs Interpret the Mode for the "Average Woman"

Skirts hovered at the knees—and both Simplicity and Motion were employed with abandon! "Motion" was provided by a variety of draped or pleated flounces, by panels, godets, circular cuts, tiers, and even apron effects. The graceful, clinging look of Vionnet's bias cut was everywhere. Fluttering handkerchief hems floated from catalog pages—and adaptations of the petal skirt. Tiers, tiers, and more tiers fell in graceful ruffled flounces—or pleated rows! Bloused bolero effects were worn for both day and evening—and cape effects added dash! Jabots continued to flutter from many frocks and the beloved vestee often went below the low waist at this time. Exhibiting an eighteenth century look, tunic frocks opened to a lowered waist, showing a contrasting underskirt—they were worn for both day and evening. Also chic was a Marie Antoinette-ish sleeve that was tight from shoulder to elbow, and wide and flowing from elbow to wrist.

"Chanel" shirring was universal, and scallops retained their popularity at waists and/or hems, as did "zig-zag" triangular points. Girdles and hip yokes were more modish than ever. Couture's "Compose," the use of contrasting fabrics and/or textures in two or more shades of the same color, was adopted. "Attaining a striking prominence" were satins and satin-backed crepes; they were worn for day, afternoon, and evening events. Contrasting bands of trim were seen, as "applied bands break the straight silhouette." Tucks and pleats, stitched vertically and/or horizontally, "are combined in many smart frocks." Long, tight sleeves, short sleeves, and no sleeves were most worn, but Chinese Lantern and Dolman sleeves continued. *National's* cried: "The Dolman sleeve is all the rage" (some Dolmans adopted couture's rows of buttons from neck to cuff).

For day, "The ensemble concept is again strong in the mode"—street length and seven eights length coats were shown—with linings, sleeves and cuffs to match their "very simple and tailored" print frocks—or "plain frocks that match or blend with the predominating color of the coat". Jersey knits remained "smart for daytime." Sleeveless frocks were now common for sport. *Vogue* remarked:

> *we have watched sleeves disappear from tennis frocks and other types of sportswear, but now, many chiffon and printed silks don't even have the suggestion of the cap sleeve... though charming for afternoon, sleeveless frocks are "incorrect for street wear.*

Popular accents were decorative belts (both wide and narrow); two narrow parallel belts were shown on some models.

Pleats of all kinds were prevalent—especially popular for sport was the "Chanel" inverted or kick pleat. Necklines were square, "V," bateau or even asymmetrical (couture's new "irregular neckline", cut on the diagonal). Narrow Mandarin necklines often extended to long ties that were either tied in a bow or left trailing and described as "Chanel-inspired".

1927 Fashions

Women's Day Wear 1927

Frocks for Day Wear were much shorter by 1927—as Lord & Taylor advised:

> *At the fall openings the Haute Couture decreed that daytime frocks will be worn just below the knee, while evening gowns beguile the eye into accepting added inches through the use of the uneven hem line. These style tendencies are reflected in our Women's and Misses' frocks at prices ranging from $25.00 to $195.00* (October 1, 1927 ad, *Vogue*)

As you'll note in *National's* selection of day dresses for 1927, couturiers continued to vary the silhouette in many ways, including the very important "Bloused Bodice." New bolero effects focused attention on the natural waistline and wide, tight girdle waists emphasized the hips. Long tight sleeves vied with sleeves that ballooned from elbow to wrist, and Dolman sleeves were a smart novelty. Curves were also emphasized by shirrings, "tucks," and narrow belts. Vestee effects (including the "underfront blouse") were favored, and asymmetric "trimming to one side" was new. Skirt portions were straight, flared, and/or pleated (including the new "stitched down plaits"). "Dainty" embroidery, convertible collars, and streamers continued—and narrow belts with buckles or "ornament" clasps were modish. Prints were becoming more and more important.

A) Shirred Flare: *Dainty embroidery and exceptional becomingness! Modish sleeves are shirred above the elbow and gathered into narrow cuffs are adorned with contrasting embroidery. The skirt is softly shirred in front. Self material girdle effect is contrastingly piped and finished with a handsome pin ornament. Contrasting color edges the becoming collar and form the modish tie ends; self sash ties in back.*

B) Bolero/Eton effect: *The new Eton effect one piece frock is the dress that every miss will adore... The waist is attached to a contrasting color self material underfront trimmed with fancy braid, and giving the stylish Eton effect as pictured. The skirt has a softly shirred front. The straight line back has self sash belt; self-tie ends and fancy buttons are smart features.*

C) "English Print" Vestee: *This tailored one piece dress cleverly simulating a two-piece style is all silk tub silk with attractive English print design. It has a finely pleated skirt front finished at bottom with solid harmonizing band. Notice the smart Vestee effect front trimmed with fancy buttons and outlined with solid piping. The straight back is finished with self sash belt.*

D) "Tucked" style: *"... bloused in front and subtly tucked like the newest Paris imports... New inverted tucks cleverly trim the front of waist section. Similar tucks trim the sleeves and supply a soft fulness for the skirt front.*

E) Dolman Sleeves: *Here's a stunning one piece frock with Graceful Dolman Sleeves and softly shirred skirt front... the waist is*

Inside illustration labels:

$6.98

(A) ALL-SILK FLAT CREPE Gooseberry Green
(B) ALL-SILK FLAT CREPE Flemish Blue
(C) ALL-SILK TUB SILK English Print Pattern
(D) ALL-SILK FLAT CREPE Flemish Blue
(E) ALL-SILK FLAT CREPE Goya Red

Gorgeous Colorings

Adorable Styles

(F) ALL-SILK FLAT CREPE Goya Red
(G) ALL-SILK FLAT CREPE Rose Beige
(H) ALL-SILK FLAT CREPE Gooseberry Green
(J) ALL-SILK TUB SILK Queen Blue
(K) ALL-SILK FLAT CREPE Athenia

$6.98

"Never were dress styles more beautifully simple or delightfully becoming to youthful figures than they are today!" The 1927 *National Style Book* described fashion's newest features, picturing "Adorable Styles" for day wear, available "... in new shades that are bright and gay as youth itself... Goya Red, Flemish Blue, Gooseberry Green, Rose Beige"! All but two are of satiny "All Silk Flat Crepe"; all have slightly bloused bodices and plain "flat" backs. Note the modish girdle belts on A, E, H and F! [descriptions under illustration]

slightly bloused in front and finished with a self band which fastens with a fancy buckle. The smart collar is finished with a neck vent closing and narrow ties in front; straight back with self sash belt.

F) Buckles! *Note the skillful manner in which the waist overlaps the plaited skirt in front to give the much desired two-piece effect. Inverted tucks at shoulders supply desirable fulness. A double self belt at the waistline is finished with a metal buckle - a new style feature. Applied self straps finished with smaller buckles to match trim the smartly tailored sleeves.*

G) Shirring: *The material is so rich and dressy that the only trimming used is soft shirring at the shoulders and on the two novel pockets...*

H) Convertible Collar, Stitched Down Pleats: *Fancy ribbon in three-tone combinations trims the new convertible collar and*

forms a panel effect on the front of the waist. A self band, trimmed to match overlaps a graceful skirt with fashionable stitched down plaits.

J) Tuck-plaits: *Notice the waist section with its new style tucking, overlapping in front for a two piece effect. Skirt shows new style tuck-plaits in front. The novel pockets show bright colored embroidery and are finished with fancy braid to match collar and cuffs.*

K) Asymmetric trim: *Trimming to the side is a dominant style note in the new dresses... a deep self fold, richly embroidered in harmonizing colors and stitched down to hip depth trims the right side of skirt portion. Embroidered inserts trim the modish sleeves; a simulated pocket flap is embroidered to match. The new (bateau) collar is another smart style feature.*

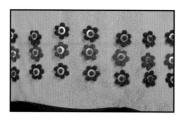

Closeup of the tiny orange and blue felt flowers that adorn the underfront, streamer ties and contrasting cuffs. These sweet little posies are hand applied; the brass centers are pronged in back.

Back view—you'll note that while the front of the skirt is pleated, the back is left "flat"; also note the chic bloused bodice effect.

Similar to *National's* "B", this smart "Flemish Blue" crepe-back satin is a one-piece frock "simulating" a three piece! This three-piece look is achieved via a smartly tailored bolero jacket effect and ecru crepe de chine "underfront" blouse with a yoked, pleated skirt portion. Four inverted pintucks at the shoulders provide bust fullness on the bolero, which features the chic convertible collar and "streamer" ties. On the front skirt portion, a wide waistband accents the low waist; it buttons at left with three large self buttons. The smart girdle effect is provided by a deep v-shaped yoke, from which smart box pleats descend to the hem. While *National's* version is just $6.98, a similar frock from B. Altman's is $25.00! Now, $300-$400

"Sylvia" proudly poses in her new satin day dress, which features a convertible v-neck, puffy cuffed sleeves, and contrasting inverted "kick pleats" trimmed with vertical rows of ric-rac. Snapshot, 1927.

Provenance: this delightful dress was worn by Mabel Short on her wedding day; in 1927 Mabel became the wife of Col. Leroy Short.

Art Deco Prints are Tres Chic!

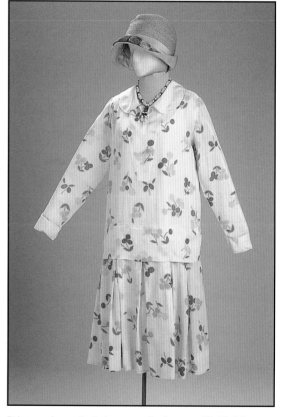

"You've Got to be a Football Hero... to get along with the Beautiful Girls!" Perched on the fender of her Tin Lizzie, this pert flapper keeps a tight grip on her handsome football hero! Showing off her glamourous gams, she wears a very short frock with a modish vestee, similar to *National's* "C," with a fetching sports cloche!

This sporty straw cloche has it all—ribbon streamers of green and blue fall from the chic tucked crown; rolled circles of multi-colored straw trim the pleated crown band in front. The back turns up smartly—like our flapper's cloche in the Football Hero snapshot. Label: *Gimbel Brothers, New York, Philadelphia, Paris.* $200-$300

Prints are increasingly important in the second half of the decade, and this modish day dress is a marvelous example, printed in a twenties favorite, colorful art deco Cherries! In cool and comfortable silk pongee, it boasts many of fashion's favorite features, including a wide cummerbund "girdle" and a wide box-pleated skirt. The convertible neck has a topstitched yoke; it can be worn open or closed. The contrasting ivory crepe Peter Pan collar and cuffs are piped in the cherries print. Four rows of pintucks at the shoulders add bust fullness. Label: *Yo-San, R&T Silks.* $200-$300. *Courtesy of T.W. Conroy.*

Lounge Wear
Informal Frocks for "House or Street"

House dresses were now versatile enough to do the housework in, and then wear out shopping! Though they were inexpensive slipover frocks, they had stylish features... including flare, kick pleats, ties, and fancy but practical pockets.

National's presents "Cool, Dainty Every Day Dresses for House or Street" in printed pongee, cotton broadcloth, and cotton "Dress Prints."

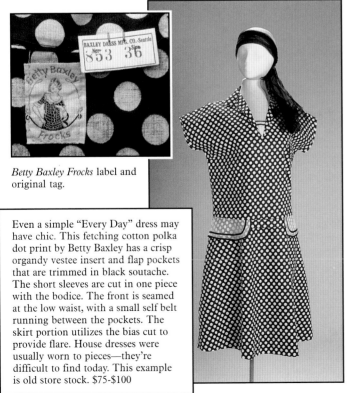

Betty Baxley Frocks label and original tag.

Even a simple "Every Day" dress may have chic. This fetching cotton polka dot print by Betty Baxley has a crisp organdy vestee insert and flap pockets that are trimmed in black soutache. The short sleeves are cut in one piece with the bodice. The front is seamed at the low waist, with a small self belt running between the pockets. The skirt portion utilizes the bias cut to provide flare. House dresses were usually worn to pieces—they're difficult to find today. This example is old store stock. $75-$100

Lounging Pajamas

Avant-garde young flappers often adopted more "Bohemian" ensembles for lounging! The lounging pajama, first worn ca. 1922, had now become such a rage that *Vogue Pattern Magazine* offered "Lounge Pyjamas with Matching Lounge Coats", asserting: "...much distinction lies in these leisure hour modes!" (June/July 1927)

So wonderfully decadent – in her Bohemian lounging pajama ensemble, this pretty flapper rests between parties. She's smoking a cigarette while reading Fitzgerald's hot new novel, *The Great Gatsby*! The radio on the table beside her is undoubtedly playing 1927's favorite tune, *Ain't She Sweet*! Note her snappy strapped pumps! Snapshot, ca. 1927.

Closeup of the *Franklin-Wear* label.

Right:
A Decadent Deco lounging ensemble in the hottest hot pink and jet black rayon jersey knit. The robe is reversible, and the fabric quite sheer, so the color beneath creates an intriguing effect. Hem and sleeve edges are piped and scalloped in hot pink; both shawl collar and revers are hot pink. Front tie closure with pink ties on the black side and black ties on the pink side. Label: *Franklin-Wear* (Franklin Simon). Then: at a store like Franklin-Simon, about $12. Now: between $300-$500.

Above right:
The pajamas sans robe. The pink pajama top features a contrasting black collar and v-necked yoke; black ribbon flowers trim each side of the snap closure and the yoke's center. A black ribbon sash encircles the waist, and the armscyes and little front pocket are piped in black. The black pajama pants are accented at the ankles with contrasting triangular pink slits. They're full cut with straight legs, and have a drawstring waistband.

To wear with her lounging pajamas, our flapper selects black kid Mary Janes with cutouts and "simulated" reptile trim; Cuban heels. $75-$125

Lounging Pajamas Leave Home *and* Go Public at the Beach

The fashion world was all abuzz as the first *fashionable* long pants for women put in an appearance at trendy beaches! At first, only the avant-garde were brave enough to wear them in public, but by the end of the decade, they had become a must.

Vogue, of course, took note of this daring trend:

> *Every modern invention, said the man who disliked TELE-VISION, "is a further invasion of privacy." And, certainly, modern life is no secluded affair...clothes reflect this trend toward publicity. Pyjamas have emerged from the boudoir to the beach, negligees serve as tea gowns or at least, as lounging robes. It is no longer enough for one's boudoir clothes to be delicate and exquisite—they must be CHIC! Chic requires a sense of the fitness of things, an ability to choose the proper costume for the proper occasion, and this rule holds good for pyjamas. Just at present, the smart woman wears **four distinct types of pyjamas** – beach pyjamas, tea time pyjamas, lounging pyjamas and sleeping pyjamas... Beach pyjamas have been worn at the Lido [Venice] for many seasons, but it was during the past winter at Palm Beach that they first became popular in America...the first and foremost rule concerning beach pyjamas is this: They must be in the sports feeling... they may be as gay in colour as you like, the bright colours are charming against the white sands...* (July 1, 1927)

Sophisticates even wore them to luncheon—*Vogue* described a typical day at Lido:

> *One leaves the hotel clad in (beach) pajamas, bathing suit and coat or summer dress, and goes to the cabins to change; then sun bathe, followed by a dip in the ocean... for luncheon, one has only to don pajamas to go to the Grotto, a restaurant especially for bathers. Then more sunning and bathing till tea time and dinner...* (May 1927).

B. Altman's presents "Replicas" of Nowitzky Beach Pajamas, which they advertise with beautifully blatant snob appeal: "Beach Pajamas distinguish the woman of traveled chic – the woman who has been to such smart places as the Lido." These chic beach pajamas have a nautical flavor, "with jolly sailor trousers in black crepe de chine." Note that Altman's Replicas are $35. Pictured in the foreground is Nowitzky's "Complete Bathing Costume" – a taffeta carrying bag, cape, suit and throw. Altman Replicas are $250, and the parasol is $50 extra. (As advertised in *Vogue*, 1/27)

In Paris, Mary Nowitzky, at 82 Rue Des Petits Champs, Place Vendome was *the* place to go for Beach Pajamas. As B. Altman exclaimed, "Nowitzky and the Southern Beach Mode are Inseparable"!

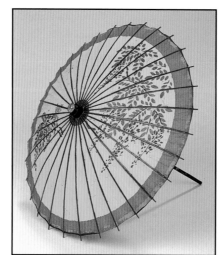

A charming bamboo parasol – strikingly similar to Suzanne Lenglen's.

A marvelous press photo of tennis champ Suzanne Lenglen strolling along the beach at Lido. The copy reads: "Queen of the Courts in New Pose! Suzanne Lenglen, soon to come to America to play professional tennis, seen wearing the fashionable Beach Pyjamas on the Lido, near Venice, Italy." One of the most famous style setters of the decade, Miss Lenglen was dressed by Jean Patou both on court and off. Note her smart bamboo parasol, trademark sweatband, and stylish beach slippers! *Photo: Henry Miller News Picture Service, Inc., 519 Thirteenth St, N.W., Washington, D.C.*

A superb art deco Beach Pajama
ensemble in silk crepe de chine,
including a jacket, sleeveless blouse,
and full cut trousers bordered with the
jacket's print. The trousers are fitted at
the waist in front with two topstitched
darts at each side, and at back with
elastic. This set is exquisitely
fashioned; the pattern is meticulously
matched, and all seams are French
seams. Though there's no label
present, the jacket's bold cubist pattern
is similar to artist *Sonia Delauney's
bold geometric designs and vibrant
primary colors. $800-$1200

Back view of the jacket's superb print!

Note the tendency for legs to grow ever wider, echoing men's wide Oxford Bags. In their May 1927 issue, *Vogue* raved over wide beach pajamas by Vionnet: "Vionnet creates Beach Pajamas in three tones of burgundy crepe de chine with OXFORD BAG TROUSERS, extremely chic because of their subtle coloring and design...". By the thirties, these delightful wide-leg pajamas had become commonplace, with legs that were almost elephantine!

*Russian born Sonia Delaunay was one of the era's most successful artists to transfer art to fabrics. During the teens Sonia and her husband Robert developed their theory of "simultaneous color" or *Simultanes* – bold innovative "color rhythms" of geometric circles, squares, and triangles in vivid, electric hues that predated the "psychedelic" designs of the 1960s.

Prompted by a desire to influence fashion via her artwork, Sonia produced her first "Simultanist" dress ca. 1913. Her creations were designed to complement the wearer when in motion. They were so innovative that a friend thought they would revolutionize fashion, claiming they were "...no longer pieces of material draped according to current fashion, but coherent compositions, living paintings of sculpture, using living forms." Sonia lectured at the Sorbonne on *The Influence of Painting on the Art of Clothing*, explaining her theories and noting the social changes that resulted in the new freedom in women's clothing. She was an advocate of *Pret-a-Porter* (Ready to Wear).

By 1922, Sonia had opened a boutique on the boulevard Malesherbes, and she soon established her own print workshop—her fabrics were often marked Atelier Simultane on the selvedge. Her prodigious body of work included cushions, carpets, curtains, lampshades, panels, screens, tapestries, handbags, scarves, and other accessories. She created a plethora of fabric designs and fashions—dresses, coats and sportswear, including swim wear and BEACH PAJAMAS! She also designed for plays and motion pictures, and clients like Gloria Swanson wore her designs both on stage and off. Nancy Cunard, shipping heiress and leader of avant-garde society, often wore Delaunay designs. At the 1925 Art Deco Exposition, Sonia exhibited her *Simultaneous* dresses and fabrics at the Boutique Simultane she shared with couturier Jacques Heim.

Three darling young Harlem girls show off the latest styles for tennis... "inevitably chic" frocks that are "free and unrestricting." Snapshot, ca. 1927.

Sports Wear For "Active Sports"

By the second half of the decade, many couturiers had opened boutiques at fashionable sports playgrounds, prompting *Vogue* to observe: "At three famous playgrounds of Europe, Biarritz, LeTouquet and Deauville, fashion triumphs! Never could sports costumes be observed to more advantage than at the aperitif hour and on the golf links and tennis courts in the afternoon..." (June 1926)

"Practicality Rules the Mode of Active Sports!" headlines the 1927 August/September *Vogue Pattern Book*. Shown are three simple styles for tennis and golf that meet *Vogue's* criteria:

> The qualifications for active sports frocks are plain and outstanding. Such frocks must be, first of all, comfortable and easy to wear. They must be free and unrestricting. They must be severely simple. They are most satisfactory if they are made of washable fabrics. And, when they are all of these things, they are almost inevitably chic!

They also recommend that "no scarfs or tie ends impede the player" – and advise "all models are sleeveless versions, since a lack of sleeves is both correct and comfortable for active sports wear... A chic point to note is that the tennis frocks are all in white." To complete an ensemble: "...white canvas shoes, thin lisle stockings; hats with close fitting crowns and turned-down brims. A wool sweater worn after the game may match the hat band."

Frock No. 8950
The hemstitched tuck above the belt of this white piqué sports frock simulates a bolero. Designed for sizes 16 to 20 years and 34 to 42. Size 36 requires 3 yards of 36-inch; price, 65 cents

Frock No. 8955
A linen frock with side pleats below the belt is trimmed with hand drawn-work. Designed for sizes 14 to 20 years and 32 to 46. Size 36 requires 3 yards, 36-inch material; price, 65 cents

Frock No. 8949
(Left) A second linen frock with a round sweater neck is trimmed with hand drawn-work. Designed for sizes 16 to 20 years and 34 to 46. Size 36 requires 2⅞ yards, 36-inch; 65 cents

Frock No. 8883
(Right) A yoke, buckled belt, and inverted pleats are features of this English broadcloth frock. Designed for sizes 14 to 20 years and 32 to 44. Size 36, 3⅝ yards, 36-inch; price, 65 cents

Perfect for tennis or golf! This white cotton sports dress features snappy print piping around the yoked neckline, armholes, and belt. Four carved green glass buttons adorn the closure; the belt buckle is clear carved glass. The front is seamed at the lowered waistline, with a center inverted pleat and wide box pleats to provide ease of motion. The back is cut in one piece, with no seam at the waist. This ready-made sports frock is labeled: *Fast Color, Made in U.S.A.* Then: summer sports frocks similar to this were priced between $5.75 and $12.75 at B. Altman's in 1927. Now: $125-$200

A very sporty green straw "fedora" cloche, with a pleated two-tone ribbon pinwheel, and braided ribbon trim around the brim. Note the chic "square-top" crown. $250-$350

Golf

For golf *Vogue* advised:

The silhouette for golf should be perfectly straight in repose; the two piece mode is recommended. It should be broad shouldered, and the skirt should not be too full or too pleated... Best of all for this purpose is the simple inverted pleat beloved of Chanel... With sweater, blouse and skirt, the player's silhouette when she stands is like a boy's; when she bends, it provides a certain kindly camouflage for too-feminine curves. Add a scarf and masculine hat with a front brim to shade the eyes. For rainy weather there is a reversible suit with rubberized crepe, with a zip fastener up one side of the blouse to the neck and smaller ones on the pockets... Bystanders are expected to wear a bit more formal clothes of course. Chanel costumes with pleated skirts and matching striped sweaters (some with loose tie necks) abound. (6/26)

The epitome of *Simplistic Chic!* This fetching white linen golf ensemble has a red gingham overblouse that can be slipped on for luncheon after the game—it's cut in a deep "V" to the natural waist, and sports two small white linen welt pockets that are just the right size for golf tees.

The frock's v-neck is trimmed in matching gingham with snappy ties; the armholes are piped in gingham. Note its superb Deco lines; diagonal pintucks radiate across the bust in a Sunburst pattern. The shoulders are also pintucked, as is the back of the neck.

A closeup of the snappy diagonal gingham overblouse!

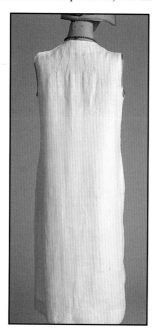

Both frock and overblouse are labeled ★Sacson. Then: this sports ensemble may have been priced around $15. Now: $350-$500

In this view of the dress alone, note the four large pleats, topstitched six inches down, that provide ease of motion on the front's skirt portion.

Back view of the frock – note the back is cut in one piece and falls straight from the shoulders. The skirt portion is not pleated. Tiny pintucks at the back of the neck provide ease of motion.

"To Shade the Eyes," our golfer selects a cool Panama cloche with a squared and ridged crown. The brim is asymmetrical, curving around the face and coming to a modish point at the right side. Around the crown, a pleated tropical print silk band adds a splash of color.

The label pictures a svelte golfer on the links with her roadster and the country club in the background. *"Golden Glow Sports, Made in Los Angeles."* Then: similar hats are priced between $3.75 and $8.00 at New York's better shops. Now: $200-$300

Yachting

Ever So Chic – and perfect for Yachting! The importance of the smart pleated skirt and jacket combination simply can't be overstated—fashion's mandates of Simplicity and Versatility combine in this popular ensemble to make it "Almost a Uniform." Today, separates like these are very rare!

"It is very smart to lunch on such hospitable yachts as *la Resolue, Liberty* and *Finlandia*... aboard ship, Madame de Gainza (left) wears a white pleated skirt, beige jacket and beige felt hat. Madame Martinez de Hoz's costume is in marine blue shades...". Here, *pochoir* artist Pierre Mourgue depicts the smart yachting set in coordinating skirts and jackets for *Vogue*'s May 1927 issue. At B. Altman's New York shop, similar ensembles are priced around $18 - $25.

"Ready to Sail – *SS St. George*, Bermuda, April 28th, 1927". For her trip, this sophisticated lady has donned the era's favorite sports combination. You'll note that the ubiquitous fox neckpiece is still MUST. As *Vogue* advised: "The smart world wears a fox scarf..." Socialites may purchase theirs at Kurzman's exclusive Fifth Avenue import shop; their ad proclaims: "Silver Fox is important this Spring – to wear it is to possess a definite cachet". Their "Silver Fox Collection" is priced from $175 to $675!

For the average woman, *Bellas Hess* offers this "Trig" version of "The Uniform." Their short, blazer style jacket: "Velveteen is one of the most fashionable fabrics this year and New York women wear jackets like this for street and general wear as well as for sports. Double-breasted jacket is made from silk faced velveteen and has mannish notched collar. Two flap pockets and white pearl buttons. Unlined. $5.98."

The pleated skirt: "A fancy plaited skirt of heavy quality All-silk Flat Crepe attached to a white bodice (frock skirt). The fine plaiting in front is stitched part way down. In white, Mother Goose tan, flesh pink or black." Note the skirt is a combination of wide and narrow pleats.

Styles for the Races

Even in the days of Napoleon and Josephine, the racetrack was a popular place to show off one's finery... especially hats! Horse racing has long been called The Sport of Kings, and crowds in the 1920s dressed accordingly.

The latest fashions are paraded at tracks like England's "Glorious Ascot". At Ascot's opening, these three fashionable ladies show off their chic new print frocks with full skirts that flutter around their knees as they walk. The most magnificent (and extreme) millinery is worn at Ascot, and all three ladies have heeded *Vogue*'s advice: "There is, however, only one correct hat to wear with the chiffon frock, and that is the hat of large proportions... the large hat is chic with a FLUTTERING FROCK"! (June/July 1927)

This press photo copy reads: "OPENING OF GLORIOUS ASCOT. Ascot opened to-day June 18th in a blaze of sunshine which did ample justice to the thousands of brilliant fashion worn. THE PICTURE SHOWS SOME EXAMPLES." It's stamped: Central Press, London, 115 Fleet Street.

Hats

For all occasions, even sporting activities, hats were pictured as an ensemble's finishing touch. The cloche was so firmly entrenched that milliners concocted imaginative variations like these pictured in *Tres Parisien's* 1927 *pochoir* portfolio. Many of the styles introduced ca. 1924 had become favorites. (See Chapter Six in my companion volume *Roaring '20s Fashion: Jazz.*) Included in this portfolio is a commentary on the latest millinery by Fany Greges:

It is difficult and even bold to pretend to find words to describe the new creations of the latest Paris modistes. The following sketches will better accomplish this purpose and will indicate more accurately and clearly than mere phrases could do, the great creations of Reboux, the personality of Suzanne Talbot, the delightful modernism of Agnes, the acuteness of Alex, the originality of georgette, the delicate taste of Le Monier,

Lewis, Camille Roger, Elaine, Helene-Thibault, Marthe Regnier, Jeanne Vivet, Marguerite and Leonie, and the other artist creators here represented forming a galaxy of the leading modistes.

The mannish style of the unadorned felt hat with its utter lack of character has come to be for the past few seasons the sole interpretation of chic and elegance. Lacking both embellishment and imagination, these hats are not so similar as to create almost a mania of uniformity... Today both the nature and the shape of the hats have changed. They have, moreover, a tendency to become larger... sometimes the brim is turned up, either at the back or on the side to set off the profile... The crown is still of a large size and very high; it is folded up from the front to the back, or on the side, but it is seldom quite plain. The crown is intended to show its suppleness and the dainty handicraft of shirrings, plaitings, and stitchings of all kinds give character to the individual note of each firm...

This exquisite *Tres Parisien* tissue *pochoir* depicts the latest creations of such legendary milliners as Agnes, Maria Guy, Caroline Reboux, and Suzanne Talbot. Note the crown treatments – draped, pinched, tucked, creased, ridged – and the chic tall flat or "square" crown. Draped tam-turban-"berets," like Reboux's (lower right) are also very popular.

At a prestigious New York store like B. Altman's, copies or replicas of couture wide brims are priced between $10-$12; smaller hats range between $5 and $10.

Un chapeau d'AGNÈS, en velours noir incrusté de velours rose, coulissé et formant ruban.
Une grande capeline de velours vert ornée de rubans du ton est créée par MARIA GUY.
De REBOUX ce simple et élégant chapeau de velours noir.
En velours froncé, voici un chapeau de SUZANNE TALBOT, orné d'un pouf fantaisie.
Ce béret plein d'allure créé par REBOUX est en velours rouge.

From AGNES. Black velvet hat, inlaid with sashed rose velvet, shows a ribbon effect.
A broad brimmed hat of green velvet trimmed with ribbons of the same colour. From MARIA GUY.
REBOUX has made this plain but elegant hat. Uses Black velvet.
Here is a hat, made by SUZANNE TALBOT, in wrinkled velvet trimmed with a fancy puff.
This beret hat created by REBOUX in red velvet, is a high feature.

Below:
The creased crown! Here's a nice example of the ridged or creased crown so popular in the second half of the decade. This hat is rose-colored straw trimmed with flocked velvet flowers and straw soutache "squiggles." These creased crowns are difficult to find today; their creases were often damaged in storage, and people have sometimes attempted to steam the creases out—not realizing they're supposed to be there. The frayed rayon lining is embroidered OZQ(?). $200-$300

The ever popular wide brim capeline or "Picture Hat." This fetching example is a flecked "tweedy" straw that's perfect for Ascot or the Kentucky Derby. It's so chic for summer, its only trim being the original green velvet crown ribbon and bow—draped and tied for a simple yet elegant effect. Note the deep crown and the brim's popular "Poke" curve. Rayon lining labeled *Trixie Hats, Paris, New York*. $300-$400

1927 "JANUARY SALE"! This smart flapper gal is waiting for the shop to open so she can scoop up the January Sale bargains. She's undoubtedly selected which of the tempting hats in the window she'll try on first. Note her pocketed day dress, Louise Brooks' bob, and Mary Jane pumps!

"Life is Just a Bowl of Cherries" in this smart black satin and velvet tam-turban-beret! It's trimmed with overlays of silk soutache latticework and scalloped embroidery on both the wide front band and modish puffy crown, which is draped to the left and caught with a tempting bunch of celluloid cherries. You can tell this charmer was a favorite; there's quite a bit of nap wear to the velvet. It's lined in black rayon and no label is present. $250-$350

Presenting a NEW IDEA – A Matching Hat and Bag! This tall square-crowned cloche's "Top Hat" ancestry is evident – but it's been given a modern art deco twist with magnificent stylized flowers worked in a technique similar to ancient Trapunto embroidery (the felt flowers are hand-stitched between a rose felt base and an outer layer of sheer pink silk georgette). The tall "square" crown alone is 5 1/2 inches high. The matching flat envelope purse has a felt change purse and snap closure. These tall "toppers" alone are rare, but with a matching bag – a real treasure! $500-$600

A closeup of the hand-worked art deco flowers. The tiny brim is tucked flirtatiously over the right eye and trimmed with a sweet little bow.

Hats in the News

People in the news inspired styles that caught on like Wild-fire—and no one was in the news more than Charles Lindbergh. Even women's hats commemorated his historic flight!

The 1927/28 *Chicago Mail Order* catalog jumps on Lindy's bandwagon with: "A rhinestone aeroplane pin ornament – all the rage since Lindy made his sensational flight, twinkles against the band of wide satin faced Bengaline ribbon on this charming model of lovely Silk Faced Velvet and lustrous Rayon Faille..."

"A NEW CHAMPION COMES BACK TO EARTH! September 21, 1927, Los Angeles, California." Flag Pole sitting was one of the zaniest stunts of the twenties – and in this super press photo Miss Bobby Mack, "The New World Champion," poses in a sassy draped crusher she popped on for a press photo when she came down to earth. The copy reads:

Miss Bobby Mack, 21 years old, of Los Angeles, wins the world's championship for flag-pole sitting by perching on a chair suspended from a flag pole for 21 days. When she came down she was awarded with a loving cup and $2500.

At her side is her fiancé, Tom McNamara, and "the bouquet and the smile were forerunners of the wedding that followed. *By Wide World Photos*. (The famous "Shipwreck" Kelly later broke Miss Mack's record, spending twenty-three days and seven hours aloft)

"IT'S THE LATEST FAD!"—Make your own CRUSHER! As *National Bellas Hess* illustrates, creative (and/or frugal) gals could buy kits to "Make Your Own Felt Hats... for only $.89! In an hour, you can cut it out, fit it to your head, embroider and make it... [it's] easily cut to fit any head size."

Packable Crusher Cloches

Foldable, packable cloches called "CRUSHERS" were very popular – they were both chic and practical!

Chicago Mail Order offers the "AVIATOR" Crusher. At just $.88, it's: "One of the biggest bargains ever offered, and very fashionable. Smart little crushable Aviator style helmet of Wool Felt Cloth, with Swagger two-tone eartabs on both sides."

Louise, our "Merry Widow," models a similar style crusher—though hers is a Mourning Bonnet. Though twenties mourners still wear black, the old Victorian mourning rules have been greatly relaxed*. This stylish black satin crusher folds flat to fit in one's pocket or purse, so it can be slipped on just before the services and tucked away immediately after. This helmet-type bonnet is shiny black satin, with a pleated crown that's trimmed with flat grosgrain ribbon. Three modish horsehair circles trim the front, and center back is marked by a small grosgrain bow. A narrow band of tightly shirred black crepe forms the tiny brim, and wide satin bonnet ribbons tie under the chin. $175-$250

*Note that many women, especially for mourning close family members, continue to add crepe veils to their mourning hats.

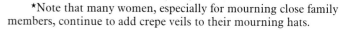

Hatboxes and Hatstands

"Paris Midinettes," ca. 1927. Wearing sassy smiles and ultra short day dresses, young Parisian apprentices march down the streets of Paris with a supremely confident air, hatboxes in hand. Note their shoes – Mary Janes and T-straps, and their stylish bobs. Noted on the reverse: Midinettes, Paris Dressmakers... from the collection of O. Mandelstamm, Hollywood, Calif.

"CHICK" (Chic) HATS! This lithographed cardboard hatstand depicts a twenties "Marie Antoinette" in a short panniered *robe de style*—carrying a large hatbox! These adorable little stands were a great way to keep one's favorite cloche close at hand. $40-$50

Great graphics adorn this twenties hatbox. On one side, an elegant lady, hatbox in hand, is about to step into her chauffeur-driven limo. On the other, a stylish lady and a gent walking his dog stroll by. $75-$100

A super hatbox by Sport Hats! Each side has a different sports scene: ladies playing golf, tennis, "motoring," and lunching! On the lid is a beach scene. $75-$100

Afternoon Frocks

For Afternoon: "While daytime frocks continue the straight silhouette, afternoon frocks introduce motion and grace. Drapery and tiers are becoming... and skirts with tiny pleats...!" (October/November 1927 *Vogue Pattern Book*)

Below left:
At luncheon at the Ritz, all heads would have turned to the stylish woman wearing this lavish lace dress and coat ensemble! Lace-making machines that replicated ancient hand-made designs were employed to manufacture the exquisite laces used. In this ensemble, two laces are combined: bands of Leavers machine-made Italian filet needle lace in a rose pattern and heavily embroidered floral panels on tulle produced on a Schiffli "Through Machine."

On the coat, very detailed Schiffli embroidered tulle panels form the body and sleeves of the coat, which features a small Medici standup collar in back, and long, tight sleeves. In front, the embroidered panels are slightly shirred to mark the low waistline. Three inch wide scalloped rose filet borders the front opening, with embroidered flowers from the Schiffli panels extending onto the rose filet. Scalloped rose filet also borders the hem, and matching rose filet insert lace forms a vertical center panel in back.

Below middle:
The dress is formed of alternating bands of insert rose filet lace and Schiffli embroidered tulle panels. The front features a five inch wide embroidered lace center panel, which falls straight from neck to hem. On each side of the center panel, bands of insert rose filet alternate with panels of the embroidered lace (the embroidered panels on the dress are slightly different than those used on the coat). Scalloped bands of rose filet adorn the armscyes and form the low waistband. Below the waistband, bias tulle godets provide the essential "flare." The neckline is the ever-popular bateau, piped in tulle. The original peach silk slip is cut straight over the bust, with delicate tulle straps based to size; its hem is bordered in matching scalloped rose filet. Coat and Dress Ensemble, $800-$1000

(The wide brim Battenburg straw hat is pictured on page 206 of *Roaring '20s Fashions: Jazz*.)

Below right:
Back view of the coat, showing two distinct lace panels used.

Art Gout Beaute's lovely *pochoir* pictures two charming afternoon frocks with "Motion and Grace!" At left, the green and black frock has a two-piece look; note the stylish sleeves puffed below the elbow and the chic "skirt with tiny pleats." The stunning dress at right is lavishly trimmed with lace; triangular bias panels lend "motion" to the skirt. In 1927, similar frocks range between $25 and $50 at New York's exclusive shops.

Wax Mannequins

Just outside Paris, a new, chic and highly sophisticated race is appearing, with sculptors as creators, wax and paint as materials, and the spreading of good taste as a purpose in life... The young women are sophisticated and slim, but there are also matronly ladies, bald gentlemen and Flappers! There are types and Personalities... any one of them suggests an entire character – with a past and a future... Here and there among this population, one sees a cold steel face with features reduced to the merest stylization, but among the ordinary population, one meets with all the familiar and various types of human beings one knows... (Article, "Siegel Mannequins," January 5, 1929 *Vogue*)

Breathtaking couture frocks were often displayed on wax mannequins from the decade's premier mannequin manufacturers – Siegel's and Pierre Iman's!

Pierre Iman's extremely rare 1927 wax mannequin catalog featured both the new "stylized" art deco mannequins and the more realistic "highly sophisticated" wax ladies! Here are two of Iman's fashion "representatives"

Pierre Iman's stunning deco catalog cover, 1927.

The elegant art deco "Raphaele" in an afternoon gown from Jean Boos.

The sophisticated "Paulette" models a marvelous evening frock with beaded girdle waist and beaded "car wash" fringed skirt.

Evening Wear

Evening frocks of 1927 exhibit fashion's latest features as they dazzle the eyes with beads and sequins.

VENICE. Stylized art deco mannequins, similar to Iman's "Raphaele," pose in Wanamaker's window in 1927. The evening frock at left has the chic cape back and bias-flared skirt; accessorized with a huge ostrich fan, slave bracelet, t-strap pumps, vanity bag, and turban headdress. The gown at right is perhaps a burnout velvet on georgette. This window display photo is part of Permaflector Lighting's portfolio (they note this lighting was installed in 1926).

"Lovely Party Frock with Beads and Rhinestones!" The chic *Chicago Mail Order Catalog* offered this spectacular frock in their 1927/28 issue – with this enticing ad copy:

As you swirl with the strains of the latest dance music, the full flaring skirt floating about you as gracefully as fairy gossamer, the sparkling rhinestones that dot the stunning beaded pattern flashing colorfully under the evening lights – Yours will be the loveliest frock on the floor if you choose this PARIS-INSPIRED creation of All Silk Georgette Crepe. For less formal occasions, just put in the cap sleeves that are sent with this dress. Rayon slip included. Black with pink slip, peach with pink slip, French blue with pink slip, or all white... In two lengths, Regular and Short.

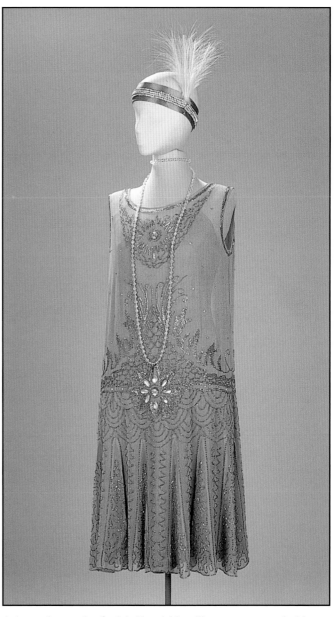

Closeup of the exquisite rhinestone flower at the low waist's center.

The back of the gown is almost as spectacular as the front!

Closeup of the skirt's beaded gores.

A devastating evening frock in French blue silk georgette, covered with thousands of silver bugle beads and rhinestones, and designed to "Swirl with the strains of the latest dance music!" The bateau neck boasts a *trompe l'oeil* bib necklace, and silver bugle beads extend in a flame pattern above the low waist, where a dramatic art deco rhinestone flower blossoms. The skirt portion's flirty flare is achieved via seven triangular bias cut godets – all beaded in a vermicular design. It's shown with a faceted crystal necklace and evening bandeau formed of period materials. $1000-$2000.

"Car Wash" Hem Beaded Frock

Highly desirable then (and now) were frocks with beaded "Picot-edged Tabs"—fringe-like panels designed to swing and sway to the beat of the Charleston! They may have been inspired by Roman soldiers' attire, though today, they're sometimes referred to as "Car Wash" dresses—which seems rather mundane when compared to *Chicago Mail Order's* original description...

Chicago Mail Order's original description is pure MAGIC!

T'WOULD SEEM THAT FAIRY FINGERS FASHIONED IT OF STAR-DUST AND MOONBEAMS! This heavenly creation – and its luminous beauty and radiant loveliness will hold you spellbound. Fine as mist, yet strong, it is the All Silk georgette used, its translucent charm embellished by glittering beads, clear-as-crystal, and brilliant, flashing rhinestones. Cut-outs in the back intrigue you, and PICOT EDGED TABS, back and front, sway gracefully with each movement of the figure, revealing a bit of the georgette underskirt, hung on an all silk tub princess slip in self color.
Sashes at sides; sleeve caps to insert if you want them. In coral, white, black or orchid. 2 lengths. $19.98.

Note that this 1927 *Chicago Mail Order* ad is an actual photograph! The model has accessorized with a single ostrich plume fan.

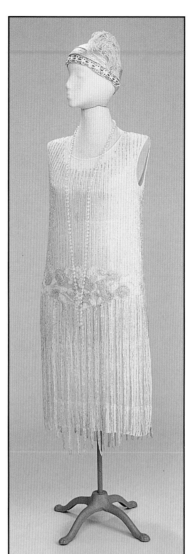

This spectacular white silk georgette evening frock has a skirt portion formed of "beaded picot-edged tabs," designed to "sway gracefully with each movement...!" The georgette underdress is visible beneath the tabs, which are longer in front and back and shorter on the sides. On the bodice, the gown's tubular lines are enhanced by narrow vertical rows of bugle beads on the bodice. The low waist is, of course, the focal point – its beading is worked in a design of exotic orchids formed of silver, pink, and rose bugle beads. $1400-$1600. Her evening turban is formed of period silver lamé, beaded band, and a pink ostrich tuft.

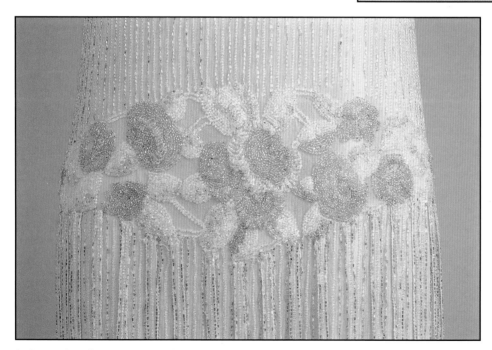

A closeup shot of the gown's magnificent orchid beading!

Complimenting our gown is an extravagant pink ostrich fan, mounted on a single faux tortoise stick with bracelet loop—it's similar to the *Chicago Mail Order's* fan! This large fan is 27 inches long (not including the bracelet loop). $250-350

132

Uneven Hems and Tailed Gowns

By 1927, couturiers were employing the "uneven hem" – various tails and draperies to lengthen the hemlines. As Lord & Taylor's prestigious New York store advised: "...Evening gowns beguile the eye into accepting added inches through the use of the uneven hem line..."; their evening gowns are priced up to $195, or approximately $2000 today!

Right:
"New Evening Frocks Make a 'Point' of Drapery!" *Vogue Pattern Book* for December 1927/January 1928 features three lovely gowns with fashion's latest features. Note the blue frock at right has a fluttering "handkerchief" hem, as well as a floating Cape Back—so flattering a look that it lasted well into the thirties. The handkerchief skirt is praised as: "...an exquisite grace of movement is contributed to this chiffon evening model by the skirt section, which has circular sides ending in long points, with an added point in the back." Note the front view, showing the deep v-neck with vestee.

At the center is a versatile Cocktail dress: "In this three piece ensemble, the separate Cocktail Jacket ties over an evening frock with a sleeveless overblouse that ties at the left hip and a separate skirt, circular in front and straight in back."

The rose pink frock at left features: "...A petal shoulder flower and double belts with jeweled buckles are interesting details of this crepe satin frock. The skirt with long drapery at one side joins the blouse under the lower belt." These "petal shoulder flowers" were extremely popular through the end of the decade. That double belt effect was one of the methods clever couturiers used to raise the waistline.

Label: *Grande Maison de Blanc!*

Far left:
The back view of our exquisite lace and sequin gown echoes the lines of the figure at right in *Vogue Pattern Book's* illustration!

Eight gored panels of coral sequins alternate with silk coral "spiderweb" blonde lace to comprise the handkerchief skirt of this spectacular evening frock from New York's exclusive import shop, Grande Maison de Blanc (538-540 Fifth Avenue). A wide scalloped band of sequins delineates the low waist. The lace bodice portion features a very deeply V'd neckline, also bordered with coral sequins; the lace-trimmed satin underdress forms the vestee effect. The flattering new cape back of scalloped, picot-edged lace extends to below the girdle. $800-$1000.

Her evening bandeau is adorned with a velvet and lamé rose surrounded with ostrich fronds. $150-$200

Left:
Front view of the gown showing the deep sequin V-neck, lace vestee effect, scalloped waist, and lace and sequin gores.

Wedding Attire 1927
Robe de Style

 The picturesque *robe de style* remained a favorite during the second half of the decade—its skirt often short under long panniers, or short in front and longer in back. It was a romantic look that was a favorite with younger women—perfect for weddings, garden parties, and teas!

Spring and a Lady
BY HELEN DRYDEN

*'Tis a wise shepherdess who carries her most becoming lamb . . . .
and a clever woman who wears silk that enhances the beauty of her eyes!*

Stehli Silks

Copyright 1927, Stehli Silks Corporation · 200 Madison Avenue, New York · Paris · London and Zurich

SPRING AND A LADY! Helen Dryden's art deco illustration of a twenties Marie Antoinette tending her sheep graced the back cover of the June/July 1927 issue of the *Vogue Pattern Book*. Her "Wise Shepherdess" is wearing a ravishing Stehli Silk *robe de style* with DEEP décolletage! Note her chic top hat and voluminous shawl.

A closeup view of the lovely ribbon flowers and the gown's exquisite lace.

Perfect for a garden wedding, this beautiful frock was a bridesmaid's gown, ca. 1927. This marvelous example of a late twenties *robe de style* echoes its famous ancestor, an eighteenth century open robe with full side panniers and ribbon rose trim. The body of the dress is a straight chemise of embroidered lace in a floral trellis design. Its original pink silk slip is attached at the shoulders. The full pannier overskirt is changeant taffeta of pale green to pink; it's lined in shell pink (visible at the back of the wide scalloped hemline). Exquisite ribbon roses with metallic trim emphasize the low waist, curving over the panniers to meet in a deep V at center and trail to the hem. The wide bateau neck is piped in changeant taffeta, as are the armscyes, hem, and cuffs (formed of eight inches of pintucked lace). Both the dress and attached slip feature a left side snap closure. $600-$800. *Courtesy of Amanda Bury.*

1927 Bridal Gown

Bridal gowns incorporated fashion's loveliest features! This lovely wedding gown is no exception - and it came with an original portrait of the bride and groom!

Our beautiful bride's gown is *tres chic* – with all fashion's latest features, including the famous handkerchief hem. Its lavish lace skirt is cut very full, ending in a pointed tulle border. The long satin torso is exquisitely beaded—crystal, white, and silver bugle beads are applied in an art deco floral pattern. The low waist is asymmetrical and scalloped with self-piping; the bateau neck and armscyes are also self-piped. One of fashion's latest accents, a trailing "shoulder bouquet" adorns the left shoulder. The veil's wide lace border matches the dress. $700-$900

The Bride and Groom in their wedding finery, June 1927! The groom wears white tie and tails; his bride, this stunning gown and headpiece. Her long veil has been carefully draped to flow around them both on their Day of Days! Sadly, no one thought to identify our happy couple.

A closeup of our bride's original tulle headpiece, trimmed with prong-set rhinestones, with two cockades of lace and wax orange blossoms at each side.

A closeup of the lovely satin and chiffon shoulder bouquet – note the pearl stamens! These popular drooping bouquets are known as "Raggedy Anns."

A closeup of the exquisite floral beadwork, and scalloped asymmetric waist.

Chapter Five

1928 Women's Fashions

Timeline

In 1928, Alexander Fleming discovers penicillin. Three U.S. homes now have "television." The Health Department announces that moonshine or bootleg liquor is to blame for over 1500 deaths, many more have been "blinded" by bad liquor.

March 21: Charles Lindbergh, "The Lone Eagle," is awarded the Congressional Medal of Honor.

May 11: General Electric introduced the first television programming—the first televised tennis match is held on July 12.

June 10: In New York City, the Board of Health stops a dance marathon, the "Dance Derby of the Century", after 428 hours. Ninety-one couples started; only nine remained. The Board of Health became concerned when one contestant began vomiting blood.

August 22: Governor of New York, Al Smith, "The Happy Warrior," accepts the Democratic presidential nomination, which is simulcast on both radio and television.

November 6: In the presidential election of 1928, Republican Herbert Hoover wins by a landslide over Democrat Al Smith.

At The Movies

Silent films of 1928 included the scandalous *A Woman of Affairs* with Greta Garbo as Iris Storm; it was based on Arlen's book, *The Green Hat.* King Vidor directed *The Crowd. The Wedding March* starred Erich Von Stroheim and Fay Wray. Joan Crawford danced her shoes to shreds in *Our Dancing Daughters; Street Angel* won a Best Actress for Janet Gaynor. Chaplin was hilarious in *The Circus.* Alfred Hitchcock directed a thrilling trio: *Champagne, Easy Virtue,* and *Farmer's Wife.* On March 15, Mickey and Minnie Mouse starred in a young Walt Disney's silent animated feature, *Plane Crazy* – with Mickey portraying Charles Lindbergh.

"**Talkies!**" *Steamboat Willie*, the first sound animated feature, debuted November 18 at the Colony Theater in New York—it starred a talking, whistling, and singing Mickey Mouse, whose favorite tune was *Turkey in the Straw.* On July 15, Warner Bros. released their first All-Talkie, *Lights of New York.*

Hollywood was thrown into mass confusion as it became increasingly apparent that the Day of the Subtitle was over— "Talkies" were here to stay... even though the need for the cast to stay close to the microphones created comic catastrophes! Stars raced to take elocution lessons; many made the transition to sound, others fell casualty to this new phenomenon. Charlie Chaplin was the last silent holdout, releasing his classic *Modern Times* in 1936.

Favorite New Recordings

Hit records included "Diga Diga Doo" by Duke Ellington and his Cotton Club Orchestra; "West End Blues" and "Muggles" by Louis Armstrong; "My Man" by Frannie Brice; "That's My Weakness Now" by Paul Whiteman—with new crooner, Bing Crosby; "I Wanna Be Loved by You" by Helen Kane, and "You're the Cream in My Coffee."

In Literature

New novels included Thornton Wilder's *Bridge of San Luis Rey;* Erich Maria Remarque *All Quiet on the Western Front*; Aldous Huxley's *Point Counter Point;* and Claude McKay's *Home to Harlem.* Of course, D.H. Lawrence's "sexational" *Lady Chatterly's Lover* was banned.

In Fashion 1928—
Short & Sassy vs. Long & Feminine!

Skirts for sports and day wear were the shortest yet—barely reaching the knees, and the most daring flappers wore them to the tops of their knees! When the very short skirt had reached its apex, however, its replacement had simultaneously stepped into the fashion spotlight—it was a silhouette that emphasized feminine curves, natural waistlines, and the longer skirts ushered in by the uneven hemline. Hemlines were "erratically uneven" and "Full skirts often dip at some point, especially for afternoon and evening." The long "Peacock" tail was beginning to draw attention—*Women's Home Companion* praised this "modishly erratic hemline which descends almost to the heels in back only to achieve knee length in front" (September 1928). Then, in the midst of all these tails, dips, and points, *Vogue's* June 1st cover astounded fashionable women by depicting a dress that was *long* all the way around! (Pg. 160.)

As this new tidal wave of femininity rushed in, many women expressed concerns about losing their beloved "Simplicity in Dress"... though they ought to have known by now that, "**Like the tide, Chic waits for no woman**"! (*Vogue*, April 1928)

Couture Trends

Vogue trumpeted:

A full, fluttering, flaring mode comes in with Spring!... Femininity is important, but it is neither fancy nor fussy – a paradox that makes great fashion skill essential to true chic. It is apparent in ruffles, drapery, bows, soft necklines, cascades, jabots, flying panels and fluttering ends.

They also noted:

The Jutting Silhouette is the Newest Note in Paris... the most exaggerated form of the ever-present note of fulness. It is used most frequently in afternoon and evening models, and, in many instances, the fulness springs from under a fitted hipline... This fulness may take the form of flares, tiers, flounces, pleating, godets, circular pleating, godets, circular inserts, ruffles, and puffed effects, sometimes massed at one point, sometimes continuing all around.

A fine example is Louiseboulanger's evening gown, "Model 98 ... Like a brilliant metal lily, the petalled girdle of this pink-and-silver lamé gown frames the tightly wrapped hips, also accented by the blousing of the bodice. The skirt repeats Louiseboulanger's full, longer-at-the-back triumph"! Also exhibiting many favorite new features is Martial et Armand's "*Historie de Rire*" – a black and white print afternoon dress: "three curved tiered flounces trim the bodice, and the lower part of the sleeves are treated in this same chic fashion"; on the skirt portion, "both the tunic effect and uneven hemline are represented in a slim, curving overskirt which is open to the hip on the right, from which a full, flaring panel dips to midcalf. A draped girdle molds the hips and ties in a soft bow on the right."

"Fulness" was of utmost importance, "Every Type of Fulness Lends Distinction to the Mode", and *Vogue* announced that "The use of fulness in the modern sense is based on the **Principle of the BROKEN SURFACE**... All of these tiered, flounced, cascaded, and draped effects, whether on skirt or bodice are produced by a layer-like treatment in which they appear to hide under or issue from one another, thus giving, in certain exaggerated cases, a fir tree silhouette – and in all cases, an interesting and never unflattering Broken Surface!" Redfern's layered "*Conquete*" was pictured: "The uneven hem-line is achieved in this instance by a circular panel with rounded edges that runs on itself and falls from beneath a curved yoke-like band. The long sleeves wrinkle softly at the wrists." It was imported to Lord & Taylor. (April 1928)

The "moulded" hipline was most modish—as *Vogue* advised, it "may take the form of a wide wrapped girdle – or a still more frequent detail of a yoke from which the skirt fulness flares." (June 1928) These snug "hip yokes" continued as a popular alternative to the draped girdle; they eased the waistline's transition by providing a double-waisted effect, a method that will endure well into the thirties. The fact that the waistline was "rising" was also noted: "Waistlines are higher, seldom all the way around; nevertheless their position is rising. Many girdles reach the normal waistline at some point. For afternoon and evening, the smartest waistline starts high in the front or at the side and slopes low in back in a curving, fluid line, bringing about the in-evitably moulded hips from which all fullness flows"! Drecoll's "*La Roulette*" was a spectacular example as it combined many feminine features, including: "A circular bolero, a deep oval décolletage, tightly girdled hips, and flowing panels of unequal length... all go to prove that the dress that flutters flatters"!

For afternoon and evening, bustle effects continued as drapery, "smartly placed at the back," facilitated the new, longer hems—there were also bows, loops, and poufs in profusion! Patou used Bianchini black taffeta for "*Thais*" – a "crisp model with flat bands" – pleated bands that arched in opposite directions diagonally across the bodice and girdle. The skirt potion featured a bustle effect with "a diagonally flowing train and looped ends." Rippling "apron" flounces were another favorite feature; they were flaunted in front, in back, or both.

Even Day Wear might have shown "here and there, the natural waistline introduced into the straight, slim silhouette by means of a series of horizontal darts." *Vogue* praised Chantal's model, "*Glozel*," with "moulded hips" achieved via "a series of radiating darts on one side from hip to waist;" in Bianchini printed silk crepe. It was imported to Best. Chanel's printed ensembles were outrageously popular. The Tailored Woman, an exclusive New York Shop, offerd a replica, "exact in every detail", of Chanel's new printed "long coated ensemble with Chanel's new low-placed fullness; cordings scallop the coat and the sleeveless frock in a way that requires real skill in reproduction;" this *Reproduction* is $118! Ensemble coats are of "every length – short jackets, hip length, full length, three quarters, and of course, seven eights." Couture couldn't get enough of prints this year; polka dots were ultra chic. *Vogue* noted they were "sprinkled over the frocks for 1928"!

The Art Deco influence was everywhere—it was evident not only in the cut of fashions, but in the BOLD NEW PRINTS as well! Printed fabrics with "jagged geometric designs of contrasting colors... diagonal bands and chevrons" exhibited fantastic Art Deco style. Silks and rayons had dramatic Deco designs as did sporty knits. *Vogue* praised Chanel's "very smart suit of knitted wool;" in several tones of her favorite beige, it was woven in rows of horizontal waves, and worn with a "simple beige blouse tied at the neck and waistline" (modeled by the Comtesse Elie de Gaigneron). Jane Regny showed a decidedly Deco zigzag knit sweater, worn with a pinched "gigelo" cloche and "slightly flared circular skirt."

For sport, *Vogue* advised: "Every variety of costume is shown in the early Paris openings – skirts with sweaters and jackets or cardigans, one-piece sports dresses with coats of seven-eights length, tailleurs, and the simple sweater with a skirt to match or contrast." Though pleated skirts prevailed for sport, they were "sometimes replaced in the new collections by a circular cut, or godets", as "plain sports skirts are varied by a certain movement and flare." Couturiers also facilitated skirt fullness via "deep and various underlapping pleats in flat skirts." Sports clothes were most often belted at or near the natural waistline, though "the low waistline is shown on many sports models." The rage for "Mannish tweeds" continued for sports and "country" day wear.

Smart Shops and Catalogs Interpret the Mode for the "Average Woman"

Women's Home Companion announced that while evening gowns and dressy afternoon frocks were *longer* than ever, "Tallieurs and Runabout frocks ("Trotteurs") are *Shorter* than ever." (September 1928) The simple tailored "Runabout" frocks that *Vogue* advocated for a wide variety of daytime activities were popular; many were belted at just below the natural waist. The versatile ensemble remained a staple in every woman's wardrobe. Favored were: "printed crepes and jerseys that come in sets" – a skirt, hip-length sleeveless sweater, jacket, and long coat comprised the smartest sports ensembles. For day, the use of contrasting colors and/or textures was stronger than ever – and "Prints, prints and more prints" were all the rage. Printed frocks often had matching or contrasting scarves. Polka dots of every shape and size had been captured from couture – they were "sprinkled all over" pattern books and catalogs.

The stylish *Chicago Mail Order* catalog's style consultant was Ella Van Hueson, "Miss Universe – Beauty Queen of the World!" She declared, "I am amazed that any store is able to offer such adorable styles in coats, dresses, hats, etc. at such low, money-saving prices!" She noted that "The mode is swaying back toward the softly feminine... emphasizing once hidden curves by delicate, though effective changes in line, and bringing forth from their hiding places frills, laces and all manner of dainty trimmings". *Chicago* headlines: "NO NEED TO GO ABROAD FOR THE 'Frenchiest', OUR CATALOG DISPLAYS THEM ALL!"

"An Emphatic Success" was announced – "The Huge Merger of National Cloak & Suit Co. And *Bellas Hess* & Co. ... Now, Fifth Avenue Sweeps Clear Across the Continent"! The new *National Bellas Hess* boasted "The same styles that well dressed New York women are NOW wearing – at a fraction of the cost." Styles shown were "Typically Parisian, yet *Americanized* to become the fashionable American woman." Couture's two-tone color concept was adopted—"*Two Colors for Chic says Fashion – and Here They Are*" – a lace vestee and tunic insert added contrast to a crepe de chine dress; and "graceful jabots of solid color fall at either side of a dainty lace vestee." Practical "removable" sleeves were advised: "In these days of multiple activities, it is well to have dual dress that will serve more than one occasion. This frock may be worn in the afternoon or evening, for the sleeves are easily removed if you stay in town for dinner and the theater...". Fabric flowers sprouted from shoulders and/or hips... the chrysanthemum-like drooping blossoms were known as "Raggedy Anns" (see page 137).

Couture's asymmetrical look had been adopted; very popular that year, it was shown on both bodices and skirts. Bodices often featured diagonal surplice drapes that fell across the front from one shoulder to the waist; and most bodices continued to be "slightly bloused." Bust emphasis was evident: "Note the clever manner in which fullness is taken care of at the shoulders – with tiny inverted pleats, decorative in themselves," another couture feature. The vestee was eternal – it was more popular than ever. For afternoon or evening, the lace vestee predominated; for day/sports wear, the newest vestee was plain and double-breasted. A clever "convertible" frock featured a collar that could be left open to show the vestee – or it could be buttoned up to "change the entire appearance of the front." Also offered was the "latest two-way collar" – buttoned up to a high Directoire look, or left with one side folded diagonally, with facings of a contrasting fabric to match the collar and cuffs. V-necks and rounded jewel or bateau necks were favored, as were turnover collars; couture's chic asymmetrical neckline was often seen too. "Chanel" tie collars endured, many were in contrasting colors. "Paris' latest 'flowing sleeve'" (an eighteenth century retro version, open and slightly flared) was often seen... though the most popular sleeves were bloused above the banded cuff, or long and tight. There was also a new art deco sleeve that flared with a piped, diagonal cutout narrowing to a tight cuff (see page150.) For the almost mandatory Bridge game, "Bridge Frocks" were shown in dressy afternoon styles.

On skirt portions, both couture's "girdle" belts and hip yokes were employed – and skirts exhibited couture's "newest flare lines." Fullness was achieved via circular flares, which "fall gracefully over the skirt beneath the wide picoted girdle." Pleats continued too, the newest were "stitched part way down;" also chic was "the new fan pleating" (narrow pleats that flared out at the hem). Tiers remained as "The three-tiered skirt gives lovely softness to the stylish silhouette;" they were often finished in scallops edges, and most modish were the narrowly pleated scalloped tiers. Godets and attached panels, often shirred at the top, were smart; they lent fashionable fullness and ended in the chic uneven hems. Shirring added decorative touches almost anywhere, and continued to be a very important fashion feature.

"Rayon" (formerly "synthetic silk") was used in frocks more and more; *National Bellas Hess* claimed it was "ideal for summer wear because it is absolutely perspiration proof"! Couture's use of metallic fabrics for sports wear was promptly appropriated—*National's* offered a chic ensemble with a "metallic knit overblouse," crowing: "The blouse can be worn with other skirts – the skirt can be worn with other blouses, and the separate coat can be worn with any dress – all are yours for $19.98!" *National's* suits were "trimly tailored with a hint of Mannish style to exactly fill your needs – becoming to almost every type of figure"! They boasted straight or pleated skirts (or a combination of both) that came to the knee, and were most often shown with short, boxy, double-breasted jackets ending just above the hips. Some skirts were "wraparound style," opening on the left side.

1928 Fashions

Life in 1928!

Just an Old-fashioned Girl

"Just an Old Fashioned Girl," _LIFE_ magazine reflects the lifestyles of 1928 in Russell Patterson's witty cover. His "Old Fashioned Girls" are dressed in the shortest dresses yet – _above_ the knees. Huge exaggerated bows add sass at the low waists—and at the left, emphasize the derriere in a bustle effect. One of the new "peacock tail" dresses is pictured at far right – short in front and trailing to the floor in back. Naturally, all these flamboyant flappers are smoking, which is almost as popular as drinking and necking!

Real life counterparts: Equally sassy vaudeville actresses from the Ted North Players pose in front of the Regent Theater in a variety of fetching frocks – all above the knees! The gal at the left, in a fluttery tiered number, points out a "No Parking" sign; the gal beside her wears a straight tailored dress, and the two gals at the right are very chic in bold art deco prints and stylish cloches (note the matching hatband at the far right). All wear jazzy Mary Jane pumps but the gal at right, who's opted for snappy tie oxfords. Snapshot 1928.

Sensational New Shoes

With skirts at their shortest, shoes were very important accessories—lattice work cut-outs and intaglio "underlays" did their best to keep in step with the latest frocks—and spike heels and rounded toes were in.

YOWSA! This starlet's gorgeous gams are emphasized by a pair of extremely high spike heeled pumps—and her skirt's so short her "Come into my parlor said the spider to the fly" garter shows! Her perky frock boasts a modish bolero, flared bias skirt, and fluttering "peekaboo" panels. This photo's entitled "Flapper Fashion," by International News Photos, 235 East 45th St., New York.

"Fascinating Models in tune with Fashion's Latest Decrees!" *Chicago Mail Order* offers a dazzling selection, described with their usual panache: "The splendor of this footwear truly defies description... such a lavish use of trimmings, underlays, appliqués, bows and scallops!" As you'll note, Black Patent Leather is all the rage. Clockwise from upper left: 2J94, A fan-shaped version of the classic Colonial tongue pump trimmed with "Fancy Gold Manchu Leather – a new and beautiful vari-colored leather a-glisten with tiny flecks of gold..., round toe and Cuban Style heel". 2J148, This flat "college" heeled shoe is a "...conservative oxford for general or street wear... the sort of footwear that never goes out of style and of which one never tires..." 2J126, Spicy spike-heeled Mary Jane pumps with Manchu Leather trim, "for social or street wear where something really dressy is desired...". 2J89, black patent opera pumps with an art deco flair, "of soft chrome tanned patent leather, a bit of the new and a dash of the up-to-date added. Dame Fashion, always original, has shaped the quarters to overlap the vamps and beneath the cutouts at either side and covering the heels has employed the newest Paisley colored kid with a most charming result." 2J91 Spike-heeled "Fancy Oxford Ties... the kind of footwear that makes a woman glad she is a woman, so she can wear something so entirely delightful and charming! Dame Fashion is to be commended for her clever treatment of the side cutouts and the fancy underlays which lend them unquestioned smartness...". 2J85, Mary Jane pumps with inlays and cutwork of "Patent with Reptile Grain Leather... The man who made these slippers was not only a shoemaker – he was a designer and a skilled artisan who realized the style possibilities of combining black, soft Patent Leather with grayish Snake Grain Leather..."

CMO Shoes

Where else but Rip-Roaring Chicago, home of Roxy Hart, could you find shoes she might have killed for! For flamboyant flapper shoes, *Chicago Mail Order* simply could not be beat.

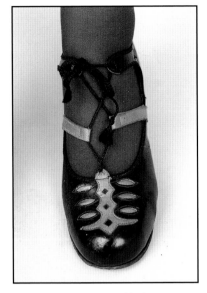

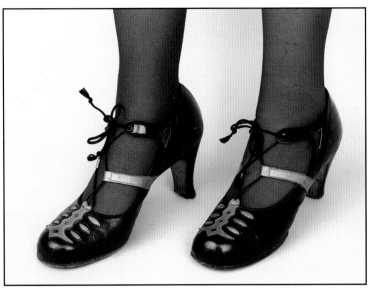

A closeup view of snappy black patent Ghillies with cutwork and intaglio designs in rose pink leather, with matching pink instep straps and spike heels. Ghillies, a traditional Scottish or Irish shoe, were another style set by the Prince of Wales.

Side view of the Ghillies, showing the instep strap and modish spike heels. Well worn and well loved, this pair has no legible marking on the insoles. $150-$200

The classic Colonial tongue pump in black patent, updated to an art deco look with chic black and white enameled buckles. Cuban heels. $75-$150

Roxy Hart Fetish Boots! A sexy twenties version of the ancient "Roman Sandal" in black patent with lattice cutwork sides, bronze cuffs, new rounded toes, and three inch spike heels! $250-$350

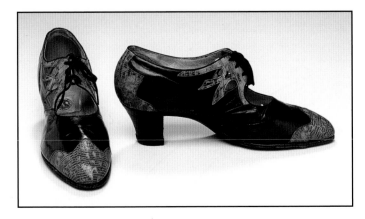

Sporty black patent oxfords, with simulated "Reptile Grain Leather" trimming the toe caps, heels, and sides in art deco geometric designs. Popular chunky Cuban heels. Insoles are stamped: *Natural Bridge Arch Shoe*. $150-$250

Day/Afternoon Frocks for 1928

The frocks of 1928 for day/afternoon events were stylish, short, and flirty!

"What the SMART MISS Wants – Stunning New York Styles!" from the newly merged *National Bellas Hess* catalog for Spring/Summer 1928. Frocks with fashion's newest features were originally described: A) The New Asymmetric Look: "Filmy and youthful, as lovely as summer itself... solid contrasting color self material cuffs and trimming on the all around draped girdle accentuate the beauty of the figured material. Two picot-edged shirred flounces attached to the skirt diagonally across the front are new and smart. A novelty ornament holds the girdle. Self material shoulder flower." B) The Modish Handkerchief Hem: "The very spirit of youth dominates this lovely frock of finest quality georgette crepe. In designing this model, no important youthful fashion idea is forgotten. For here is the new neckline trimming – and self material drapery which gives such a lovely graceful movement from waistline to bottom of skirt and supplies the ultra-modish uneven hemline. 'Handkerchief' cuffs give the same charming finish to the sleeves... adding further beauty to the dress, a wide band of the material exquisitely embroidered in soft colored and metallic threads finishes the bottom of the skirt and underside of the cuffs; it also forms the draped girdle." C) Flared Skirt Frock with waist "slashed at left side, faced with contrasting color georgette and turned back to disclose the contrasting color georgette insert and button trim plaiting... Cuffs are of plaited georgette to match... draped girdle finished at left with bow and fancy ornament..." D) Tiered ruffles! "The georgette crepe frock, always chic and dressy, is in greater demand than ever this season. And in this Misses frock of all silk georgette, you of youthful figure secure a very smart, delightfully girlish model... Paris stresses draperies, for she likes their smartness and becomingness, and here you have an extremely attractive version with two tiers of it adorning the front of the skirt and giving a very distinctive air..." E) The Bolero: "A new version of the Bolero Dress... the cleverest combination of pintucking and plaiting that have been shown on any model. The bolero effect waist hangs loose over the finely pintucked section all around... the finely plaited front of the skirt and slight flare at the bottom give the fulness now demanded of the most fashionable frocks." F) The Ultra Chic 2-Piece Knit: "There's such a flair this season for soft knitted wool overblouses worn with silk skirts that we had this favorite made up... Almost without limit are the daytime occasions on which you can wear this chic two-piece combination... The overblouse may be worn with other skirts and dresses and the skirt with other blouses. Light weight overblouse is knit from fine soft all-wool worsted yarn and is set off with a contrasting silk and METALLIC border... Skirt is of good quality all silk flat crepe, plaited in front and attached to a bodice top waist; plaits are stitched part way down." G) The Chic Cape Back "... follows the new silhouette with cape like drapery flowing down the back... three-tiered skirt with shirring imparting the new slightly draped effect at left... A delightful dressy touch is added by velvet appliqué and jeweled ornaments at shoulder and waistband". H) Classic Tailored Frock: "Smart Simplicity for Juniors ... the essence of the simplicity that typifies the season's styles...! Pin-ticking, the trimming that fashion favors so greatly, is used with particularly good effect on the front... Double collar and cuffs – the lower part of contrasting color flat crepe and the upper of plaid rayon taffeta. Skirt is plaited in front; buckled all-around belt of self-material." K) Shirred Girdle, Pleated Skirt: "There's heaps of smart style in this youthful model... a striking note of contrast that is such a dominant feature of the season's dresses is given by collar and rever facing of contrasting color flat crepe, also used for the tab in handkerchief effect... a close row of contrasting buttons and loops adds its bit of smartness to the bloused waist front. Skirt is shirred and plaited in front in the newest style." L) Scallops... "One of the latest and most fashionable New York models, created especially for the young miss with a penchant for what is truly smart... Notice the skillful way the pin-tucking in scalloped outline trims the waist front, which blouses over the shirred font of the skirt. Contrasting color outlines the neck, trims the sleeves and jaunty shoulder bow streamers; sash ties finish the one piece back."

144

Tight Girdles and Tiers

Similar to Figure "D" opposite, this flirtatious lace and georgette afternoon frock is "Up to Date in Every Detail!" It's so sassy and sexy it might have been worn by Loreli Lee to Cocktails at the Ritz in Paris... you can almost hear her squealing, "Paris is *Devine!*" (Loreli is the heroine of Anita Loos' hilarious new novel of 1928 – *Gentlemen Prefer Blondes*.) The lace bodice portion is slightly bloused at the low waist. A smart draped scarf effect is created by a scalloped lace panel attached to the round neck at the shoulders. In back, it hangs to a cape effect, draping down to focus attention to the natural waist before continuing up to the left shoulder, where it ends in a smashing burst of lace "tassels." The wide, tight girdle band of blue georgette emphasizes the low waist; it closes at center front with a stunning art deco clasp. Beneath the clasp, shirring provides the essential flare – and *action aplenty* is provided by two circular cut tiers of blue georgette, which flutter and flirt over the lace skirt like little panniers. A matching rayon underslip is attached at the shoulders. $500-$700

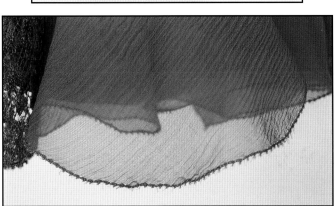

A closeup of one of the skirt's georgette flounces with the twenties favorite picot edging.

Back view showing the draped lace cape-drape and tight girdle belt – which obviously accentuates every wiggle and jiggle!

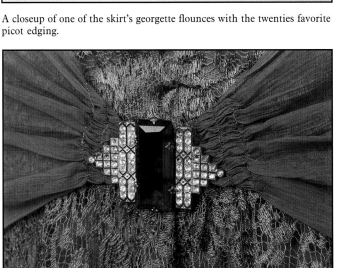

The fabulous art deco rhinestone and "sapphire" clasp.

Complementing our lace afternoon frock is this enchanting pair of pale gold brocade slippers in a floral pattern accented in sparkling metallic silver. Bands of silver kid with gold lacings trim the vamps and ankle straps, which fasten with tiny rhinestone buckles. The silver spike heels are three inches high. From Saks-Fifth Avenue, $200-$300.

Handkerchief Hems

Right:
A twenties favorite—The Handkerchief Hem! Similar to *National Bellas Hess's* Figure "B," this fetching butter yellow afternoon frock is a delightful example of the "deceptive simplicity" couturiers strive for – and of their dogged determination to lower the hemline – in this case via the uneven "handkerchief hem." This frock has a complicated, almost architectural cut: on the skirt portion, four bias panels float in points to the hem; they're topstitched to the very short underskirt in dome-shaped arches that draw attention to the hips. The low waist is emphasized by a wide girdle, which ties in front in a sassy bow. The bodice portion is stylishly simple; its self-piped neckline is rounded in front and dips to a daring "V" in back. The narrow shoulders are smartly shirred, and small bust darts also provide subtle shaping. Hems are picot-edged. It's accessorized with a crystal bead necklace-purse (below), and scalloped brim cloche formed of horsehair circles and trimmed with a flocked velvet dahlia. Frock, $250-$350; Cloche, $150-$250.

Far right:
This back view shows the low v-neck as well as the skirt's graceful handkerchief points.

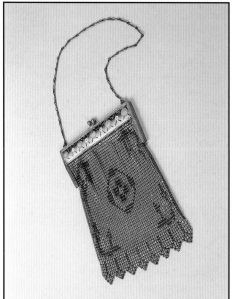

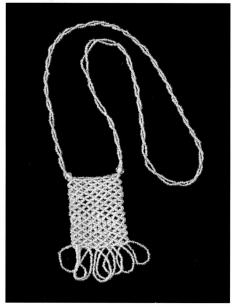

We've accessorized with this jazzy Whiting & Davis "Peaches" bag. The frame is enameled with peaches and blossoms; the armor mesh body features four succulent peaches surrounding a purple pansy. The vandyked border has a small orange flower at each tip. $250-$350

Sharing a sweet embrace, this jazzy couple is stylishly dressed. She wears a handkerchief hem frock with a bold print bodice; the waist is pointed to compliment the hem. Her handsome beau wears a white shirt, white linen plus-fours, and very snappy plaid socks! Snapshot, 1928.

A pretty and practical accessory – a tiny necklace purse of crystal beads. It measures only two inches by three inches, just the right size for a trolley token! $75-$100

Tiers and Flares

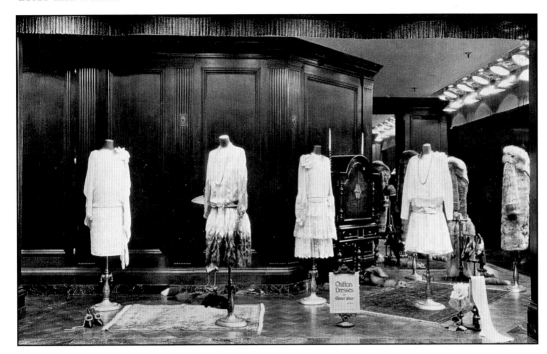

"Chiffon Dresses, Third Floor!" These short, sassy frocks for 1928 are part of a window display by Crowley, Milner & Co. of Detroit, Michigan. Pictured left to right are: a tailored frock with draped side panel and shoulder bouquet; a frock with skirt of fluttering bias strips; a frock with the ultra chic tiered skirt; a full-skirted frock with bloused overblouse. Note the coats at right, and stocking display in the right foreground. From Permaflector Lighting's portfolio.

"Three Generations!" Dolly, daughter, and Mom are all decked out in their finest. Mom's wearing a modish frock with a tiered skirt similar to the one in Crowley Milner's window. Snapshot, 1928.

This lovely day dress features several of couture's latest features! Take note of the popular new Asymmetric neckline (cut diagonally lower at left); also it is very full, with a flouncy skirt and snugly draped girdle. Best of all, it is screen printed in seductive cherries. The fabric is the sheerest navy silk over a pale pink rayon underdress. The sleeveless bodice achieves its "slightly bloused" look via the shorter pink underdress; the wide pleated girdle ends on the left in a sassy trailing drape. The asymmetric neckline is accented with a corsage of composition cherries. $300-$400

This closeup photo shows the skirt's circularly cut flounces and the print's delicious cherries.

147

Floating Cape Backs

"Ain't She Sweet?" asks one of the decade's most popular tunes. Artist Barbelle's flirty flapper wears a frock that flares around her pretty knees as she prances "Down the Street." Partial lyrics are:

> There she is! There's what keeps me up at night.
> Oh, gee whiz! There's why I can't eat a bite.
> Those flaming eyes! That flaming youth!...
> Gaze on it! Dog-gone it!...
> *Now I ask you very confidentially – Ain't She Sweet?"*
> (Yellen & Ager, 1927)

"Ain't She Sweet" personified—a sweet young flapper in a pose so like the sheet music it's uncanny! She's also wearing a floating chiffon dress... though hers has the modish new "cape back" which flutters in the breeze. Snapshot, ca. 1928.

Chicago Mail Order presents their version of the "Stunning New Cape Style... Dripping and drooping in repose, or fluttering as you move or a gentle breeze catches it, a pointed cape falls from beneath a yoke of embroidered ecru silk net... accordion pleat skirt trimming to the front... and a yoke of silk net... and so (the front) might not feel in the least slighted, a novelty pin at the front of the shirred, all around belt..." (Fall/Winter 1928/29)

The New Cape Style is so fetching that it will remain a favorite well into the thirties! This delightful sheer silk georgette frock is screen printed in art deco daisies; fluttering Butterfly sleeves continue around to form a chic cape back, which ends at the natural waist to focus attention there. The fluttering ties that border the small back yoke are a smart accent. The skirt portion's flare is achieved via bias cut godets. Attached red rayon underslip. Dress, $250-$350. It's worn with a red straw cloche with a bouquet of blue berries; its brim is medium width in front, narrowing to nothing at center back, $250-$350.

A front view of the frock showing the slightly bloused bodice, graceful butterfly sleeves, and wide, self-piped v-neck.

The Chic Poke Bonnet

Another very popular hat that's worn with floaty summer frocks is the twenties version of the Victorian "Poke Bonnet." It's a deep crowned hat with a wide brim in "fascinating curved and drooping shape." *National Bellas Hess* offers this "Youthful" example, its crown trimmed "in sections of all-over novelty lustrous Braid and silk and rayon," and "handsome flowers and foliage..." (1928)

A very rare wide brim "Poke Bonnet" cloche! This stellar hat is an extreme example of the popular "Poke" – with an asymmetric twist (the asymmetric look is so popular it's even seen on hats). As our "Agnes" illustrates, this intriguing brim dips dramatically lower at the right to flatter one's profile. This hat is fine red straw; the deep crown is adorned with overlapping pleated grosgrain bands. On the right is a bouquet of blue morning glories, forget-me-nots, blueberries, and orange "foliage;" streamers tipped with forget-me-not bouquets trail to the brim's edge. The top of the poke brim is trimmed with alternating pleats of white and red crepe; the underbrim is solid red crepe. The original lining was badly shredded; the label illegible. $500-$700

Front view of this exceptional "Poke"!

Closeup of the poke's stunning bouquet!

New Asymmetric Frocks

"Paris Proves That a Diagonal Line is the Shortest Way to Smartness!", *Vogue* announced as couture promotes the Asymmetric Look. (October 13, 1928)

This marvelous custom-made dress exhibits many features that simply scream *COUTURE* in the smart new asymmetric skirt, decorative hemstitching, bloused bodice, and new asymmetric sleeves. On the bodice portion, a deep vertical pleat at left from the silk floss hemstitching to the low waist provides ease of motion. The modish bloused look is achieved via a shorter matching camisole top, which is attached at the waist and snapped at the shoulders. The sleeves are both "bloused" and asymmetric—they're cut diagonally from just below the elbows to the wide hemstitched cuffs that fasten with a row of six covered buttons. The front of the skirt portion is straight to the dramatic diagonal hemstitching, where smart box pleats continue the asymmetric lines (the skirt is constructed in wrap-around fashion with no right side seam; it meets the straight back on the left at a wide side pleat). The frock is self piped at bateau neck and sleeves and has a self belt. It's in fetching "Rose Glow." Label: *Jeanette L. Cobb, Syracuse, N.Y.* $500-$700

The back view shows the plain "flat back," asymmetric sleeves, and cuffs.

Above:
Spring/Summer 1928 *National Bellas Hess* concurs, presenting their new asymmetric frock:

> *...Diagonal lines, one of Fashion's pet style features, distinguish this charming model in both waist and smart two-tone yoke on skirt; bloused waist and sleeves; shoulder flower to harmonize....the front of the skirt is box-plaited and the back is plain... In Rose Glow and Briar Rose or Mother Goose Tan and English Oak.*

Note her deep crowned cloche with its smart turned down brim—it's one of the favorite styles of the late twenties!

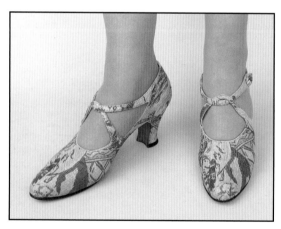

To accessorize this stylish frock, a lady may have selected these exquisite shoes in a ribbed raw silk fabric with a tropical design similar to some of Rodier's. The clever overlapping "figure eight" straps were popularized by Perugia; they fasten with grey pearl buttons. Medium 2 1/2 inch heel. Stamped in gold on the insoles: I. Miller & Sons Inc., New York-Chicago-Brooklyn; Beautiful Shoes, Made in New York. $500-$700.

To compliment our asymmetric frock, this light-as-a-feather Baku straw cloche is just perfect! With lines similar to the cloche *National Bellas Hess* shows, it has the very deep crown and modest turned down brim that's favored by many modish women. It's simply but smartly trimmed with two pleated chiffon crown bands, one rose beige and the other lilac; they're threaded through piped slits in the crown to end in a smart tie at right. Baku hats are extremely popular in summer; they're fashioned of an open weave straw "made from the unopened leaf stalks of the talipot palm of Malabar and Ceylon," according to historian R. Turner Wilcox. The rayon lining is labeled: Model by Apfel, New York, Paris; size 22 (an arrow points 'Front'). $300-$400

The Chrysler Building and The Chrysler Building *Dress*

As the decade progressed, futuristic art deco prints were more desirable than ever... and what could be more Art Deco than New York's famed Chrysler Building!

In 1928, work began on New York's beloved Chrysler Building—one of the most famous examples of Art Deco architecture in existence. This Machine Age Miracle, designed by architect William Van Alen, was destined to become the undisputed King of 42nd Street on Manhattan's east side. When auto magnate Walter P. Chrysler decided to establish his corporate headquarters in New York, he told Van Alen to design the most spectacular, most modern, and of course, the TALLEST skyscraper in the world. On October 15, 1928, work began on the site with the demolition of the existing structure, the former Bloomingdale Brewery.

The Chrysler Building's seventy-seven stories were to be topped by a 185 foot seven-story spire Van Alen originally described as: "surmounted by a glass dome which, when lit, will give the effect of a great jeweled sphere." This famous spire, clad in Nirosta stainless steel, was constructed inside the building, in secret. In November 1929, it was hoisted to the top and, as its triangular windows glowed in the night sky, it fulfilled Van Alen's dream, becoming the brightest star in New York's skyline. For several glorious months, the Chrysler Building was also the proud victor in the notorious Skyscraper Wars (it was superceded on completion of the Empire State Building in 1931).

Naturally, Chrysler's skyscraper boasts automobile themes galore. The dome's distinctive arched tiers and triangular windows are said to have been inspired by the hubcaps used on Chrysler cars—and with a salute to ancient Gothic architecture, art deco eagle gargoyles, representing Chrysler hood ornaments, peer proudly from the base of the tower. The classical era is also represented – Mercury's Winged Helmets are "Art Deco-tized" Winged Radiator Caps! A stunning brick frieze of auto hubcaps and mudguards graces the 31st floor.

On its completion in July 1930, Chrysler declared the building "A city within a city!" Its interior boasted a lobby of red Moroccan marble and a ceiling mural by Edward Trumball depicted airplanes circling the building. Its thirty-two Otis elevators were veneered in ash and walnut in fabulous art deco designs. A private restaurant, The Cloud Club, was housed in the tower just below the spire; prominent businessmen paid yearly dues of $300 for the privilege of lunching there. Though on its completion, opinions of the building varied (conservatives considered it somewhat "gaudy"), fellow architect Kenneth Murchison had the most apt description: "It teems with the Spirit of Modernism!"

The Chrysler Building *Dress*! With stylized arches and triangular "windows" that mirror the splendor of Chrysler's famous spire, this day dress is the "most spectacular" and "most modern" (if not the tallest) of art deco dresses! It's Nile green China silk, screen printed in bright orange and deep turquoise, outlined in white. The stripes accenting the cap sleeves and *trompe l'oeil* bib neckline add an Egyptian "moderne" flavor. From the low waist's vivid striped border, the deco triangles rise to the level of the natural waist, placing emphasis there. The smart pleated skirt portion is just ten inches high; box pleats alternate with tiny knife pleats all the way around. A narrow belt was optional; belt loops are placed slightly below the natural waist (the belt, most likely a narrow self-belt, is missing). $500-$700

The reverse of this period photo postcard notes:

The Chrysler Building – A modernistic Georgia Marble and Indiana Limestone building which rises 1046 feet from the ground to the top of the steel mast. A truly great achievement of modern architecture!

CHRYSLER BUILDING, NEW YORK CITY   50

14844

These two lovely African American flappers show off their glamorous gams and garters! The gal on the right wears a dress with a fantastic art deco border. Snapshot, ca. 1928.

This Whiting & Davis "Skyscraper" bag is the perfect accessory for our Chrysler Building frock! It is enameled armor mesh in shades of turquoise, orange, and black on cream, with "city lights" surrounding a towering skyscraper that rises from the vandyked border to the top of the embossed silver frame. $250-$350

Cocktail Dresses and Evening Frocks

Cocktail dresses and evening frocks for 1928 shimmer in the city lights.

Art deco at its finest... The "State Street Window" of Marshall Field's in Chicago! Against a sensational background, two wax mannequins model frocks featuring couture's favorite TIERED SKIRTS! From Permaflector Lighting's portfolio, 1928.

The *Wisteria* Frock! Even more stunning than the frocks in Marshall Field's window, this sophisticated little number is just right for cocktails... and perhaps dinner at the Plaza! This French blue silk georgette frock has it all, including the extremely popular short-tiered skirt. Its three scalloped, pleated tiers are picot-edged; they're attached to a matching georgette underskirt. Scallops, piped in silver lamé, are repeated at the low waist. A wide self belt, also piped in silver, accents the waist; it fastens with an embossed brass buckle. The bodice is heavily embroidered in metallic silver Wisteria branches. The long tight sleeves are accented with blue ties at the cuffs, which are piped in silver as is the round neckline. Rows of shirring at the shoulders provide proper fullness at the bust, and a French blue shoulder bow adds a nice finishing touch. This dress is fully lined in French blue georgette. $600-$800

This closeup photo shows the exquisite art deco Wisteria branches of silver lamé... how they must have glowed in the early evening light!

A back view of the frock's fanny-flattering tiers.

Spectacular Beaded Evening Gown
Beaded, tiered evening gown with popular "keyhole" or "peekaboo" neckline.

TIERS AND MORE TIERS! Two heavily beaded tiers accent this stunning evening frock of white silk georgette—the tiers are bordered in silver bugle bead fringe, designed to Shake and Shimmy! The all-over beading is worked in a Persian motif; it includes both mercury glass beads and silver bugle beads. In front, the skirt is softly shirred for DANCING! The low waist, also fringed with bugle beads, is fashionably scalloped. The bodice portion features a stunning "keyhole" neckline with a center medallion of mercury glass beads (these keyhole necks are very popular; they're often placed in back; though here, tiny darts indicate the front). Another mercury bead medallion accents the natural waist; at its end, two swags of mercury glass fringe swing over the fringe at the low waist. The matching slip is attached at the shoulders. $1000-$1200

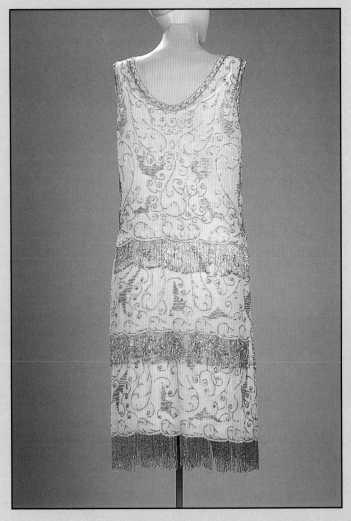

In this photo of the back, you'll note that the beaded neckline dips to a sensuous, low "U."

A closeup of the front's beaded keyhole neck, waist medallion, and silver fringe.

Though couturiers were now promoting a longer look for evening via pointed drapes, tails, and even peacock hems, many women preferred short frocks – especially for dancing! *Vogue's* "Viola Paris" questioned the practicality of the new longer look:

> *When are Long Dresses Smart?... This is generally conceded to be a dancing age, in which people have to be much amused by more active diversions than conversation and evenings spent in homes...Yet, the greatest dressmakers in Paris all have seriously proposed dresses that trail on the ground. Viola Paris has several such dresses, but she will never be seen hopping out of a taxi, seated in a theatre, or dancing in a night-club, struggling with these dresses... For informal wear – restaurant dining, theatres, and cabarets, she wears her shorter evening dresses. Chanel has made her several beautiful dresses of this type...* (October 13, 1928)

SCHIAPARELLI!

Flamboyant newcomer Elsa Schiaparelli was making her presence felt by 1928. The date of her first success, the fabled *trompe l'oeil* sweater, varies from late 1927 to early 1928 according to various historians – though all agree it made an instantaneous impact on the World of Fashion!

Italian born Elsa Schiaparelli considered fashion an art. Collaborating with Surrealists like Dali, Cocteau, and Berard, she would create some of most witty yet sophisticated fashions of the thirties and forties.

"Schiap" was born in Rome in 1890, and by the mid-teens, she'd begun to design clothing for herself and her friends. In 1922, after an unhappy marriage, she moved from New York to Paris, where she met many influential friends, including Poiret, Steichen, Beaton, and Man Ray. In 1925, backed by an American friend who'd admired her sports wear, she opened a small shop, Maison Lambal, on the corner of rue Saint Honore and rue du Juillet, near the Place Vendome. Maison Lambal's sports wear and "daytime ensembles" were striking enough to be mentioned in *Women's Wear Daily* in January 1926. When Maison Lambal closed due to lack of financing, Schiap operated out of her apartment, showing Display No. 1 in January 1927, which included handmade sweaters of Rodier's stretchy Kasha fabric, trimmed with innovative buttons, and paired with jackets and skirts of crepe de chine.

In Spring 1927, inspired by the new Surrealist art movement, Schiap created the design for her famed *Trompe l'oeil* butterfly bow sweater. She then had to turn her design into reality—so when she saw an American woman wearing a smart knit pullover, she inquired about it. The lady gave her the name of "Aroosiag Mikaelian," the Armenian woman who'd made her sweater. Schiap tracked her down and asked if she thought she could incorporate a butterfly bow design into the knit of a sweater. When it was made up, Schiap wore it to luncheon at the Ritz. It impressed a visiting buyer from Lord & Taylor, who ordered some forty sweaters with matching skirts to be delivered in two weeks. Her first private customer was author and socialite Anita Loos. Mainbocher, then editor-in-chief of French *Vogue*, thought the sweater sensational and featured it in French *Vogue*. In December, American *Vogue* followed suit, with a sketch entitled "Artistic Masterpiece."

By 1928, both *Vogue* and *Harper's Bazar* were featuring Schiap's creations. She opened *Pour Le Sport* in January 1928 at 4 rue de la Paix, and followed her *trompe l'oeil* sweater triumph with innovative crossword puzzle items and bridge sweaters with caps to match. In July 1928, she exhibited Display No. 2, which received rave reviews: the *New York Sun* noted sailcloth beach pajama ensembles, pants so wide they "resembled a skirt;" wrap-around skirts, hand-knit tunics in deco motifs and jersey pants, and culottes with knit pancake berets. A *New York Herald* article, two weeks after Display No. 2's debut, exclaimed "...comfort, perfect suitability and undeniable smartness are qualities not often happily united in garments really designed for sports... but Schiaparelli sports clothes are admirably adapted to the use for which they are made."

In January 1929, Schiaparelli presented her first major collection. In February, the *Paris Times* proclaimed her "...one of the rare creators of the fashion world." She had only just begun.

Of course, it didn't take long for something as spectacular as Schiap's *trompe l'oeil* bows to "inspire" imitations, and they soon appeared on a variety of items, including Cocktail Dresses!

Vogue's sketch of Schiaparelli's *Trompe l'oeil* Triumph!

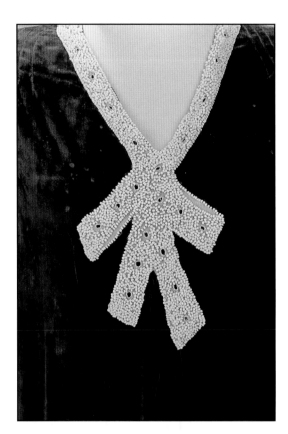

A Schiap inspired *Trompe l'oeil* bow graces this luscious cocoa brown velvet cocktail dress! This very detailed bow is worked in milk glass seed beads on ecru chiffon, with pierced accents.

This lovely cocktail dress is a slip-on style, with the popular double waist effect or "yoke;" there's a waist seam slightly below normal level, and another seam at the hip line which is pointed. Ten triangular gored panels give the skirt its modish flare; the hem is picot edged. You'll note that the long tight sleeves feature matching beaded half-bows; two darts at the elbow provide ease of motion, and the cuffs have snap closures. This frock is ca. late 1928-32) $400-$600

Note that velvet was very fashionable at this time—as *Mallinson's* advised: "Fashion's world wide demand for velvets far exceeds that of many years in the past, and never before have velvets shown such bewitching variety and such marvelous beauty!" (*Vogue* ad, 10/28)

Schiaparelli's card advertising Pour le Sport from the October 13, 1928, issue of *Vogue*. This issue also features a stunning Schiaparelli sports ensemble from New York's exclusive The Sports Shop for Women.

"Tails" Frocks

Despite women's penchant for the very short frocks, couturiers continued to lengthen the hemline. Their various drapes and "tails" were beginning to catch on as "NEW HEMLINES HAVE THEIR UPS AND DOWNS AND 'POINT' TO GREATER LENGTH!" (*Vogue*, October 13, 1928)

The "Uneven Hemline," couture's clever way to induce women to accept the new longer hemlines, is depicted by these two chic evening frocks with tails described as "cascades" and "volants." Pictured at left is: "A becoming evening frock of velvet brocaded chiffon has cascades on the blouse and the skirt... The skirt joins the blouse beneath the top belt." Note the new asymmetric neckline. At right: "Shaped volants are set on at the sides and fall below the edge of this crepe satin frock, creating the very smart uneven hemline. There is a slight blouse above the tight-fitting hips." *Vogue Pattern Book* December 1927/January 1928.

This devastating autumn afternoon dress is panne velvet, screen printed in a dramatic deco "Machine Age" motif! The richness of the velvet, with its mix of vibrant and subtle shadings – claret, ecru, teal and brown – is impossible to describe. Its chic uneven hemline is achieved via two trailing bias tails or "volants," similar to the figure at the right in the illustration. A corresponding jabot drape, smartly shirred at the top, descends from the left shoulder to the low waistline. The jabot, volants, and hem are faced with ecru silk crepe, and the round neckline is similarly piped. Multiple rows of shirring adorn both shoulders and provide bust emphasis; shirring continues around the neckline in back. The back is otherwise plain, as is common at this time. The long, tight sleeves are shirred at the elbows for ease of motion and fasten with rows of self-covered buttons. The inset waist/hip yoke is asymmetrical—it's wider on the right, and tapers at left to shirring where it joins the bottom of the jabot. The skirt's flattering flare is achieved with the bias cut. Note that these printed velvets are rare; many are very fragile, and tend to split easily. $500-$600, noting light wear.

Far left:
A marvelous Mandalian Peacock bag compliments our print velvet frock! On a French vanilla background, two proud peacocks perch on stylized branches—the male's spectacular tail spreads to the fine link fringe (several strands are missing). It has a silver repousse cathedral frame and chain handle. $300-$350

Left:
A closeup shot of the printed velvet's spectacular "Machine Age" deco motif.

Note that these new printed velvets were very desirable: "PARIS PRONOUNCES ANY WARDROBE INCOMPLETE WITHOUT, AT LEAST, ONE GOWN OF PLAIN OR PRINTED VELVET – AND NEW YORK ACQUIESCES!" (*Vogue*, 10/28). At this time, "simulated silk" (Rayon) velvets were often used.

This dramatic custom-made evening gown "Makes a Point of the New Length" with a flared side drape at right that dips to a trailing train. Its bold Cubist theme is provided by insets of shell pink slipper satin which provide a startling contrast to the gown's lush black silk velvet. The many focal points "point-counterpoint" in complimentary rhythm - the "tail" on the right corresponding to the bow's trailing ties at left, and the bow in turn complimenting the raised "step" at the natural waistline - topped by the bodice's satin side inserts which repeat the cubist motif. Beneath is its original black silk crepe slip, which is tacked to the dress at strategic points along the low waistline to insure it hangs properly; tulle straps are attached at the shoulders. $700-$900

Provenance: this stunning evening gown was worn by Emily Knight MacWilliams Huntington. Mrs. Huntington, a prominent socialite, was president of the Junior League of Syracuse; she resided on Teall Avenue in Syracuse, New York, from 1925-35.

Evening "Tails"

"THE EVENING MODE... in which it is very evident that new lines Sweep Clean and that it's never too Low to Flare"! (*Vogue* waxes witty over the new tailed evening gowns, October 13, 1928.)

Vogue advocated these trailing trains, advising:

> *Trains are favored by Chanel, Vionnet, Paquin, Lanvin, Molyneux, Cheruit and Callot... They provide an excellent suggestion of movement... They're part of the Return to Elegance, and though nobody suggests that you should leap from taxi to taxi, from party to party, and from dancing partner to dancing partner in them, these dressmakers suggest there is more to modern life than that. And they are right... Molyneux, Lelong and Patou have all been busy with the scissors, cutting pieces up, joining them together, emphasizing the seams, making panels of them – and letting them flounce off!* (October 13, 1928)

In this side view, you'll note the geometric treatment under the arms, which corresponds to that at the waist.

A New LONG All Around Frock!

In June of 1928, a HARBINGER OF THINGS TO COME appears on Fashion's Horizon...

What a sensation Bolin's cover must have caused when it first appeared on the June 1, 1928, issue of *Vogue*. Against New York's skyline, his white dress shines like a beacon! Though he's cleverly hidden its fluttering hem in the art deco foliage, it's clear that this dress is *LONG... ALL THE WAY AROUND*! Its slightly bloused bodice accents the natural waist, and the low tight yoke ends in points that emphasize the hips. The skirt falls in graceful triangular bias panels, perhaps to near ankle length. She's accessorized with a deep-crowned "picture hat" with a wide transparent brim.

Like the dress on *Vogue*'s cover, this lovely transitional afternoon frock shows a dramatically lowered hemline. Its marvelous skirt echoes the city skyline with double-peaked bias panels that are set at different levels – higher at the sides and lower in the front! These triangular panels are topstitched, and the full, floating hem is picot-edged. The fabric is the sheerest silk georgette, screen-printed in a delightful deco floral pattern. The bodice portion features a piped V-neck in both front and back. Rows of shirring at each side both provide the chic bloused effect and emphasize the natural waist. The lilac rayon underslip is separate. The label, attached to the left side seam, reads: *Persky Bros. Inc., 265 West 7th St.* $300-$500

It's shown with a wide brim horsehair picture hat that's entirely covered with squiggly vermicular soutache and trimmed with a lavender tulle crown scarf. Store stock, $250-350.

This view of the georgette frock shows the skirt in motion, fluttering in the breeze!

This lovely long afternoon dress would have been perfect to wear to a summer wedding.

1928 Formal Wedding

This beautiful formal wedding gown incorporates many of 1928's favorite features, including a spectacular asymmetric hem and long scalloped cathedral train. Couture's favorite decorative shirring plays an important role: rows of shirring at center and sides drape the modish cummerbund "girdle;" the shirring begins at the natural waistline, hinting at its growing importance. At the shoulders, shirring provides the modish bust fullness. The long, tight sleeves are shirred at the inner seams, from just above the elbows to a bit below the wrists. Beneath, a camisole top is attached to the bodice at waist and shoulders. A sweet traditional touch trims the left hip – a spray of wax orange blossoms and buds. A huge bow perches pertly on the right hip; its draped folds cascade to the hem. The asymmetric hem is short in front, dips lower at the sides, and continues around to touch the floor in back. In back, the cathedral train is joined at the low waist with rows of shirring at each side of a center "arch," which extends into the bodice; the train billows almost six feet to the wide, scalloped curves at its hem. Tiny bouquets of orange blossom buds wrapped in tulle accent the train's scalloped curves.

This front view of the gown shows the shirred, draped girdle and skirt that's short in front. It was photographed at Lorenzo State Historic Site in Cazenovia, New York, where it was featured in their 1995 exhibit, *Something Old...Nothing New – A Century of Bridal Fashions, 1840-1940.*

A closeup of the orange blossom bouquet on the left hip and the hand-stitched shirring.

Cupid Stockings
Something shocking – a glimpse of Stocking!

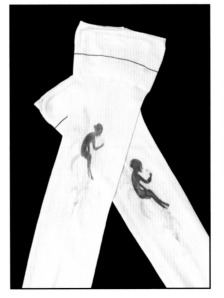

The bride's seamed silk stockings – with romantic "Cupid" silhouettes! The cupids, placed almost thigh high, were meant to be seen by the bridegroom only! $75-$100

Back view, showing the curved cathedral train, enormous draped hip bow, and shirring on sides and sleeves.

This lovely gown is heavy rayon satin. The shoulders show a bit of wear, which is reflected in the price estimate of $400-$600.

Chapter Six
1929 Women's Fashions

Timeline

The Museum of Modern Art opens in New York to great acclaim, exhibiting works by Van Gogh, Cezanne, Gauguin, and Seurat.

January 17: Popeye cartoons debut; the popular Sailor Man's created by Elzie Grisle Segar.

February 14: One of the most infamous gang murders in history, the St. Valentine's Day Massacre, takes place in Chicago, as seven members of Al Capone's gang (three posing as policemen) gun down five members of Bugs Moran's gang. Bugs Moran, who arrives late, escapes the massacre – commenting to reporters *"Only Capone kills like that."* Capone, of course, was vacationing in Florida at the time. Public outcry caused Hoover to issue orders to arrest Capone however possible. Two years later, Capone was arrested on charges of tax evasion.

February 18: The first Academy Awards are announced.

August 19: Amos n Andy, a popular radio comedy, debuts.

October 29: On Black Thursday, one of the most desperate days in history, the stock market crashes, ending the exuberant optimism of the Jazz Age, and beginning The Great Depression. By the end of the day, millions have lost their life savings, and eleven Wall Street financiers have committed suicide. Stock prices had more than doubled since mid-decade; buying on margin, easy credit, and the popularity of the Installment Plan all contribute to the crash. Banks are soon forced to call in loans and foreclose mortgages, but many fail regardless. By 1932, one out of every four Americans will be out of work. Bread lines and apple sellers will soon replace streets that were formerly bustling with prosperous men and women. Many of the newly homeless will live in cardboard box shacks in "cities" called Hoovervilles.

November 28: Thanksgiving Day explorer Richard Byrd and his three-man crew complete their perilous flight across the Antarctic, fulfilling Byrd's desire to be the first navigator to survey both poles by air.

December 31: Guy Lombardo plays "Auld Lang Syne" for the first time... ending the decade that will never "Be Forgotten..."

At the Movies

The first Academy Awards were presented this year (for 1927-28 films); winners for Best Production were *Wings* and F.W. Murnau's classic *Sunrise*. By 1929, all studios agreed that "Talkies" were here to stay. By 1929, nearly 5000 theaters of-fered Talkies; many stars of the silent screen debuted in their first talkie this year.

Mary Pickford starred in *Coquette* (which won her an Academy Award), and Joan Crawford in the steamy *Untamed*. Doug Fairbanks' first talkie, *The Iron Mask*, was a big hit. Louise Brooks created a sensation in her finest film, *Pandora's Box*. The zany Marx Brothers' first talkie was *The Coconuts*; Laurel and Hardy starred in *Big Business*. Gary Cooper starred in a hit Western, *The Virginian*. King Vidor directed *Hallelujah!*, the first Hollywood film with an all black cast. Fanny Brice starred in *My Man*, and Texas ("*Hello Sucker*") Guinan played herself in *Queen of the Night Clubs*. Sound fostered a group of new musicals: songbird Jeanette MacDonald and French heart throb Maurice Chevalier starred in *The Love Parade*, and crooner Rudy Vallee made his film debut in *The Vagabond Lover* – singing the title song he made famous by singing nasally through his megaphone. A fabulous singing and dancing extravaganza, *Broadway Melody*, won an Academy Award for "Film of the Year."

Favorite New Recordings

Hit records included "What Did I Do to Be So Black and Blue" by Louis Armstrong also "Black and Blue" by Fats Waller; "Am I Blue" by Ethel Waters; "Nobody Wants You When You're Down and Out" by Bessie Smith; "Button Up Your Overcoat – Baby It's Cold Outside" by Helen Kane; "Makin' Whoopee" by Eddie Cantor; "You'll Do It Someday, So Why Not Now" by Rudy Vallee; "I'll Get By As Long As I Have You" by Aileen Stanley; and Hoagy Carmichael's immortal "STARDUST" by the Isham Jones Orchestra.

In Literature

William Faulkner's classic *The Sound and the Fury*, heralded as a "*tragic fable*" of Southern angst, was published in 1929—also Hemingway's *A Farewell to Arms*, Thomas Wolfe's *Look Homeward Angel*; as well as *Dodsworth* by Sinclair Lewis and *Magnificent Obsession* by Lloyd C. Douglas. The first Nancy Drew mystery, *The Secret of the Old Clock*, debuted, written by Mildred A. Wirt Benson, one of several authors that wrote under the *nom de plume* "Carolyn Keene" for the Stratemeyer syndicate. Mildred had a lot to do with developing Nancy's intrepid character—feeling that young girls needed heroines that weren't "mamby-pamby," she gave Nancy a lot of spunk and independence! Feminist Virginia Woolf published her controversial *A Room of One's Own* this year, exclaiming: "a woman must have money and a room of her own if she is to write fiction... thanks to the toils of those obscure women in the past, of whom I wish we knew more, thanks, curiously enough to two wars, the Crimean which let Florence Nightingale out of her drawing room, and the European War which opened the doors to the average woman some sixty years later, these evils are in the way to be bettered."

In Fashion 1929—
The Return of the Woman!

It was a **Best of Times** decade – a decade of heady new freedoms, constant celebrations, clandestine speakeasies, and daring new dances. As it came to a close, you'll note that 1929 was a year of marked transition. Rapid fashion changes occurred as new styles accompanied more "womanly" attitudes. As our sassy young flapper became a feminine yet sophisticated woman of the world, her boyish figure changed. She now exhibited definite curves – a bosom, waist, and hips! Fashions hugged the figure at the bust, natural waist, and hips – and longer hems swirled gracefully as flirty flapper gamines were transformed into adult women, women who would have to be mature enough to deal with **The Worst of Times** – The Great Depression of the Nineteen Thirties.

Jean Patou was the couturier most credited with launching this new "rounded body" look; he had sensed that women were beginning to grow tired of the *garconne* and were in the mood to "dress up again." On presenting his new collection, he paced the floor, nervous at the dramatic changes he had made – until his assistant came in to report that women in the audience were tugging at their short skirts to cover their bare knees! *Vogue* took note of the new look, trumpeting:

> *...here is the first dramatic change in dress that has occurred since the garconne mode came in. Women are as womanly as ever they can be... What looked young last year looks old this season, all because longer, fuller skirts and higher waistlines have been used so perfectly that they look right, smart and becoming.*

This change in fashion had come about gradually, as part of a continual evolution. It had begun around mid-decade with hints of a natural waistline, "bloused" bodices, and "dipping" uneven hems. As 1929 began, the extremely short styles were generally reserved for sports and casual wear, while for more formal afternoon and evening events, the new feminine styles were setting the stage for the curvaceous clothes of the thirties. They were heralded as *"the most feminine fashions in years!"*, prompting one commentator to rhapsodize: *"How marvelous it would be to be naked with a cheque book in order to buy the new figure revealing fashions"*! Not everyone welcomed the new look however; *Harper's* Marjorie Howard, noting that the longer skirts and tighter bodices were introduced by male designers rather than female, cried: *"I suppose they cannot bear it any longer that our clothes should be so much more comfortable and easy to get into than their own."*

Couture Trends
"The transformation goes on; clothes are becoming more feminine. True genius lies behind this transformation, controlling and directing its onward march...," *Vogue Pattern Book* observed as the new silhouette solidified. (August/September 1929) Feminine features that had been merely hinted at were now PRONOUNCED. Femininity was embraced with *"New Soft Touches"* in all the latest clothing – with bows, lacy lingerie touches, jabots, scallops, bindings, pipings, and hemstitching – and "wings, loops, ends and puffs" were everywhere.

Flora McFlimsey praised the new Femininity, noting that "The clever woman... can intimate by a few telling touches so many things that are best left unspoken – those saucy streamers that say, 'Suivez-moi, jeune homme' (Follow me, young man); that diabolically innocent collar on an evening wrap that hides everything but a charming nose and two mocking eyes, that coquettish and ridiculous little muff... do they not put ideas into the heads of the least susceptible males?" (*Vogue*, March 1929)

CURVES from Neck to Hem
Bigger bust lines were emphasized with a variety of pleats, tucks, shirrings, darts, and asymmetric diagonal lines. As "DIAGONAL LINES LEAD UP TO SPRING CHIC," asymmetric necklines and surplice wraps continued in the mode. Bodices continued to be "slightly bloused for fullness" – they were now bloused to the natural waist. Couture's new shirred or "puckered" seams often accentuated curves down center fronts and/or on the sides of bodices. Boleros, Berthas, Jabots, and Cape effects were used more than ever to focus attention on the upper body. As *Vogue* noted, "The Cape Collar is a soft, becoming detail." Trailing "Scarf Collars" draped many necklines, as did smaller "Handkerchief Jabots." Smart diagonally pleated inserts often filled a squared neckline.

For evening, Stehli Silks advertised white satin gowns with deep décolletage in both front and back to show off sunkissed tans: "Now copper-toned shoulders greet the evening... fashion's habit of following the sun has made the pink and white complexion as absurd as bathing stockings..." Décolletage was most often deep "U" or "V" shaped and it was often draped or caped in back. And, as *Vogue* observed, "the new sharply square décolletage is very smart."

Rising waists/"moulded" hips: The transition to the natural waist was made via the "molded hip" and "Moulded hiplines are achieved by divers means...," including girdle effects and hip yokes. Girdles were now often draped asymmetrically and tied on one hip. The important inset waist-to-hip yoke emphasized both the natural waist and the low waist with lower seams that were horizontal, diagonal, curved, asymmetric, or v-shaped (see pg. 186). Peplums flared from many hips. Flounced or pleated, they were "Youthful and Slim"! To "mark the natural waistline", shirring, inverted pleats or a "cluster of tucks" were often placed at one or both sides of the waist. "Curved inserts" or godets (sometimes shirred at the top) often flared from one hip – or both hips – and from back and/or front. Pleats continued to be of utmost importance, the newest skirts were "stitched to accentuate the fitted hip line." Asymmetric pleated or tucked bands provided interest on many frocks; Lelong created a dress with diagonal insert bands on both bodice and skirt. Belted a bit lower than the natural waist, it was worn with a straight jersey coat that was lined in a lighter shade of jersey than the dress.

Longer Skirts: To segue into the longer fashions, the uneven hem was more modish than ever – dips and tails prevailed! Frocks' hems dipped anywhere and everywhere, and commentators noted: "Flared fulness is important in all phases of the mode"! Layered looks were ultra chic, and floating side and/or back panels often combined to create a feminine "fluttering line." Couturiers "achieve the desired look with circular panels that dip in back to 'follow an interesting down-in-the-back line'." Circular flounces, and even "spiral" flounces, kissed the floor and double flounces were "deftly swathed and draped." Flounces, layers, and tiers were often asymmetric, and tiers also dipped as "tiered circular flounces are longer in back." For afternoon and evening, the ultimate "Dip" was provided by long "Peacock" or "fish-tail" gowns; many had layered, looped, and bowed back accents so extravagant they rivaled the Victorian era's bustles!

For day, even casual frocks "dipped," though not as dramatically as evening or afternoon dresses. Cape collars were seen on day dresses as well as evening gowns. On skirts, *Vogue* advised that "sectional pleats are smarter than all-around;" and pleats stitched down lower than usual were preferred to "those released too soon, on account of the persistency of the moulded hip line." Especially chic were frocks with diagonal-topped "inserted pleated sections" on the skirt's front. Since "All Paris speaks of the 'Frock with Softness' for afternoons," Golflex "interprets" Chanel's latest, headlining "Chanel Bows and Plaits Appear for Afternoon... Stitched plaits to deep yoke depth – and the introduction of godets – give a modish ripple to the skirt. The tight 'young' swathed hipline is retained while the deeper belt with its Chanel bows is distinctly new. In colors that go well with sun tan – Nattier blue, Zeppelin gray... and a subtle new red that suggests tomato. $35.00." The new blouses also exhibited femininity, winning "feminine hearts as they are becoming and utterly different from those masculine creations women wore not so long ago... jabots, bows, hemstitching and tucking have wrought the miracle"!

Couture's affair with the tailored ensemble continued. *Vogue* pictured "an all-white suit from Schiaparelli; the coat and skirt made of Ondamoussa, and an unusual woolen material with eyelet holes in it is used for the blouse, the lining of the jacket and the scarf." Available at Lord and Taylor, this smart suit was knee length, with a large inverted pleat at the skirt's center providing ease of motion (January 1929). And Jane Regny created a spectacular four-piece "yellow and black sports ensemble for 'traveling, motoring or town wear'... an exceptionally smart tweed in a mixture of yellow, black, and white is used for the loose seven-eights coat and for the skirt which has a slightly circular movement. Black lamb is used for the fur trimming. The sweater is of a yellow and black mixed jersey exclusive with Jane Regny. The cardigan and scarf are black knitted angora wool." The hip-length blouse was belted with a narrow belt slightly lower than the natural waistline; the seven-eights coat had a slightly flared skirt. (March 1929)

The versatile "Runabout" (or *trotteur*) dress was extolled as "a dress that will lead you smartly by the hand from late summer to crisp autumn." It was available in jersey, silk or wool crepe, and in "smart tweeds in modish patterns" of triangles, diagonals, small and large checks, speckles, herringbones, criss-crosses, and zigzags. "Add a new close-fitting hat and classic one strap shoes, fling a fur scarf about your shoulders and walk from your door with all the self confidence in the world, for you are a picture of chic from head to foot."

For warm weather, *Vogue* advised: "Indulge in summery prints, sleeveless tennis dresses, light afternoon dresses that fit in so charmingly with country club backgrounds, and beach clothes that were never so enticing as this year." Also, "flowered or plain chiffon frocks with jackets to accompany them are a delightful summer fashion."

Smart Shops and Catalogs Interpret the Mode for the "Average Woman"

Catalogs had to move quickly to keep up with 1929's fashion changes. They offered many of the very shortest frocks, though the longer, feminine look crept in more tentatively with adaptations of new couture features. "Paris takes us 'Back to Femininity this Season' with the most charming, graceful flares!" headlined the Fall and Winter 1929/1930 *Chicago Mail Order Catalog*! Their consultant for 1929 was "Miss France," Germaine Laborde, "acclaimed the most beautiful and best dressed Girl in Paris." *Chicago* cried: "Even in Paris there are no smarter styles...as French in spirit as any Dumas novel, telling such a story of unusual charm, and revealing such a perfect understanding of things fashionable as to pique the interest of every style-adoring human!" Their ad copy was superb! A dipping *robe de style* was "...as spell binding in beauty as a Rivera night." Of the chic ensemble suit *Chicago* declared, "*Vive l'Ensemble* – Cries Paris! – Long May it Reign echoes America!... wear it nonchalantly all day long, sure you're garbed *'a la correctivement'!*"

Hemlines shown lagged a bit behind those of haute couture; in most cases they reached the knee – though the ubiquitous "dip" was well represented, and even day dresses often dipped at the sides or back. And, "Graceful as a Fluttering Butterfly's Wing," couture's cape collars were everywhere!

Not to be outdone, the 1929 *National Bellas Hess* catalog countered with: "Today you will find the smartest dressed women in the world on Fifth Avenue... New York is now without question the style center of the World!" Their ad copy was both fresh and brash: "**Styled by *National* is Like Saying 'Jewelry by Tiffany'!**" They promoted clothing for the "Woman of Today... Who is TRIGLY up-to-the-minute from head to toe!... So Smart – So Ultra New Yorkish!"

National's quickly interpreted many of the latest couture features: "Fashion Says: Cape Backs, Flares, Spirals (dresses and cuffs), Shawl Collars; Tiered Effects, Princess Lines; Trimmed Backs, etc. etc." They described an "ultra-smart" couture-inspired day dress: "The skirt is circular cut at the left side and its graceful flaring folds effect the modish uneven lower hem; the surplice front has a contrasting vestee with button trimmed jabot; the set in hip band is rounded at the left side, in satin backed crepe, with attached belt [placed just below the normal waistline]... You'd never think it cost only $7.98"! Couture's vertically shirred or puckered seams that so charmingly accent feminine curves had been adopted too—they were seen on several frocks. Also adopted: "an interesting new feature is the beltless waist front, draped by shirring into a curved low waistline, below which the circular cut skirt hangs in the fashionable flaring fullness" (see pages 172, 173).

1929 Fashions

New Millinery Trends

FROM HEAD TO TOE, A NEW LOOK ushered in the last year of the decade—and, from the top, hats, as always, were the crowing glory! The latest millinery trends were broadcast in *Vogue's Spring Millinery* issue:

> *The forehead must be revealed – hats are worn on the back off the head – width appears – brims are uneven – straw is treated like felt. Drastic changes have come about somehow... By simplifying the fronts of hats, new emphasis is placed at the back.*
> (March 2, 1929)

Of course, the new style hats had trendy new names: hats "worn on the back off the head" were known as "The Cute Eyebrow Style" or "Forehead Cloches." Snug Skulls or "moulded hats" were very chic; they complimented fashion's Molded Hips! Catalogs praised the Skull cap: "Trim and snugly fitted, it expresses Youth in every line...!"

On the hats that were brimmed, the brims have gone wild! Many now had sculptured effects – and there were perky pleats, folds, tabs, and tucks. Modish asymmetric or "uneven brims" were longer on one side than the other; the new "Earlaps" were "modishly longer" on both sides as their "drooping" brims echoed dresses' drooping hems. Inspired by the Victorian era, many hats not only had "poke" fronts, but also Victorian "curtain" backs. For the adventurous, pinched bicornes and tricornes titillated: "Beauty cannot hide or lie dormant when Milady wears this hat—it awakens every bit of latent loveliness... it's the very newest 'Bicorne'!" (*Chicago Mail Order* 1929/30). By mid-year, couture was showing tiny tricornes that would become the favorite hats of the early thirties (see pg. 186). The "Vagabond" retained its sporty smartness: "The smart set is wearing the Vagabond style... the sort of hat you just crush on your head and know that, no matter which way the lines go, you're looking very swagger"! (Vagabonds were carefree "Happy Wanderers" – Rudy Valle's "I'm Just a Vagabond Lover" was one of the year's top tunes!)

The Newest Hats for Day and Evening

Hats, like dresses, are changing drastically in 1929.

Benito captures the sleek, streamlined look of the end of the decade for *Vogue's* September 28, 1929, cover. The Eiffel Tower makes a dramatic backdrop! The cloche, which features the new exposed forehead, is the latest "Earlap" or "Dutch Boy" style.

Agnes strikes a similar pose beside a wonderful deco hatbox, signed *L.P.B.* from *Daniels and Fisher*. The clock tower in the background seems to remind one that this incredible decade's time is running out. Agnes models 1929's favorite Earlap cloche that *Chicago Mail Order* heralds as: "*EXTRAORDINAIRE*! Rare *Beauté*! So raved the French *modiste*. It is a perfect bit of chic... inspired by Ancient Egyptian Headgear – sleek, sophisticated and subtly exotic!" Ours is soft fur felt with earlaps and "curtain back" formed of overlapping felt petals, which meet at a small bow at the center back. Earlap cloche, $250-$350; Box, $75-$100

Label: *Hotel Astor Chapeaux, Hotel Astor – New York – Paris – London.*

The year 1929's favorite styles, as offered by *National Bellas Hess*: "Triomphe Hats... Exact Reproductions of Original Models Created by Leading Parisian Designers...""! As you'll note, many new features are often combined in one hat. Original descriptions, clockwise from top left:

Earlap Cloche: *copied from* **Lanvin**... *the brim cut away in front, draped up and drawn across the crown at left side. The right side of brim is cut longer, folded over, and held with a rhinestone pin ornament...just as chic on the smart American woman as it is on her French cousin!*

Copied from **Reboux**: *A Smart Tricorne... the brim is richly embroidered across the front and sides with metallic cord and glass bugle beads.* (Reboux is arguably the most famous milliner of all time.) As Chicago Mail Order declares: "Beauty and royalty alike pay homage to the divine talent of Reboux – to whose famed shop there flocks the feminine 'elite' of every continent on the globe!" (1929)

This **Agnes** replica is: *One of the biggest successes at the recent fall openings... Agnes' new version of the ultra chic swathing Skull style Hat... Fashion says: 'the two sides of a hat must not be alike' - so this charming model has a pointed dip of the left ear and a jaunty long loop with a beautiful rhinestone pin at the right side.*

A pleated **Patou** "Skull": *The 'Skull' Hat in a New Model... while the crown retains its skull like lines, the dip over*

each ear gives a vastly more becoming line... a new note is struck in the folded brim of two color Lyons velvet....

Tallien's "New 1929 'Vagabond': *a style that the smartest followers of the sports model have adopted for general service as well....*

A **Louison** replica, with chic curving brim and pleated earlap and Victorian "Curtain" back is: The Very Latest Poke... *Louison gave the always flattering poke shape a new silhouette in this latest velvet hat...lustrous wide satin ribbon with moiré back forms the smart plaiting at right side and back...*

Copied from **Molyneux** is: *A Glorified 'Sou'wester'... Among the first to see the artistic possibilities of the fisherman's sou'wester, Molyneux presented this glorified version to his clientele in both Paris and New York... with brim rolled up sharply in front and drooping low at each side, it follows the sou'wester lines until it reaches the back, where it is cut shorter to fit snugly into fur collars...*

Talbot's beaded, embroidered replica: *Shows Talbot's clever use of all-over embroidery for dressy hats... the design carried out in either gold of silver metallic cord, metallic thread, small glass beads and spangles, covers the crown and turned up brim.*

Note that while these *Triomphe Hats* are $4.95 each, prices for couture "Replicas" at stores like B. Altman's range from $7.50-$12.50.

The most popular hat styles of 1929!

Far left:
This modish "Beaver brown" felt Fisherman's Sou'wester exhibits the latest asymmetric lines—its sculptured brim droops lower over the right ear; just behind, a large felt bow adds "Swagger." A bit left of center, the crown is "cunningly cut" into the brim, and accented with a bakelite and rhinestone tulip pin. The black rayon lining is labeled: *Blower's Hats, Syracuse, New York.* $250-350

Left:
This marvelous forest green felt combines many new features – it's a Bicorne-Sou'wester-Forehead-Asymmetric combo! The close skull crown has a creased ridge; the applied, sculptured brim dips over the left ear to a Napoleon-ish bicorne pinch that's topped by original Egyptian celluloid birds. From center back, a wide velvet half bow continues to the right to meet the long Sou'wester droop over the right ear. The green rayon lining is marked only with a size tag: "23." $250-$350 (Also see page 174.)

This fetching flapper hat stand is a real beauty—she's wearing a chic Forehead Sou'wester that's as smart as Billie Dove's, with a pert turned up brim that droops devastatingly at the sides. Green felt leaves trim the left side, and her matching rayon neck bow adds panache. Note that her blonde mohair hairdo is correspondingly longer, as the new more feminine look mandates. She's hand-painted composition on a painted wood stand, stamped *Made in Germany*. Old store stock, $300-$400 (similar examples with light wear, $100-$200)

The "Skull" is one of most popular styles of 1929—by the next decade, it shrinks to segue into the chic little "Juliet Caps" of the thirties! It's easy to picture this chic art deco Skull at cocktails, "In Some Secluded Rondevoux...!" This black velvet hat has an Egyptian border of gold kid leather, with hot pink and metallic gold floss embroidery. Just left of center, a cartouche of hot pink roses and gold kid leaves adds panache! It's asymmetric, dipping lower on the right. Of course, it's couture; lined in black silk, it's labeled: *Antoinette, 332 Rue Saint Honoré Paris, Made in France.* $350-$500

This beaded evening skull is "As French as the Seine!"... and so *soignee*! It's the softest imaginable black fur felt, with a wide applied border of silver bugle beads in dramatic art deco swirls. The rayon lining, which pictures a flapper with two huge hatboxes, is labeled: *Sacks – Germantown at Chelten Ave.* $300-$350

Molyneux's modish Earlap-Curtain-Skull is THE Hat of the Future, presaging those chic little hats of the thirties – hats that *Vogue* will praise as "...beginning to take shape and form, to reveal some independence of character..."! This is an "Exact Reproduction" of one of Molyneux's smartest creations, knitted in cotton tweed (tweed, of course, is *ultra chic!*) Fitted very closely to the head, its smart little brim turns up from center back around the face; then turns down at right, dipping to form a smart pleated "Earlap-Curtain" that ends at center back. $175-$250

Label for a licensed replica of Molyneux's sporty tweed hat: *Reproduction, MOLYNEUX, 5 Rue Royale, Paris*

A beaded Evening Skull that's as ROMANTIC as Romeo and Juliet! *Chicago Mail Order* describes a similar Evening Skull with their usual panache:

> *Can you perchance guess the inspiration for this heavenly bit of millinery, milady? Seek for it in fairy-tale lore, for it's most like the ravishing "jewel-cap" worn by some lovely princess dressed to receive her "Prince Charming" – and yet, it's as new and modern as TELEVISION AND "TALKIES!"* (1929/30)

Ours is gold lamé on tulle net, with faceted multicolor "jewels," bugle beads, and gold soutache braid in a streamlined deco design. $200-250

Famous film star Billie Dove chats on her candlestick telephone in a chic Sou'wester-Earlap-Forehead cloche! Note that not only are her eyebrows exposed, but also most of her forehead! It's "moulded" to her head, the smartly tucked asymmetric brim is longer on the left, and pleated, like the Lanvin model opposite (top left). Note Billie's "Swagger" outfit – a mannish shirt and tie.

Day Wear, 1929

At the beginning of 1929, many women were wearing the shortest hems yet... it was their swan song just before *The Fall*! As noted, the new longer styles have already debuted – though more as toes tentatively dipped in fashion's waters than being truly "in the swim"... though by Autumn, both hemlines and hairstyles will come spiraling down with the stock market.

"THAT'S MY WEAKNESS NOW"! This cover illustrates why so many guys went weak in their own knees at the sight of dimpled knees like these! This tune is "Successfully introduced" by Helen Kane, who bears a striking resemblance to the illustration. "Weakness" has many choruses, both male and female, including this rather risqué last chorus:

> *He's got a 'ha-cha-cha'*
> *I never liked a 'ha-cha-cha'*
> *But he's got a 'ha-cha-cha'*
> *AND THAT'S MY WEAKNESS NOW!*
> *What's more - What's more -*
> *I know he knows what 'ha-cha-cha' is for!*
> *He likes to 'ho-de-o-do'*
> *I never liked to 'ho-do-o-do'*
> *But he likes to 'ho-de-o-do'*
> *AND THAT'S MY WEAKNESS NOW!"*

(Green & Stept, 1928)

HO-DE-O-DO! Three lively ladies enjoy a cruise aboard the *City of Honolulu* out of Los Angeles in 1929 – all wear sweet smiles with their sassy frocks! The gal at left has selected a frock with a scalloped hem that's belted at just below the natural waist; her companion at right wears a flirty flared dress, and one of the new "eyebrow/forehead" cloches with an asymmetric brim.

Montgomery Ward's window display, ca. 1929... a delightful array of flares, tiers, and shirrs with very short and sassy skirts! On a hanger at center foreground is a frock with the new shirred bodice that heralds *The Return of the Bustline!*

"WEAKNESS!" This little number must have knocked 'em dead as it sashayed down the street flashing legs up to here! This perky print of poppies on silk georgette boasts huge semi-circular cape sleeves that are bias cut to flutter in the breeze; they end at the natural waist, providing emphasis there. A self belt, held in place with attached belt loops, also highlights the natural waist. The tight yoke or "inset hip band" focuses attention on the low waist—it's delineated by the curved topstitched seam that joins it to the skirt. The bias cut provides the skirt's fetching flare and flirty uneven hem. Then: about $10.98 in smart catalogs. Now: $200-$300.

A back view of the dress, showing the cape sleeves and back of the haute couture Marie Alphonsine straw hat.

A rare treasure! This extreme example of a late twenties asymmetric poke is a haute couture creation by the famed Marie Alphonsine. Its daring brim is short on the right to provide a provocative peek at the profile; at left, it's tantalizingly long! The leghorn straw is so fine that its texture resembles linen. Additional drama is provided by the "simple" trim – a wide black satin bow at left extends from beneath a straw pleat to continue up the crown, where it juts through half way up.

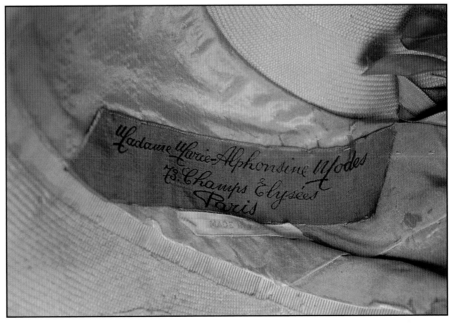

As you can see in this interior closeup, this hat is partially lined, and the back is marked by a small bow. The original label reads: *Madame Marie-Alphonsine Modes, 73 Champs Elysees, Paris, Made in France.* This hat was never worn; as it's price tag attests, it was imported to R.H. Stearns Co., written in script: Marie A. Style 160, (original) Price $65.00 (comparable to about $600 today). $600-$800

Day Frocks for 1929

"Smart frocks" for day wear, 1929...

Louise Brooks, Paramount's precocious vamp, poses in a sporty plaid tweed ensemble that comes to just above her knees; it's belted at almost the natural waistline. Note that chic cloche and those sporty spike-heeled oxfords! *Vogue* refers to such casual, all-purpose fashions as "Runabout Costumes." In 1929, Louise stars as "Lulu" in her finest film, *Pandora's Box*.

New Shoe Styles

Spike heeled oxfords, like those Louise Brooks wears, are THE shoe for sports and casual day wear!

National Bellas Hess offers dramatic lattice oxfords in "New Cut-Out" design, noting: "The fan-like cut-out quarter of this chic, dressy oxford is of reptile-grained leather." They're available in your choice of the new high spike heel or the practical chunky Cuban heel. (1929)

The 1929 *National Bellas Hess* frocks are "Styled in the Modern Manner... We Rest Our Reputation FOR STYLE LEADERSHIP On Smart Frocks Like These!" Rather conservative by necessity, their hemlines hover at the knees. Waistlines are slowly creeping up – and many frocks spotlight both the natural waist and low waist with double waistline effects. At lower left is a sporty "3-piece Ensemble" that's similar to Louise's. At lower right is another of the latest styles – a frock which utilizes shirring at the bust and torso to hug those new feminine curves. Note the modish "drooping" cloches.

Ever So Chic! These fetching oxfords are navy gabardine with fantastic patent leather lattice cutwork; they're accented by discreet white topstitching all around. The sassy spike heels are a full 3" high; the original rayon laces end in tassels. Size 4 is stamped inside, there's no other label present. Never worn, they're old store stock. $150-$200

New features to note, as originally described in the 1929 *National Bellas Hess* catalog (opposite page):

Top row, left (10E822):

Beautiful cape back with modish irregular lower edge; typically French...with the new cape falling over the back in soft ripples.... [Asymmetric] wide draped band at waistline... fashionable uneven lower edge [handkerchief hem].

Top row, second from right,(10E824): A smart asymmetric style with the double waistband effect:

Circular cut front of skirt flares gracefully below the wide pointed inset hip band trimmed with novelty buttons... details of the new mode include dainty vestee of ecru lace and looped bow which make the trimming on the slightly bloused bodice surplice style waist front.

Lower left (10E826): This "trig" 3-piece tailored tweed ensemble is:

One of the smartest of the swagger new fall ensembles is this well-tailored 3 piece model with coat and skirt of handsome novelty silk and wool tweed and the blouse of all silk flat crepe. The coat shows a modish trimming in the curly Krimmer fur cloth used for the collar, revers, cuffs and patch pocket trimming... Has all-around buckle trimmed belt. The plaited skirt, made on a bodice top, and the blouse are equally smart worn without coat, or the blouse, skirt and coat may each be worn with different costumes.

Bottom right(10E829): The New Shirred Look, similar to the Vionnet creation opposite:

Nothing so chic as black velvet with a touch of fine lace for contrast – comes the word from Paris. And one of the handsomest dresses in our entire line of styles for the smart woman features this favored combination. It's a very new model of rich black chiffon velvet that follows Fashion's vogue for graceful flaring lines. A button trimmed tab at the neck which shows soft shirring, holds in place the petty jabot beautifully trimmed with the same fine lace which finishes the sleeves in pointed line. The waist section shirred at center front gives a modish draped effect that harmonizes with the graceful rippling lines of the all around flared skirt which has circular cut shirred godet at center to achieve the fashionable uneven lower edge. This sensuous shirring will carry over well into the thirties.

Shirred Vionnet *Adaptecheune* Frock

This forest green crepe frock is a Madeleine Vionnet *Adaptecheune* – a licensed design by Vionnet purchased by manufacturers for an upscale retail market. Vionnet, of all the era's couturiers, most influenced the look of the late twenties and thirties – and this dress is a veritable Triumph of Transition! With its very complex construction, it exhibits many noteworthy new features, from its chic deco collar to the flattering flared hem.

In this full photo of Vionnet's design, you'll note that on the bodice, Vionnet accents feminine curves with a "Skyscraper" look – a startling shirred spire that's divided by a row of twenty-four covered buttons! The spire's peak extends onto the sailor collar, to the top of the wide v-neck. From the base of the spire, its sides descend to a low waist in curved, topstitched seams (period magazines often describe this style as "Princess," though the lower waist is partially seamed). The wide sailor collar is two-tone – spring green and forest green meet in embroidered "flames;" it's also embroidered in contrasting ecru and forest green "sprigs," which provide a "moderne" touch of the past. The sleeves too are dramatic; they're pouched from elbow to wrist via two rows of shirring (they're seamed at the underarm only, but shirred on both sides). Three diagonal inverted pintucks placed at the insides of the elbows provide ease of motion, and the tight piped wrist is adorned with a row of four covered buttons.

On the front of the skirt portion, a narrow pointed godet at center begins at the bottom of the bodice's buttoned spire, to fall from the natural waist to the hem. On either side of this long pointed godet, seven triangular topstitched bias panels, their points at varying heights, continue around to a straight narrow center panel at back.

Label: *Madeleine Vionnet Adaptecheune*

Closeup of the bodice's incredible detailing – the shirred, buttoned "Spire"!

In back, a smart bolero highlights the natural waistline—attached at the shoulders and side seams, it floats free at the waist. A self sash ties at the natural waist, spotlighting the curves of the derriere. In back, the collar is attached only at the shoulders, allowing a peek at the four inverted pintucks that shape the rounded neckline. Note the pouched, shirred sleeves.

This delightful dress is quite similar to the *National Bellas Hess* frock at the bottom right – perhaps they too were "inspired" by the fabulous Vionnet!

Then: note that while the *National Bellas Hess* version is $14.98, at an exclusive New York shop similar frocks might be priced around $25-$30. Now: a licensed Vionnet *Adaptecheune* might be priced between $500-$700 (noting some old repairs at underarms, and slight wear at v-neck)

Accessories, a Sou'wester Cloche, & an Elephant Purse
An exotic Elephant Clutch Purse adds a touch of whimsey!

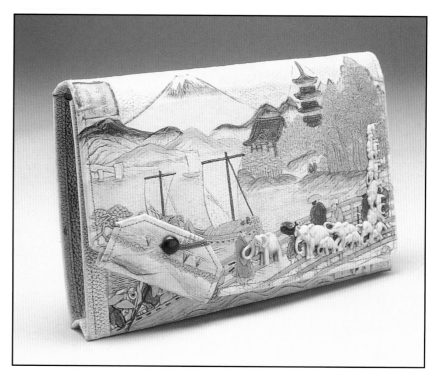

A *PACHYDERM PARADE*! Carved celluloid elephants march along the front of this enchanting envelope clutch! It's simulated embossed leather, hand-painted with scenes of Japan – people, pagodas, sampans, and mountains. There are additional scenes beneath the front flap and on the reverse (under the carrying strap). For a quick makeup check, a gal simply snapped open the flap at left and pulled out a concealed mirror. Inside, there's a rayon moiré lining with two pockets and two compartments separated by a zippered pouch, and a flat section for cards or notes. This charming bag, made for export, is signed in Japanese at the bottom right. It was owned by Hattie Susong of Jonesborough, Tennessee – a maiden lady who traveled extensively after the deaths of her elderly parents. $100-$150

The scene on the back of the bag is partially hidden by the carrying strap.

Here's a closeup of the carved celluloid Egyptian birds that grace her green felt sou'wester cloche. (See also pg. 167)

174

Checked "Runabout Frock

READY FOR TAKE OFF! This smart gal is about to board a Goose Air Lines Inc. flight, dressed in a natty blazer and short checked skirt. Her accessories include a chic cloche, handled bag, and strappy pumps! Snapshot, 1929.

This smart slate blue chemise with a navy windowpane check is a practical style that *Vogue* dubs the "Runabout" – it's perfect for shopping, travel – or the office! Ours is the softest wool flannel imaginable to ward off chilly fall winds and features a sporty sailor collar with "Swagger" satin tie, long cuffed sleeves, two roomy welt pockets, and a self belt. $150-$200

New Shoe Styles

Perfect to wear with our blue flannel checked "Runabout" frock! These chic Deco Spectators are black kid with white perforations – and a sexy 3" spike heel. No store or maker's label is present; a numbers series is stamped inside the quarters. $100-$200

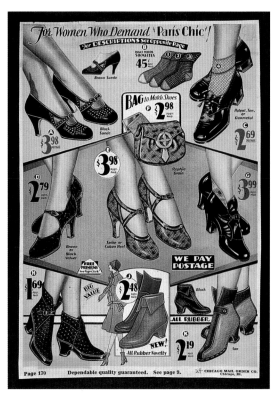

"For Women Who Demand PARIS CHIC," the 1929 *Chicago Mail Order* catalog offers this smart array of the latest shoes! The "Bag to Match Shoes" at center is a new trend. With their usual panache, Chicago describes: A) Spectator pumps "as exquisitely feminine as Cinderella's famous glass slippers, but much more practical – a perfect replica of a favorite Paris model." B) The new "Sockettes:" "Follow the Paris fad: wear sockettes over your hose for street and sports, and you'll be smartly dressed! They're good looking, sporty, and protect your ankles from cold!" C) "Swagger Street Oxfords" (with sockettes): "reptile grain leather forms the smart tongue. Perforated quarters, creased vamps, semi-square toes add that note of style so appealing to the discriminating woman!" D) Dressy Mary Janes: "Velvet moiré slippers in a richly self-color embroidered fabric; covered spike heels...round toe last." E, F) Mary Jane Pumps and "BAG TO MATCH! ... A masterpiece in fine footwear, in reptile grain leather, the leather sponsored by style-wise Parisians, trimmed with glossy patent leather on vamp and quarter." Of the matching bag, Chicago exclaims: "Paris dictates color harmony in the complete ensemble – that of course includes the purse, but retail shoe stores ask such outrageous prices for such combinations – so we bring you this popular pouch style bag...at less than you've paid for just any old kind of leather bag. Clever celluloid snap closing ornament. Back strap handle." G-K), the latest boots are: "The latest Paris interpretation of the swanky boot – the novel footwear that has captured the fancy of American women." J) These boots are: "The latest Parisian innovation! Brillant-colored gaiters – that cheerfully take the gloom out of rainy or snowy days, and keep your feet cozily dry! Popular automatic fastener closing (Zipper); snap fastening strap. Cuffs may be turned up."

Sports Wear for 1929

New Fashions for Golf

At the Fifth Hole, September 1929! is noted on the back of this fabulous golf photo! It pictures stylish attire for both men and women golfers. The two gals at left wear flared knee length frocks; the three at center, chic sweaters and skirts. Two of the guys have donned sporty plus fours, while the tall, slim man at far right has opted for cutting edge flannel bags and a cricket sweater.

This photo is a companion to the golf photo (this gal is the lady at right in the group photo). It's her turn to tee – and she's wearing a very chic two-piece ensemble that's perfect for GOLF. Her smart striped sweater tops a trim skirt with inverted kick pleats that provide ease of motion. And check those checkered golf stockings!

Sporty ensembles like these are seen at such famous couturiers as Patou, Chanel, Jane Regny, and Mary Nowitsky, to name a few. At upscale New York shops like B. Altman's, two and three-piece "knitted sports suits" are priced between $16.95-$25.00; separate pullovers and cardigans are $5-10; separate skirts, $10-$15.

By 1929, Schiaparelli's spectacular *trompe l'oeil* sweater had been interpreted in many ways! This delightful example, perfect for golf, is rayon boucle knit with *trompe l'oeil* simulating a jacket with an asymmetric side closing, and two-tone collar and cuffs. These original late twenties to early thirties *trompe l'oeil* sweaters are so rare today that there are too few extant for price comparisons. Buyers should be aware, however, that in the 1970s similar sweaters were very popular.

This photo from the Rotogravure Picture Section of the September 22, 1929, *New York Times* pictures the latest golf shoes for women – snappy oxfords trimmed with "Genuine Alligator." (At B. Altman's, a similar pair is priced at $9.75.)

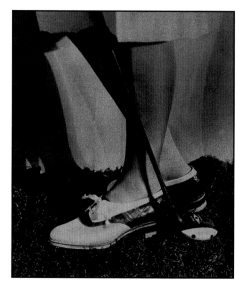

Riding and Aviatrix Attire
Breeches for Riding – or Flying!

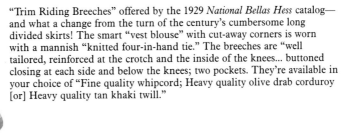

"Trim Riding Breeches" offered by the 1929 *National Bellas Hess* catalog— and what a change from the turn of the century's cumbersome long divided skirts! The smart "vest blouse" with cut-away corners is worn with a mannish "knitted four-in-hand tie." The breeches are "well tailored, reinforced at the crotch and the inside of the knees... buttoned closing at each side and below the knees; two pockets. They're available in your choice of "Fine quality whipcord; Heavy quality olive drab corduroy [or] Heavy quality tan khaki twill."

Classic late twenties breeches or "jodhpurs:"
These sporty pants are heavy tan whipcord with protective suede knee patches; inside, the crotch is lined with soft chamois. They feature a four-button closure at each side, and two diagonal welt pockets. Below the knee is the traditional stepped closure – four buttons, a jog, then two additional side buttons. The white pique cotton blouse has a pintuck/diamond weave, and features a Peter Pan collar and wide waistband. It's worn with a brown striped rayon knit tie – a Mannish MUST!
Whipcord breeches, $55-$75; Pique blouse, $45-$55; Knit boucle tie, $20-$30.

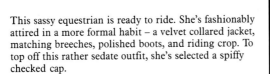

This sassy equestrian is ready to ride. She's fashionably attired in a more formal habit – a velvet collared jacket, matching breeches, polished boots, and riding crop. To top off this rather sedate outfit, she's selected a spiffy checked cap.

177

Breeches were also worn by women pilots or "aviatrixes."

Just before hopping into her cockpit, plucky Patty Willis poses for the camera in 1929. She wears breeches, boots, an open-necked shirt, and leather jacket – and a leather aviator's cap and goggles! Patty was a friend and flying buddy of such daring women pilots as Bobbie Trout, Pancho Barnes, and Amelia Earhart. She flew with many other "Lady Birds" in the famous "Powder Puff Derbies" in the late twenties and thirties. Patty was featured in the January 1930 issue of *The Pilot, Women's Activities in Aviation* section. The article noted "Patty's desire to fly goes back to the time her father was an infantry captain in France... [during WWI]; only seven years old, Patty was convinced her father was a pilot!"

Patty realized her dream, taking her first flying lesson on November 9, 1928. She soloed the following month on December 27. At nineteen, she obtained her pilot's license, and was hired by Angelus Aero Corp. at Los Angeles' Metropolitan Airport.

Since many people still thought that being a pilot was not a proper "feminine" occupation, *The Pilot* article goes on to describe Patty as "...a diminutive pilot, about 5' tall and 100 lbs, she is exceedingly feminine in all her ideas and is about the last person in the world one would suspect of being a capable and fearless pilot."

This photo is courtesy of Patty's son, Lee Seely, and his wife, Jeannine. Lee was kind enough to share a story that typifies Patty's plucky spirit: *Near the end of her life, probably a month before she passed away – I simply asked Mom if she could still fly an Airplane... Get it up and down safely? Her answer was, 'HELL, YES! I can fly the crate that it was shipped in!'*

Skiing and Skating

Both skiing and skating were popular winter sports, with fashions that were both chic and comfortable! Matching sweater/hat/glove sets were favored, and though both knickers and breeches were still worn for skating and skiing, at trendy ski resorts skiers were beginning to adopt the full length ski pants that would become the rage in the thirties!

Adrienne's glorious couture ski sweater and matching gauntlet gloves! It's a rare treat to find a photograph of the original owner wearing existing period clothing – so it's wonderful to see how chic Adrienne looked in her stylish ski set. It's a beautiful, vivid "Monet Blue" wool, with a marvelous deco diamond-checkerboard collar, cuffs, and border. Couture Sweater and Gloves set: $400-$500

We've paired Adrienne's sweater with heavy, lined wool "Norwegian" ski pants that are a subtle tweed that combines "Fog" (dark bluish grey) and "Wombat Grey" (a medium gray resembling wombat fur color). These baggy pants with their tight buckled cuffs are a longer version of knickers. $75-$125

This smart skater's ensemble includes a sweater and cap similar to Adrienne's – but since our skater has opted for breeches instead of long Norwegian pants, she's wearing matching socks!

Skiing in Lausanne, Switzerland! Pictured at left is Adrienne Bessie Steinhard Unger, who was seventeen and attending the Pension Roseneck when these photos were taken during the winter of 1929-30. Adrienne bought much of her wardrobe in Paris—the spectacular ski sweater, cap, and gauntlet gloves she's wearing are from la maison du tricot! Note that Adrienne and her friend are both wearing the new long, baggy ski pants that *Vogue* describes as "Norwegian trousers that bag at the ankle..." (January 5, 1929) This photo and couture sweater set are courtesy of Adrienne's great niece, Patricia St. John, who notes that the matching knit cap has vanished with the years.

A closeup of the sweater's label: *la maison du tricot.*

Adrienne's matching gauntlet ski gloves.

179

Blue Jean Overalls

OVERALLS were *FASHIONABLE* in 1929; they had become yet another stylish type of pants worn by women by the end of the decade.

"Blue Jeans Fox Trot Song" – As this rural beauty illustrates, formerly overalls or "blue jeans" were heavy duty WORK PANTS! (Sheet music, 1920 by SamFox Pub. Co.)

Four Flapper Humpty-Dumpties! Perched atop the garden wall, these flapper gals illustrate the newly FASHIONABLE overalls for women – a trend that will carry over into the thirties. Snapshot, 1929.

Swim Wear

By the end of the decade, swimsuits were more daring than ever!

This original 1929 Jantzen swimsuit box depicts late twenties sun worshipers in a colorful array of their latest suits. Note the Oriental parasols, swim caps – and the sexy rolled thigh-high stockings on the woman just left of center! Green striped changing cabanas dot the background. The side of the box bears Jantzen's famous legend: "The Suit that Changed Bathing to Swimming," and a paper label glued to the bottom states: "Hudson's Bay Company, June 26, 1929, Clerk No. 12." Box, $100-$150

Two beach bound beauties speed off in their snazzy roadster, bound for Fun in the Sun! Note the thigh-high rolled stockings on the gal getting into car – and the snappy headache bandeau on the driver. Since the steering wheel is on the right, these "Bright Young Things" may be headed for Brighton Beach and Amusement Park on England's south coast! Snapshot, ca. 1929.

Note that by the end of the decade, many woman were omitting stockings for beach and even resort wear... Sommers Shoes advertises:

Special Shoes for Stockingless Ladies? – Palm Beach "says yes!"... This year, south of the frigid belt, fair ladies will cast off their stockings with quite the same abandon as they do an odd husband or so. Sans hose will be the smart thing. Why not special shoes for these modern ladies... (As advertised in *Vogue*, January 5, 1929)

Vogue recommends *Bas de soie* leg makeup for "Stockings á la mode... simple to apply, and it will not come off unless it is rubbed away with soap and water or eau de Cologne... available in three shades, Rose, Mode, and Ochre..." (March 2, 1929)

A closeup the *trompe l'oeil* belt, and Jantzen's all-American diving girl symbol. Jantzen's perky Diving Girl was everywhere – even on car windshields!

By the late twenties, bathing suits for both men and women are boldly baring what's been hidden for centuries!

Left, Man's Swimsuit: Note that while a man's bare chest was still a decade away, by the end of the twenties, men's suits had intriguing peepholes! This man's suit, a stretchy burgundy knit, features sexy side cutouts, while still retaining a vestigial "modesty" tunic. Label: *Zephyr, 100% All Wool.* $75-$125

Right, Woman's Jantzen Swimsuit: "You can slip through the waves as smoothly in a Jantzen as in your own skin"! This sensational woman's two-tone purple Jantzen suit is a one-piece suit with a two-piece look. A wonderful *trompe l'oeil* belt, knit into the design, accentuates the waistline. This woman's suit also has a short modesty tunic. With its obvious "trim fit," it's easy to believe Jantzen's claims that their suits "are so fashioned that it must fit... never stretching out of shape... never binding... never sagging. Jantzen's improved knitting process results in a lively, springy fabric of marked flexibility... hence a Jantzen suit always fits trimly – with scarcely the sign of a wrinkle." Miraculously, this splendid Jantzen has none of the usual moth bites; it was stored well! In pristine condition $300-$400; fair/good condition, $75-$150

Jantzen's ad campaigns were phenomenal: "Jantzens are favored by smartly clad folk at the beaches everywhere, here and abroad. Indeed, they're famed around the world." They had a right to boast – in 1917 Jantzen sold about 600 swimsuits; by 1930, their sales had increased to over a million and a half annually!

An interesting comparison! OLD VS. NEW... From Stuffy to Sexy in little more than a decade!

"Bathing" suit styles for men and women, ca. 1915! Though this winsome threesome sure seems to be having fun in the sun, their suits are rather cumbersome – especially the ladies'! With puffed sleeves, long skirts, and mobcaps, they're a far cry from 1929's clingy knits. The guy with the naughty hands wears a two-piece knit suit with knee length shorts and a long modesty tunic.

On the Riviera – 1929! This photo is a prizewinner—the handsome gent chivalrously holds his lady's mirror so she can attend to her bob; he's also holding her cigarette while puffing on his own. His knit suit with sexy side cutouts enhances his "manly figure!" His gal also wears a figure-hugging knit swimsuit similar to our Jantzen above.

Drastic Fashion Changes

By summer, "Fashion's Winds of Change" had swept in a new silhouette... and magazines like *Vogue* and *Harper's Bazar* were showing fashions with marked changes! Hems, even for day wear, were noticeably longer – though the waistline still couldn't seem to make up its mind. The transition to the natural waistline continued as couturiers focused more attention on the natural waistline while still highlighting the low waistline.

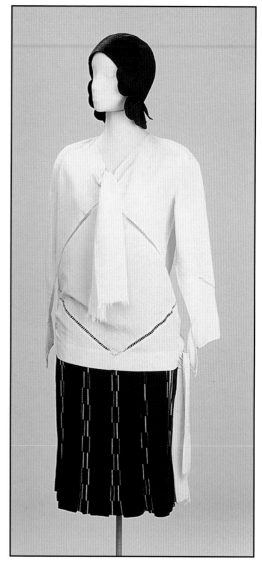

This chic rayon blouse could be worn two ways – as an tunic overblouse as shown, or tucked in. The bust, natural waist, and low waist are all emphasized – divided by a wide diamond of chic hemstitching! A mannish fringed tie compliments the v-neck. It's worn with a pleated black crepe skirt, with Petersham waistband and snap fastenings at left. Separates are rare, and early rayon often didn't hold up well; this blouse shows some deterioration at the shoulders. Blouse (with some wear), $35-$50; Skirt (excellent), $150-$200.

Three chic examples of the latest looks sketched for *Vogue's* June 22, 1929, issue. The "Jacket Costume" at left is dramatically accented at both the natural waist and low waist via the bodice's clever asymmetric draping to the buttoned tab at the natural waist. At center, this smart brown ensemble features a narrow belt just below the natural waist while the Rodier print bodice extends in points to the "moulded" hips, where it meets the skirt portion's geometric stitching. At right is a snappy three-piece ensemble with a skirt that's belted just below the natural waist; the skirt's pleats are topstitched to mold the hips and emphasize the torso. The jacket's hem is placed to correspond with the skirt's topstitched pleats. Note that similar frocks are priced between $25-$29.50 at B. Altman's.

Black kid leather Opera Pumps – so chic with these new fashions! These stunning shoes feature smart yet subtle art deco decorations - gunmetal grey zig-zags and triangular perforations on the sides. The modish spike heels are three inches high. Then, priced about $12.50 at upscale New York shops (comparable to around $125 today); Now, $150-$200 (excellent condition, never worn old store stock).

In a dramatic art deco setting, lovely Gladys Rennick poses in an afternoon to evening "Jacket Costume" – an elegant ensemble with a fur trimmed jacket, pleated skirt, and coordinating satin blouse, twice tied, and draped to accent the natural waist. Referring to her chic "Egyptian Curtain" cloche, the copy describes Gladys as "An 'Egyptian' Helen on American Streets!" She accessorizes with a rope of pearls (of course), bangle bracelets, silver opera pumps, and a smart deco envelope bag. *Photo, Seattle Sunday Times, Rotogravure Pictorial Section,* September 22, 1929.

The fashion photograph and other mementos are from Gladys Rennick's scrapbook, which follows her career as an actress and professional model from New York City. A former Miss Bronx, Gladys modeled for many companies in the twenties and thirties, including Emmett-Joyce, Merl, Inc. and Maison Simone Furs.

Among her memorabilia are clippings of her favorite "mannequin" assignments, including modeling at the Ritz-Carlton in Merl, Inc.'s "Comprehensive Fashion Review," and in the Belmont Fashion Parade. In 1929, Emmett-Joyce sent Gladys to Washington State to model at the grand opening of Helen Igor's new Seattle store, and also for Meier & Frank's Autumn Fashions T-E-A. In March 1931, she modeled "The Latest Parisienne Creations" at Madison Square Garden in a glittering gala benefit for the Israel Orphan Asylum—over 20,000 socialites attended this event, with Maurice Chevalier headlining the evening's entertainment.

During her acting career, Gladys performed in the famous Ziegfeld Follies, receiving raves for her part in "At the City Hall Steps," a skit from a 1927 Ziegfeld Extravaganza held at New York's famous New Amsterdam Theatre. Gossip columnists reported that New York's famous mayor, Jimmy Walker, was in the audience!

Gladys Rennick's memorabilia is courtesy of June Lang of Tigress Productions, New York City.

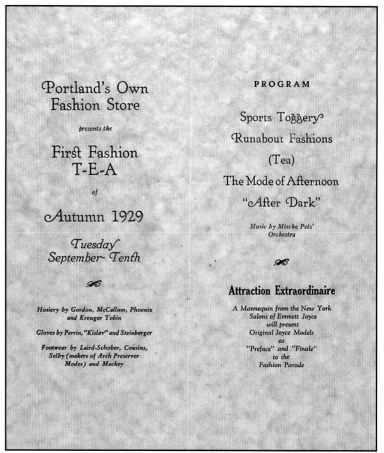

Inside is the program for their "First Fashion T-E-A," to be held on Tuesday, September Tenth. They note that as an "Attraction Extraordinaire, a mannequin from the New York Salons of Emmett-Joyce will present Original Joyce Models"—that beautiful New York "mannequin" was Gladys Rennick!

Heralded as "Portland's Own Fashion Store," Meier & Frank presents *Autumn Fashions*! On their program cover, classic art deco gazelles are printed in *pochoir* on vellum.

Gladys had a busy season; that fall she also modeled for an exclusive New Jersey shop, *Doop's - East Orange*.

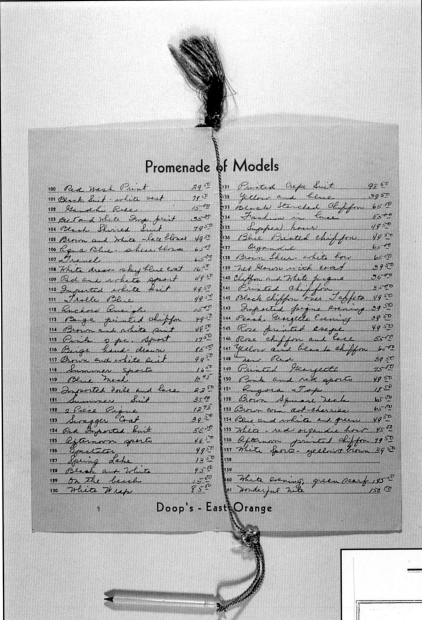

Doop's handwritten *Promenade of Models* provides a rare peek at the prices of an upscale shop. Note the imaginative names given to some of the outfits! A tiny pencil is provided for checking off one's favorites.

In Washington State, Gladys modeled at the grand opening of Helen Igor's new shop. As their announcement in the Monday, September 1, 1929, *Seattle Daily Times* proclaims: "Opening of the New Shop... Showing Over One Hundred Original Models Depicting the New Silhouette!"

Chic Coordinates – Head to Toe!

The "New Look" for 1929 – completely accessorized...

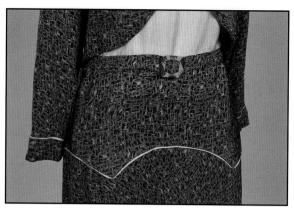

This closeup shows the art deco rose printed crepe and celluloid buckle, stamped Germany.

A "Rose Printed Crepe" like #145 on Doop's fashion list, this fine rayon print exhibits many of 1929's transitional features! It's a one-piece slip-on frock cleverly masquerading as a three-piece ensemble. The chic bolero, over an ecru vestee "underblouse," accents the newly important bustline; this bolero effect is in front only, it's attached to the underblouse at shoulders and side seams, and ties in a flirty bow over the bust. Four inverted pleats on each shoulder also accent the bust. The long, tight sleeves are piped in ecru at the cuffs and have snap fastenings. It's a nice example of the yoked double waist effect as the low waist is highlighted by ecru piping, while the natural waistline, although not extremely tight, is defined by a narrow self belt with a celluloid buckle. From the uneven ecru piping, the bias skirt flares to fall a few inches below the knees. Then: B. Altman's pictures similar "Frocks That Flare and Fall in the Newest Manner" at $16.75-$19.75; Now: $150-$200 (noting wear at the underarms of the underblouse, hidden by the bolero).

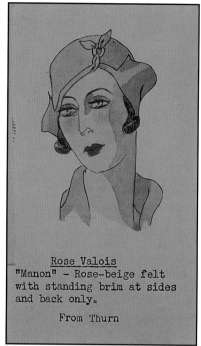

Rose Valois
"Manon" – Rose-beige felt with standing brim at sides and back only.

From Thurn

From the illustrious French milliner, Rose Valois – the shape of hats to come is sketched here for *Vogue's* March 2, 1929, issue! "Manon," her tiny "Bicorne," is available at Thurn's. As *Vogue* advises: "The fact that the bicorne is given prominence in the collections of leading French modistes indicates an important place for it in the spring mode..."

These smart leather pumps coordinate well with the bolero frock – and they match the faux marble of the Meeker bag! They're bone-colored kid, with cocoa brown lacing, and 3" spike heels. They're stamped "Fashion Plate – Johnson Stephens Shinkle" on one insole, and "The Hirsch Shoe Salon, Jack Davis Inc. Birmingham, ALA" on the other. Then: about $12 at B. Altman's; Now: $75-$100 (well-loved).

Look what's happened to the classic Nouveau tooled leather bag! While retaining its traditional laces and hand tooling, it's been given an art deco update with a faux marble insert and tooled geometric lines. Even the turnlock closure has been "deco-tized" with spectacular brown and caramel bakelite fastenings! This find is stamped "Meeker Made" on its suede interior. $150-$200

This little bicorne is fashioned of soft velvet, in a rich shade *Chicago Mail Order* describes as "Brown Sugar... a Golden Brown." Its pert curved brim is "pinched" twice; the left pinch is trimmed with a perky self bow. Black rayon lining with label: *Bergdorf Goodman, On the Plaza, New York.* Then: priced around $12 at Bergdorf's; Now: $75-$125.

Intimate Apparel for 1929

Corsets Return

Of course, the latest curve-caressing styles demanded new "Foundation Garments"... and after a hiatus lasting much of the decade, corsets (though not as torturous as former versions) were making a comeback.

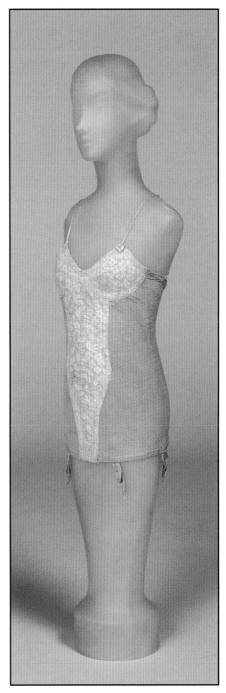

"LOVELINESS IN EVERY LINE... Models exactly right for wear under your new frocks and ensembles..." from Bien Jolie Foundations, available at Benjamin & Johnes, 358 Fifth Avenue. Note her magnificent Spanish Shawl! As *National Bellas Hess* proclaims: "The most smartly dressed New York women sponsor the vogue of the Fringed Silk Shawl for evening – or for any dressy occasion. And no wonder. It adds such grace to the wearer!"(Bien Jolie Ad, *New York Times*, March 10, 1929).

This Lalique-ish Lady is a corset counter display. She's modeling her very own sample corset, which gently shapes her waist, bust, and hips to provide 1929's new feminine curves! Her long line combination corset/brassiere is elastic net, with a lace overlaid "uplift" bust, and a front panel that's wider over the abdomen for tummy control. A ribbon rose bouquet trims the strap at left. Narrow satin straps that crisscross in back, and ribbons simulate faux garters. Frosted glass corset mannequin, $150-$200 (noting cracks in left shoulder and a break at right shoulder). Sample Corset, $75-$100 (noting that per usual, the elastic has lost some of its stretch).

Lingerie at the End of Decade

Though haute couture styles may seem to demand the return of the corset, many women refused to give up the comfortable undergarments they had become accustomed to – and wear "DAINTY UNDERTHINGS" that are sexier than ever!

National Bellas Hess offers an enticing variety of "Stunning Creations in DAINTY UNDERTHINGS" for 1929, in colors that include "Flesh-pink," "Honeydew" (Peach), "Nile green," "French tan" (Nude), "Orchid," and sensuous Black! Of particular note are:

A) A very brief "Hand painted bandeau and girdle" (garter belt) set.

B), C) "Negligee or Lounging Ensemble... a hand-painted outfit that's Guaranteed Washable... consisting of two-piece pajamas, and 'Coolie Coat' of good quality knitted Rayon Jersey."

D) A "Lovely Dance Set... Shortie step-ins and a very sexy little Uplift bandeau/brassiere which hooks in back."

M) "All-Over Chantilly Lace 'Teddy'... An exquisite piece of lingerie is this delicate 'Teddy' step-in of beautiful all-over Chantilly pattern lace – an exact copy of a new Paris model... the neck and waistline are run with ribbon typing in dainty bows in front."

R) "Rayon Jersey Slip, Embossed Flounce... You who have the annoyance of slips clinging to dresses will be delighted with this model of smooth-textured knitted rayon jersey. This material makes a lustrous, handsome, dressy and non-clinging slip...accordion-plaited flounce of self material with novelty embossed design. Plaited sides."

T) "Ruffled Rayon Bloomers!" (Yes, that popular knee-length undergarment is still kicking!) They're: "Kickaway bloomers with saddle seat permits ease and comfort in all postures!"

Introducing 1929's sexy new "underthings!"

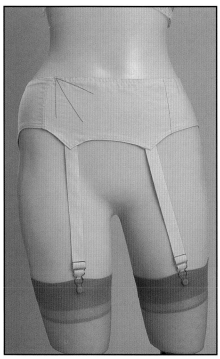

This TINY "Honey-dew" Garter Belt is "Just the thing for dancing, sports, etc!" It's fashioned of sturdy cotton coutil and features four long elastic "hose support-ers" garters. An embroidered art deco sunburst accents the right hip. In back, a wide band of elastic ensures a proper fit; it fastens with a hook & eye closing. This charming little unmentionable is old store stock, with tag labeled: Super Form, Style 248, Size Medium. $35-$45

A sensuous Black Chantilly lace "Uplift" Brassiere "for the 'modernist' who zealously guards her figure-freedom while conforming to style's demands – an Uplift Bandeau"! The new "Uplifts" are skimpier than ever – this one is a mere wisp of black Chantilly lace that's "cleverly darted" for uplift via two darts under each breast. To further accent busty curves, it's also pleated at the center front to dip between the breasts rather than being cut straight across; these pleats are topped with a sweet ribbon rose. Peach satin ribbon straps baste to fit (adjustable strap mechanisms will appear in the thirties). Hook fastening in back. It is never worn, old store stock, $75-$100.

Note that as *NBH* advises, these wispy brassieres are made for "women and misses who need only slight support for the bust...". For women who need more support, brassieres with "cupped" busts are now offered; very similar to today's bras, they have a band placed under the cups, which continues around to hook in back.

Above left:
Similar to *National Bellas Hess's* R),"A full slip of knitted rayon jersey for 'non-cling,'" is this rayon jersey slip in the ever popular Nile green! Five rows of pinked self ruffles form the fetching hem flounce. Pleats placed at the sides of the natural waist provide ease of motion. Adjustable top with cased drawstring ribbon; self-fabric shoulder straps. $35-$50

Above middle:
This Black Chantilly Lace "Teddy" Step-in is comparable to Fig. M): "A New Paris Model – an exquisite piece of lingerie is that delicate 'Teddy' Step-in!" Whisper thin, our erotic Teddy is transparent black silk chiffon with center panels of sheer Chantilly lace; its sides are "slashed" almost up to the waist. Delicate hemstitching connects a picot-edged ruffle of black chiffon around the hip slashes and bottom edges. A narrow satin belt accents the natural waist; the shoulder straps are narrow satin ribbon. The top is adjustable via a

cased drawstring, and a darling ribbon bouquet of a lavender rose with blue forget-me-nots makes a perfect finishing touch! $150-$200

Above right:
This short and sassy Chenille Robe is "Monet Blue" – a "Deep, Bright Blue" that's just electrifying! It's ribbed panné velvet – a fabric with a sheen that shimmers in the lights, and is oooh so sensuous! And although it's very modern, its wide split sleeves, dripping with six rows of ecru lace, give it a Marie Antoinette flavor; these sleeves are cut in one with the front and back. Four more rows of ecru lace adorn the "Popular Tuxedo collar," which "extends to the low waist" where it closes, surplice style, with a snap fastener at left. (These tuxedo collars with the "new long revers" (lapels) are also called "shawl" collars.) The hem is bordered with two rows of ecru lace. Inner ties ensure proper fit. Robe, $250-$400. It's worn with a peacock blue beaded Headache Band, with a chain/hook fastening. $50-$75

Lounging Pajamas and Boudoir Dolls

"THESE STUNNING PAJAMA ENSEMBLES ARE MORE POPULAR THAN EVER!" the 1929 *National Bellas Hess* catalog raved! Arch-rival *Chicago Mail Order* countered with, "ALLURING PAJAMA ENSEMBLES FOR MILADY WHO SEEKS THE EXOTIC!" – and, for proper ambiance, a flapper *must* have a boudoir doll!

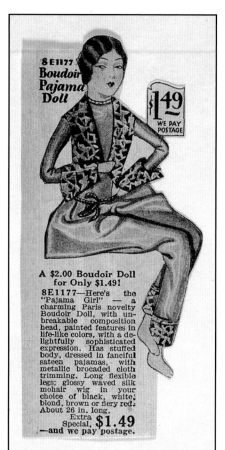

The 1929 *National Bellas Hess* catalog offers this "Boudoir Pajama Doll: Here's the 'Pajama Girl' – a charming Pris novelty boudoir doll with composition head, painted features... with a delightfully sophisticated expression." Like ours, she's wearing lounging pajamas, described as: "fanciful sateen pajamas with metallic brocaded cloth trimming."

Clad in chic lounging pajamas, this lovely flapper poses by a trellis with twining roses, ca. 1929! She's wearing low-heeled satin mules with her pajama ensemble – and she's carrying her favorite Boudoir Doll!

Our lovely Boudoir Pajama Doll is such a Sophisticated Lady! She's clad in a captivating pajama ensemble, with jacket and wide-leg trousers of printed panné velvet, and a magenta rayon crepe blouse. Her blonde mohair is set in the new longer hairstyle. She's applied very long false eyelashes, red lipstick in a "Cupidsbow," and she's painted on a naughty beauty mark! A firm believer in "Diamonds are a Gal's Best Friend," our gal wears a inset "diamond" necklace – and of course, she's betrothed – there's a huge "diamond" ring on her left hand! She has a composition head and neck, hands, and legs, and a stuffed cotton body. She wears black high-heeled pumps. Her original paper label reads: Keeneye, Pat.'s on eye & lashes, other pats. pending. $350-$500

In this full front view, you'll note that the top's v-neck ends in self streamers, the ends tipped with apple blossoms to match the border. It's paired with a pair of plain black trousers with piped cuffs which feature a yoke front waist with elastic back. Her velvet skullcap is trimmed with a huge flocked velvet butterfly (period, but not original to the ensemble).

THE CAPE BACK IS "THE CAT'S MEOW" – and this ravishing pair of lounging pajamas boasts the biggest and the best! A fine example of Opulent Orientalism, this beautiful China silk top is a color catalogs describe as "Rose Petal – a vibrant rose pink." The extravagant cape back ends at the natural waist at center, and dips almost to the hem at the sides. The cape, cap sleeves, and front collar are all trimmed with a wide border of exquisite machine made Needlepoint lace.

A closeup photo of the top's enchanting Oriental border. It's screen printed, with butterflies gathering nectar from spring apple blossoms. The sides are pleated at the bottom, and the pleats are topped with multi-colored metallic ribbon wreaths. Pajama ensemble, $300-$400.

Evening Gowns and Spectacular Shawls

Evening gowns, even more dramatically than day wear, paved the way into the thirties! B. Altman advised: "SOPHISTICATION SHIMMERS FROM SHOULDER TO FLOOR" as hemlines fluctuated with flattering floating panels, bustle effects, and proud Peacock Tails!

Butterfly Panel Frock

During her sojourn in Washington, Gladys Rennick modeled at the September 3, 1929, opening of the new Helen Igor shop. Over 100 original models "Depicting the New Silhouette" were shown – including this "Exquisite Formal Gown."

September 22, 1929

PART BUTTERFLY AND PART MOTH: AN EX-QUISITE FORMAL GOWN
This lovely creation of white marquisette trails ruffled panels on the floor and is worn with a short jacket which boasts elbow

Gladys, "Part Butterfly and Part Moth," models a beguiling fur-trimmed jacket and beaded evening gown... its modish uneven hemline is formed of overlapping panels of white marquisette which flutter gracefully to the floor. *Seattle Sunday Times Rotogravure Picture Section*, September 22, 1929.

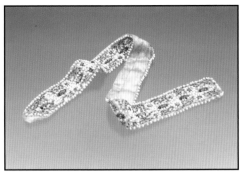

A closeup of the gown's satin straps – encrusted with rhinestones, silver bugle beads, and white seed beads. This was an extra piece, perhaps meant for a headband.

This elegant slipper satin evening gown features similar "Butterfly" panels! It's a fine example of the intricate dresses of 1929-30. More formfitting than earlier slipover styles, it molds the torso, necessitating snaps up the left side. And though the svelte torso is very dramatic, the accent here is definitely on the skirt's long, uneven bias panels. Two long triangular godets highlight the center front; the highest points to the natural waist, while the one beneath accents the hipline. The surrounding "Butterfly" effect is formed by an ingenious bias panel that's cut in one piece; it's seamed to the low waist in diagonal topstitched curves that begin at the base of the top triangle and continue around to the center back, where the gown dips to touch the floor. Though there's no belt loops, a narrow self belt with a rhinestone clasp was included. Then: B. Altman offered similar evening frocks with "charming femininity... the long bodice is vastly becoming... the unusual circular skirt is cut extremely long in back... $49.50." Now: $500-$700.

A closeup of her sequined Skull Cap! It's a sensational deco evening skull that perfectly compliments this "Butterfly" gown. It's formed of thousands of tiny iridescent sequins on a base of silk tulle; sequins of "Brown Sugar" (Golden Brown) forming the crown, and white sequins the Egyptian earlaps. It's a truly delicious confection! The chic bonnet-back is darted and bordered with a tiny white sequin "curtain." $200-$300

Note that these close skulls predate the romantic little "Juliet" caps of the thirties; they're similar, but a bit more encompassing.

Right:
In this full length photo, the back of the gown peeps through the shawl's swaying white-to-flame fringe, which is 23 inches long. The shawl itself is 45 inches square. $350-$500

Far right:
O, My Luve's Like a Red, Red Rose! (Robert Burns)
To make an Unforgettable Exit, our flapper accessorizes with a superb Spanish Shawl – with fine machine-embroidered *Red Roses* as shown in this close up!

Flounces, Shirring, and Bustle Effects

As the Flounced Silhouette's floating panels, draperies, ruffles, and uneven hemlines usher in couture's longer silhouette for evening, Victorian ancestors are often saluted with frilly Bustle Effects.

The flattering new shirred torso heralds the Return of the Bustline as exemplified by this *Flounced Silhouette* gown of Nile Green crepe. A fine example of couture's new feminine look, it boasts a very intricate cut: on each side, two bias side panels are shirred from the v-neck all the way down to the hips; inside, narrow self bands extend from the underarms to the hips to ensure the proper drape. The triangular center, cut Princess style in one from v-neck to hem, separates the breasts to emphasize the bust – and flares at the uneven hem. On the right, a sassy shirred flounce spotlights the hip; just beneath the uneven hem climbs almost to the knee before meeting the back triangular panel, which dips to the floor. Evening frock, $250-$500. Accessories include a period Art Glass and bugle bead necklace, and gold lamé jeweled skull cap (see pg. 168).

(b)
Doeuillet-Doucet
"Adriatique"

(b) Characteristic of the new flounced silhouette is this evening dress of printed marquisette. The line of the slightly bloused bodice and the unusual disposition of circular flounces are new.

(c) Here is the new front revers décolletage. Black moire, printed with multi-coloured flowers, adapts itself charmingly to the evening silhouette. The rounded apron-panel in front is bordered with black tulle; from Kathleen.

(c)
Chéruit
"Déjanire"

Vogue, enchanted by these flattering flounces, showed two fetching gowns: b) *Adriatique* from Doeuillet-Doucet: "Characteristic of the new flounced silhouette is this evening dress of printed marquisette. The line of the slightly bloused bodice and the unusual disposition of circular flounces are new" (despite the obvious resemblance to the Victorian bustle).

c) *Dejanire*, from Cheruit: a chic moiré print with a sweeping back dip. Note the "new front revers décolletage" and "rounded apron-panel in front is bordered with black tulle..." (June 22, 1929)

6/22/29

Dressed in a similar Flounced Frock, a beautiful young African American woman poses for a photo before leaving for a party! Snapshot, 1929.

A side/back view of our green flounced frock, showing the shirred side draping and long princess-cut back panel that's meant to kiss the floor. Note the deep v-neck, topped with a pert bow, with ties that trail to the hips—it focuses attention on the derriere, and provides a counterpoint to the short side flounce.

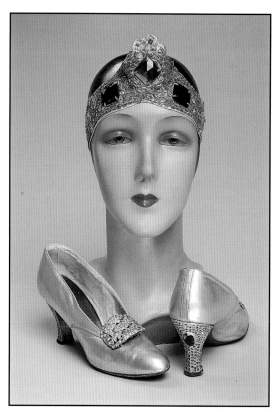

This devastating set, tiara and opera pumps, perfectly compliments our evening frock! The headpiece boasts three enormous faceted square-cut "Emeralds;" it's fashioned of shiny silver lamé that's completely covered in silver bugle beads. It ties in back with green satin ribbons tipped with steel marcasite beading. $150-$250. Her stunning silver kid opera pumps have removable rhinestone buckles and "Imported Rhinestone studded spike heels," with large, faceted "Emerald" centers. $300-$400

Accessories include...

Our gal might carry this beaded deco bag with a witty *trompe l'oeil* "Vestee and Bow!" Beadwork includes white seed beads, silver bugle beads, pearls, and rhinestones. Bracelet handle. $75-$125

"The Correct Pump for Evening Wear," offered by *National Bellas Hess* in 1929: "You'll find these dainty Opera Pumps of good quality silver color genuine kid a most appropriate compliment to your dressiest frocks. Remarkably comfortable dancing slippers too. Popular new round short vamp." Note that for an additional $3.49, you could purchase the stunning "Imported Rhinestone Spike Heels... easily attached by any shoe repairer."

A closeup photo of the stellar rhinestone and "emerald" heels!

Lavish Shawls for Summer Evenings

A "Transparent Velvet" shawl makes a perfect EVENING WRAP.

A closeup of the beautiful shimmering irises – and macramé fringe!

This sheer delight just has to be one of the most magnificent shawls of the twenties... how it must have shimmered under the stars! Multi-colored panné velvet irises glow on a background of sheer aqua silk crepe. The multi-colored silk fringe border features hand-macramé for 6 inches, then extends for an additional 21 inches. $1000-$1200

Note that these transparent velvet or "burnout" shawls are much rarer that the embroidered shawls, and command correspondingly higher prices.

HEAVEN! This flapper gal's in ecstacy – and no wonder, with such a beautiful flowered shawl draped around her pretty shoulders! French hand colored photo postcard.

Luxurious Lamé Shawl

Art Deco masterpiece! The moon turns green with envy when gazing down on this spectacular lamé shawl with huge deco poppies surrounded by rich gold Fortuny-esque pearls and swirls. It measures 42 inches with24 inch fringe. $800-$1000

197

Evening Coats

Of course, chilly winter evenings call for a more substantial wrap – and, as B. Altman's notes, the latest coats are "Cut as Elaborately as the Dresses Beneath"! Note that though the coats for evening also "Dip," they are *SHORTER* than the gowns, allowing an intriguing peek at the flounces beneath.

The 1929 August/September *Vogue Pattern Book* offers "The Chic Wrap for Evening," commenting: "Velvet or velveteen is most practical as a smart year-round fabric for evening wraps... it may either be furless or trimmed with sable, dyed furs, summer ermine, or blue fox..." Note the dipping back with its modish shirred flounce – and the cut of the sleeves, which are seamed below the elbow.

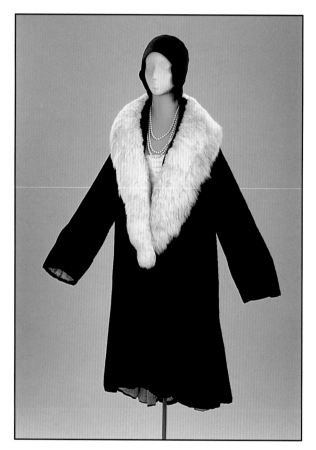

This lush black velvet evening coat features 1929's favorite dipping flounced back hem – which is circular cut for Flare! The velvet collar is smartly shirred at the neckline, and trimmed with a spectacular collar of coney simulating blue fox (it's 62 inches long). The sleeves are seamed in an intricate "U" shaped design, and softly shirred in front to flare over the wrists. There is no front fastening; one simply grasped this wrap closed as pictured in *Vogue's* illustration! The original satin lining has a shirred front pocket at right, and as is usual for linings of this period, it's shattering in many places (some collectors elect to replace shattered linings using the old lining as a pattern; if the damages is not too extensive, some elect to keep the original lining and simply appliqué a similar fabric over the damaged area). These lovely transitional coats were popular for just a short time, from the end of the decade through the beginning of the thirties, and are quite rare.

A side view shows the dipping back flounce and flared sleeves. The back dip follows the lines of the "dipping" silhouette; center back measuring a full seven inches longer than center front. Then: B. Altman's features a similar flared coat of "Kashmir Cloth with its luxurious shawl collar of wolf, its slightly fitted silhouette..." for $75.00. Now: $400-$500.

The Peacock Silhouette

The late twenties most popular style for evening is the famous Peacock Silhouette, described by *Art Gout Beaute*: "...with her dress lengthened at the back in a sort of train spreading like a peacock's tail... a woman looks like a beautiful bird with brilliant plumage." (January 1929)

Joan Crawford, star of MGM's 1929 racy film, *UNTAMED*, poses in a Peacock gown of flame red – with a sweeping tail of ostrich plumes! This cover is from *Untamed's* hit tune, "Chant of the Jungle." The "Savage" chorus goes:

> *... Hear the chant of the jungle*
> *For it sings of Savage Charms,*
> *Tropic nights and Lovers Arms...*

THE PEACOCK SILHOUETTE,
Presented by Altman's for Evening in Trailing Chiffon, Accented in Sparkling Embroidery. The Long Sweeping Trail May Be Lifted About the Shoulders to Form a Little Cape.

B. Altman's presents "The Peacock Silhouette" with a practical twist: "The long sweeping trail may be lifted about the shoulders to form a little cape!" This stunning gown, with its tail of "Trailing Chiffon" appeared in the *New York Times* Rotogravure Section (1929).

Note that today's collectors also refer to these late twenties Peacock Silhouettes as "Mermaid" or "Fishtail" gowns.

A Symphony of Symmetry! This haute couture gown from *Lucien Lelong is a masterpiece – with a tail so spectacular it's enough to make a peacock blush! It's a deep royal purple satin, with a slip-style front that's deceptively simple: the molded slip-style bodice drops to a very short tiered skirt in front; the tiers are bias cut to flare to perfection. The back, of course, is the main focal point – echoing the splendor of the "waterfall" bustles of the Victorian era. Wide ties that begin at the sides of the natural waist meet at center back in a huge butterfly bow, with ties that sweep the floor. Beneath this bow, two large pleated loops form a bustle effect which ends at the level of the skirt's front; under these pleated loops are six long trailing satin "plumes" of graduating lengths which complete this *Tail of the Twenties*! It's fully lined, with hand bound seams. $8000-$12,000. *Courtesy of Steven Porterfield*

Lucien Lelong's couture label.

Perfect symmetry from back to front! In this front view, the short skirt's bias tiers show to best advantage.

*Lucien Lelong (1889-1958) was one of the decade's most prominent Parisian couturiers. During the teens, he attended the *Hautes Etudes des Commerciales* in Paris, but his first collection was delayed due to WWI. After the war, he opened his own couture house, which was noted for its fine designs and exquisite workmanship. By the mid-twenties, the House of Lelong employed over 1,000 people.

1929 Bridal Gown

We end our twenties odyssey with ~ A New Beginning ~ A Wedding!

Georges Lepape captures the regal elegance of a formal wedding as his bride and groom descend the chapel steps to begin their lives together... the handsome groom in formal morning attire, and the bride a vision in clouds of satin, lace, and tulle...(Cover, *Vogue's Special Bridal Features* issue, March 2, 1929)

This bridal gown and accessories came from an estate in Utica, New York. Still nestled in their original box were this lovely 1929 wedding gown, breathtaking lace veil, long tricot gloves, stockings, and slippers. The box was addressed to the Mother of the Bride, Mrs. Anna Gregorio.

Flowing from a simple bonnet headdress, this cascading waterfall of fine machine made needlepoint lace measures fourteen feet long. *BREATHTAKING!* Lace bonnet headdress and veil, $1000-$1500

Our bride's splendid slipper satin gown exhibits all the favorite features of the end of the decade – including a very modish peacock tail that's quite similar to the B. Altman gown on page 199.

This back view shows her lovely gown is designed to make a spectacular exit as she walks down the aisle as a new *MRS*! The graceful peacock tail is formed by two long bias panels with triangular tops that are smartly shirred to mold the derriere; these panels are attached at the low waist only, to float free in their dip to the floor. In the center of these two shirred triangles, a large diamond-shaped insert begins at the natural waist to focus attention there; it then extends between the shirred triangles to highlight the hips. Note that the "tail" is a full twelve inches longer than the front of the gown. The back's bodice portion mirrors the waist's diamond insert with a deep "V" décolletage; a small insert of blonde lace modestly peeks from between the chic new revers (lapels). Gown only, $600-$800

A closeup of the back's hand-shirred triangular panels!

In this front view, the gown's molded torso hugs those new feminine curves, with emphasis provided by so-chic shirring! At center front, the skirt portion is cut to rise to the natural waistline in a narrow obelisk or spire that's shirred on both sides. The bottom of this spire curves into the topstitched seam at the low waist. Attention is also focused on the natural waistline via rows of shirring at the side seams. In front, the skirt portion ends about mid-calf; the legendary bias cut provides that flattering flare. The bodice features the almost obligatory bouquet of self flowers on the right shoulder. Both the v-neck and armholes are self piped. The form-fitting torso necessitates a snap closure at left.

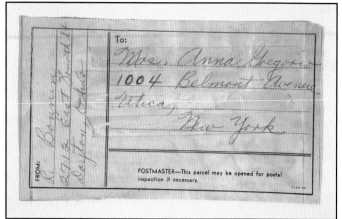

The box's original shipping label addressed to Mrs. Anna Gregorio, 1004 Belmont Avenue, Utica, New York. The box is stamped Rike's Store, Dayton, Ohio.

In this closeup of the lace bonnet style headdress, note the exquisite pearl flowers with rhinestone centers, and the delicate tulle petals also outlined in pearls – as well as the exquisite pattern of the lace.

Our Bride's Wedding Accessories!

Pumps: Cut in a smashing art deco design, the satin t-straps lace through clever ankle cutouts. Six satin "petals" extend over the tops from the soles to form the vamps; the sexy spike heels are three inches high. Lined in pink kid, they're stamped Filene's on the right insole. In "Danced All Night" condition, they show some smudges. $75-$100

Stockings: Our bride's silk stockings are seamed, of course; the seams have rows of decorative parallel stitching at mid-calf. They're cotton reinforced at the tops, toes (which have a stepped design), and squared "Cuban" heels—touchingly, our sweet bride has one small run near the back seam! $20-$25

Gloves: Adding just the right finishing touch, her long gloves are silk tricot mesh, fastening with two pearl buttons; the tops are finished with a picot-edged band. They're 22" long, and come to just above the elbow – to be worn draped a bit like our Matron of Honor's (seated at the extreme left in the photo). $45-$75

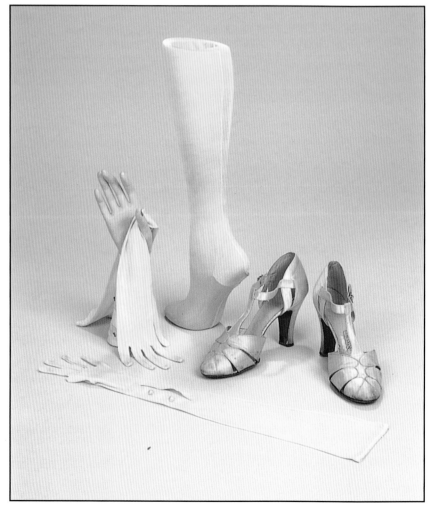

A lovely 1929 wedding portrait – including the bride, groom, and attendants. The lovely bride is wearing a beautiful bonnet headpiece and veil with long cathedral train similar to our bride's. The bridesmaids wear transparent horsehair "sou'wester" cloches – except for the Matron of Honor, seated at extreme left (note her spike heeled opera pumps and draped gloves). The groom and his men wear formal attire – white tie and tails – complete with rosebuds in their peaked lapels! Their hair is "slicked" and parted on the left.

Sadly, no one thought to identify these happy people – but we thank them for sharing this happy moment with us and hope they all had long and happy lives.

Retro Rogue's Gallery

1950s and 1960s Fashions
Often Mistaken for 1920s

Clothing of the 1950s, '60s, and '70s is often mistaken (and sold for) clothing of the 1920s. The full-skirted dresses of the 1950s, with their nylon net crinolines, imitated the twenties favorite *"robe de style"* fashions, and the short, straight dresses popular from the mid-'60s to early '70s, echoed the lines of the twenties beloved Chemise dress, and many were similarly beaded, fringed, and sequined.

The fashions in our Retro Rogue's Gallery point out the similarities and differences for the beginning collector. Two dead giveaways that dresses are post-'20s are zippers and fabric. During the twenties, dresses did not fasten with zippers, but were either slip-on style (with no fastenings) or snapped up the left side and/or shoulder. Dresses from ca. 1929 through the mid- to late '30s often fastened with snaps at the left side seam. Zippers weren't commonly used to fasten garments until the late '30s (after Schiaparelli introduced "Fashion Zippers" ca. 1935). Dresses from the late '30s through the '40s often closed with zippers on the left side seam, and/or at the back of the neck. Twenties fabrics were woven of natural fibers – silk, linen, cotton, and woolens (and combinations thereof) – with the exception of the first synthetic, rayon or "fiber silk." During the first half of the decade, this new synthetic was used mainly for underwear, but by the second half of the decade, it had been christened "Rayon" and it was used for some dresses and other garments.

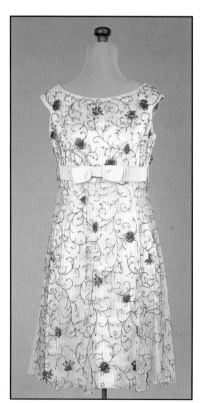 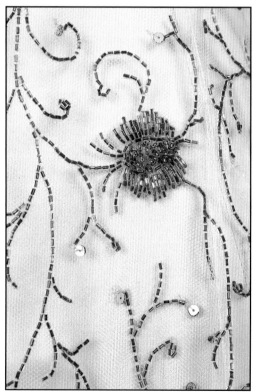 

SOOO "Jackie Kennedy!" This marvelous early 1960s sheath echoes the straight lines of twenties frocks—and its tulle overdress is heavily beaded with the twenties favorite bugle beads, accented with rhinestones. In front, its beaded tulle overdress is attached to a satin underdress at the white satin "Empire" belt; the underdress is seamed up the center front, with bust emphasis provided by two long darts that go from bust to hem. The back of the beaded overdress is gathered at the bateau neckline to fall free in an eighteenth century "Wateau" revival.

Note: The dress fastens with a metal zipper at center back—the most common method on 1950s and '60s fashions. **Fabric:** this custom made dress is made of synthetic fabrics. Heavy synthetic satin lined in a polyester/cotton blend is used for the underdress; the overdress is Nylon tulle, not the more fragile silk or cotton (nylon tulle was not commonly used until the 1950s). The bugle beads, though "silver" lined, are more uniform in size that 1920s beads; the rhinestones are sewn on sequin-style, not prong set.

Though this chic felt Carnaby Street "Bobby" hat echoes the lines of the famous twenties helmet cloches, it's pure '60s. Note the plastic strap that goes from a brass sailor button on top to form the Groovy chinstrap.

The Flappers' favorite, FRINGE – but flying this time from a late 1960s/early '70s number! In the twenties beloved "tunic" style, this dress is made like a frock skirt – with its short fringed skirt attached to a polyester underbodice. The tunic top is polyester crepe, with a scooped "U" neck and side bust darts. Seven covered buttons at center emphasize its straight chemise lines, and its sexy, swingin' fringed sleeves are cuffed tightly at the wrists. It's fully lined in polyester. Label: *"An Original Jr. Theme, New York."* Again, there's a metal zipper fastening down center back. Our lovely model is Caroline Szozda of Delavan Gallery. Thanks, Caroline!

Picture Doris Day in this wonderful 1950s Retro, Retro dress! A perfect example of fashion's maxim *What Was Old Is New Again*, it's Retro to the '20s full skirted *robe de style* which in turn was Retro to Marie Antoinette's eighteenth century gowns! Its "V" neck and tight torso (cut Princess style in front and dipping with a low waist seam in back) are straight out of the twenties. The fabric, however, is a heavy synthetic faille that's as stiff as taffeta; it's woven with shiny white polka dots (another twenties favorite). The full skirt opens to reveal a wide, button-trimmed insert of white pique; it's fully lined in a synthetic muslin-like fabric, with a wide band of polyester stiffening at the hem. It also has an attached nylon net underskirt. Deep diagonal darts provide the mandatory '50s "pointy" bust. Again, the fastening is a metal zipper down the center back. Label: *"Werle', Beverly Hills"* (often advertised in magazines like *Vogue* and *Harper's Bazar*).

Care and Storage of Antique Clothing

Included here are conservators' recommendations for antique clothing. Since the following may seem complex to novice collectors, the most important things to remember are:

1) Get antique clothing out of cellars (damp conditions cause mildew) and attics (extremes of heat and cold make fabrics stiff and brittle, leading to eventual disintegration).
2) NO plastic bags or unprotected cardboard boxes for storage.
3) NO unprotected wire hangers.
4) NO fabric glue or fusable iron-on patches for repairs.

To Wear or Display?

If you're the lucky owner of antique clothing, the choice of wearing or displaying is up to you. You should be aware though that museum conservators as well as many experienced collectors advise not wearing antique clothing. Every year the number of existing antique garments dwindles; wearing items, poor storage, and careless cleaning have all taken a toll. Wearing antique clothing puts tremendous strain on old fibers and seams, and body oils and perspiration also contribute to fiber breakdown. Replicas are suggested for re-enactments, mystery theaters, costume parties, etc. Many collectors think of their pieces as works of art, or as important remainders of their era's history, rather than as something to wear.

Pristine and/or very rare pieces, including couture labels, are best displayed on a mannequin only. If you feel you need to wear an antique or vintage piece to a special event, consider wearing something that's not in pristine/excellent original condition, but rather something that's already seen some repairs. Consider wearing the piece for a short time only – for a studio photo or portrait, for example – rather than subjecting it to strenuous activities like dining or dancing.

When displaying your treasures, rotate displays and change them often – around every one to four months. Don't display items in strong light, directly in front of a window; use indirect lighting. Display items only in areas away from cooking odors or cigarette smoke, and keep them away from food and/or drinks. Conservators also recommend wearing clean cotton gloves or washing hands often when handling antique clothing, and be sure to remove all jewelry that could catch or snag fabrics.

Storage

Flat Storage

Ideally, items should be stored in controlled temperatures and as flat as possible to avoid stress, folded as little as possible. To prevent fiber breakdown, lightly pad any folds with a small rolled piece of acid free paper or polyester batting. Lay items flat in large acid free boxes, using acid free tissue. (Non-buffered tissue is recommended for many fabrics, including silks and woolens, while buffered is suggested for cottons, linens, and metallics.) Store metallic lamés separately. Unbleached, undyed cotton muslin is also recommended for storage purposes as wrapping. Bias cuts, beaded dresses, and other heavy pieces are among the items that are most important to store flat.

Hangers

If you have a large collection, and it's necessary to hang some of the lighter items, you may want to hang them from the waist rather than the shoulders to more evenly distribute the weight and avoid undue shoulder stress. Some collectors cut a cardboard roll down the center and place it over the bottom of a sturdy hanger, taping it securely; then the roll is thoroughly covered with acid free paper, the open ends stuffed with tissue to prevent slippage. The item can then be hung from the waist, if necessary padding any folds. If the garment has long sleeves, place the cuffs over the top. If a garment is hung from the shoulders, even a padded hanger should be wrapped with acid free tissue or covered with polyester batting to provide maximum support. CHECK ITEMS YEARLY, replace acid free tissue, and look for any insect/rodent damage. Moth balls are not recommended for storage due to harsh chemicals. Some recommend placing materials such as eucalyptus leaves or a few slivers of soap in the storage box (not touching the fabric) to discourage pests.

Cleaning and Repair

Washing

Washing is not recommended by clothing conservators as it may damage old fibers, and the results are chancy at best. (Keep in mind that stains that have set for decades are not likely to come out without resorting to stain removers containing harsh chemicals, and the result may be a hole rather than a stain.) Washing can damage old gelatin/cellulose sequins or bugle beads that have coated centers. Metallic fabrics and brocades should not be washed, and woolens can both shrink and shred. Vacuuming on LOW power, with the item placed under a length of nylon tulle is suggested by conservators. To freshen garments that are sturdy enough, air them in a gentle breeze (on a covered porch or breezeway if possible).

If you do feel the need to wash, cottons, some silks, and linens are the safest fabrics; first try a test in an inconspicuous spot to check for color bleeding, shrinking, shredding, etc. Before washing, remove any delicate trim that may be damaged and any celluloid buttons or covered buttons that may rust; mark the exact placement by basting with contrasting color thread. Wash items in room temperature distilled water, soaking for around ten minutes in a small amount of Orvis paste (available at archival supply stores). Strong stain removers are not recommended; better a small stain than a hole. Rinse in distilled water until there is no soapy residue in the rinse water (about ten times). Don't wring or twist, but gently blot and smooth flat to dry (not in direct sunlight). Keep steaming/ironing to a minimum as heat leads to fiber breakdown.

Dry cleaning is NOT recommended for antique clothing, as the harsh chemicals used in the process can cause permanent damage.

Mending

Use the same fabric for mends whenever possible; look for additional fabric and/or beads in hems, seam allowances, and waist tucks. If not enough original fabric is available, use period fabrics that are as alike as possible, or transparent crepeline, with period thread, buttons, snaps, and hook & eyes (search estate sales, flea markets, and Internet auctions). HAND STITCH patches from the underside, using a larger patch than the weakened area/hole; if the surrounding fabric is weak, you'll need to take a bit larger stitches as tiny ones will pull through. NEVER GLUE OR IRON ON fusable iron on tape or patches. These will not only stiffen the fabric, they will lead to the fabric eventually tearing around the bond.

Records

Many choose to keep records of garments with a numbering system, basting a numbered fabric tag to each item in an inconspicuous place. The number is then stored with a description of the item, including a photo, any provenance (history), date and price of purchase, and approximate date the item was originally worn. Information may be stored on disk or in a file box. Some collectors simply note information in pencil on a cloth tag or piece of acid free tissue and baste it to a hem or inner seam. (Don't use pins, iron-on labels, or write directly on fabrics.)

Informative Websites

Kent State University Museum (dept.kent.edu/museum/ staff/care.html), an excellent clothing website, includes a section on care of antique clothing.
Costume Society of America (costumesociety america.com), an informative group that offers symposiums on antique clothing.
Vintagefashionguild.org, is an interesting and informative website for vintage clothing fanciers.
The Ladies Treasury of Costume and Fashion (tudorlinks.com/treasury)

Archival Supplies

Talas
talasonline.com
(212) 219-0770

Light Impressions
lightimpressionsdirect.com
(800) 828-6216

Gaylord
gaylord.com
(800) 448-6160

Archivart
archivart.com
(800)804-8428

University Products Inc.
archivalsuppliers.com
(800) 628-1912

Appendix

Listed here are some of New York's fine department stores and exclusive specialty shops that were regularly seen in period magazines like *Vogue* and *Harper's Bazar* (shown as "V" and "HB" in the following descriptions). Also included are samples of the stores' original ad copy.

Arnold Constable (Fifth Ave., 39th - 40th St.) – One of New York's finest department stores. *Harper's* October 1926 article features a Patou original evening gown with ostrich bands, imported to Arnold Constable, priced at $85.

B. Altman (Fifth Ave. at 34th) – 1927 *Vogue* article features Altman imports from Chanel, Patou, Lelong, Molyneux. In Altman's Men's Shop, a four piece "Golf and sport suit" is $55.

Henri Bendel (Fifth Ave. and 57th) – Exclusive shop offering exact copies of Paris couture as well as his own designs; Bendel also wrote for *Harper's Bazar*.

Bergdorf Goodman (Fifth Ave. at 58th) – "On the Fourth Floor, our made to order department reveals its selections from the Paris openings and its own exclusive designs for 'les chic Americaines'... on the Third Floor, a ready to wear collection... the new clever ensembles...chiffon evening gowns of infinite grace...and the Salle Moderne with the latest sports clothes... On the street floor, the most successful and magnetic hats of the season...matching bags and scarfs; smart stockings and jewelry. In each of these salons, with their spring vivacity, you will discover that inexplicable something which distinguishes art from routine." (V3/29) In 1923, Bergdorf's offered dresses from their ready to wear department, priced from $85.

Best & Co. (Fifth Ave. at 35th, 1928) – Best featured imported couture as well as their own designs; they sold sports clothes under their own "Nada" label and a line of hats under their "Fortmason" label. "Our representatives hold fashion exhibits in most of the larger cities east of the Mississippi. Write for date of showing in your town or nearby. Charge accounts solicited. Mail orders filled." Branches in Paris, London, and Palm Beach.

Bloomingdales (59th and Lexington) – Bloomingdales's enormous emporium was founded by Lyman and Joseph Bloomingdale in the 1860s on New York's lower east side as a notions shop; hoop skirts were one of their best selling items! In 1886, they moved to 59th and Lexington; by the twenties, "Bloomies" covered an entire city block.

Bonwit Teller (Fifth Ave. at 38th, 1928) – "As one would know...the most distinctive of the new fashions are found in the Bonwit-Teller collections"! (V4/28). In addition to imported Paris originals, Bonwit's touts: "Paris **inspirations** and our own 'originations'—the latest word in fashion..." (HB10/26)

The Brick Shop (18 East 56th St) – Importers, "French apparel exclusively...sports wear a specialty."

Bruck-Weiss (6-8 West 57th) – "The World's Show Place of Fashion," an exclusive shop, offered "The Total Ensemble" look: "Hats, bags, hosiery, jewelry and accessories that are perfect complements to the ensemble effect...It is our aim to interpret and express in terms of dress the personality and style of each individual customer." (HB23)

Hattie Carnegie (42 East 49th St, 1925) – "Gowns and Millinery...Clothes to Suit Your Individuality...The greatest success of Hattie Carnegie has been achieved in making clothes to suit each individual type—designed in their every detail to enhance the smart woman's own style." (HB5/23) Enterprising Hattie Carnegie sold her own house designs as well as Paris originals she bought on her seven annual trips to France; by the late twenties, she was also offering stylish ready to wear.

Deja (550 Seventh Ave) – Specialized in couture "inspired by" replicas. Also available "at your favorite shop or write to Deja...for Lanvin, Martial et Armand, Patou, Lelong, Molyneux... copies in the newest colors and fabrics will be on sale at well known shops at the uniform price of $39.50." (V9/26)

Dobbs (681 & 620 Fifth Ave) – "Sports clothes whose dash and certain becomingness are an expression of careful taste, smart Dobbs hats—costumes for street, sports and afternoon are created with Dobbs' bright, particular genius..." (HB10/26)

Eldridge Manning – Exclusive import shop often featured in *Vogue*.

Frances Clyne (Fifth & 50th) – Imported Chanel, Lanvin, and other prestigious couturiers.

Franklin Simon (Fifth Ave. 37th & 38th Sts.) – "A Store of Individual Shops!" The "New Trousseau Room, first floor" featured "Paris handmade lingeries with real laces—chemises $4.95-$59.50; step-in drawers, $4.95-$59.50." (HB5/23). In "Mademoiselle's Suit Shop, Second Floor," ensembles were priced at $155-$195; in the "French Blouse Salon, Third Floor," an "Indo-Chinese tapestry blouse" was $55. (V4/28) In addition to Paris imports, Franklin Simon offered their own patented in-house "Bramley" designs.

Gervais (16 East 48th St.) – Exclusive shop often featured in *Vogue*.

J.M. Gidding (Fifth at 56th & 57th) – Import/design house. "The latest French Spring Fashions, personally selected by Gidding Representatives abroad, are coming each day through The New York Entrance to Paris to delight the American Woman!" (HB23) Gidding's featured imported couture and creations of their in-house designer, Evelyn McHorter.

Gimbel Bros. – New York store was located near Macy's, in Herald Square; founder Adam Gimbel opened the New York store in 1910.

Grande Maison de Blanc (538-540 Fifth Ave) – An exclusive specialty-import shop.

Hickson, Inc. (Fifth at 52nd) – "Gowns created for the most superb collection of advance winter modes ever shown in our Salons…characterizing the individuality and chic associated only with Hickson apparel." (HB10/26) Hickson also wrote articles for *Harper's Bazar*.

Peggy Hoyt (16 E. 55th St.) – "Hats, Dresses, Suits, Wraps of unsurpassing beauty and originality designed and executed for America's most distinguished gentlewomen." (V28) Her exclusive shop featured her own designs as well as imports.

Jay-Thorpe (57th & 56th Sts. W) – Importers, and by 1929: "We are now couturiers—announcing the opening of a new dressmaking salon, a superior custom order department…staffed to design in the French manner and make to order dresses, coats, ensembles, evening costumes and bridal gowns of great chic and superlative hand workmanship. The Spring collection of new French imports and original models is ready now… in the Louis XVI Salon, Third Floor." (V 3/29) Resort branches at Palm Beach and Miami Beach.

Joseph Nemser (105 Madison Ave.) – An exclusive New York designer who sold to the finest shops in America.

Kurzman (Fifth, 52nd & 53rd) – Prestigious "Importer"; also featured their own original in-house designs. *[[why is "Importer" in quotation marks here?]]*

L.P. Hollander (552 Fifth Ave) – An exclusive custom/import shop with a branch in Boston. "For seventy-five years, couturiers to the Gentlewomen of America." (HB23)

Lord & Taylor (Fifth at 38th) – "We have in readiness a new collection from France…"; French imports included Mary Nowitsky, Redfern, Louiseboulanger, Cheruit, (priced around $200-$700). "Mail and telephone orders promptly filled." (V28)

MacVeady Inc. (10 East 56th) – Importer, advertising hats, gowns, sports clothes; branches in Palm Beach and Southampton (V29)

McCutcheons (Fifth at 49th) – "The Ensemble Vogue, smart for town or country, $69.50." Also known for fine imported fabrics. "Write for samples of these exclusive materials." (V2/22)

R.H. Macy (Herald Square) – Famous for moderately-priced fashions, including ready made knitted sports apparel in the $16-$25 range; afternoon and dinner gowns, between $25-$50; and "Whitby Frocks, exclusive with R.H. Macy & Co.," priced at $14.74-$24. (V23, V26)

Maxon Model Gowns (11 East 36th St.) – "Exclusive frocks and coats, half-priced! We specialize exclusively in the choicest, no two alike Original Models of the pre-eminent modistes; samples, we get them for much less and sell them at about half the usual cost." (V9/26)

Milgrim (6 W. 57th, 1925) – Milgrim's exclusive shop offered both custom made and ready to wear; they featured creations of "America's Foremost Fashion Creator," their famous in-house designer Sally Milgrim. Realizing the selling potential of the silver screen, Milgrim photographed stars like Louise Brooks in creations named for them. As the store notes: "Milgrim creations may also be obtained at the foremost shops in leading cities."

Russeks (Fifth at 36th) – "America's Most Beautiful Store," advertised "a vast assemblage of the winsome modes of youth…" (V10/27)

Saks Fifth Avenue (49th to 50th) – Saks Fifth Avenue opened in September 1924, heralding "Our collection of exquisite originals from the PARIS couturiers—and our faithful replicas— have the sure distinction characteristic of fashion by Saks-Fifth Avenue." "The personal shopping service will gladly answer inquiries or fill orders promptly." (V10/27)

Stein & Blaine (13 & 15 W. 57th) – Exclusive specialty shop. "A Creative House… Furriers Dressmakers Tailors," who promoted the in-house creations of the talented E.M.A. Steinmetz (which she also illustrated). (4/28V)

Stewart & Co. (Fifth at 37th) –"Correct Apparel for Women and Misses!" Stewart's offered "Paris Reproductions, inspired by Paris, approved by Fifth Avenue and reproduced by Stewart & Co. For the woman of discerning taste…," such as a cape for $124.50, day coat for $69.50. (HB 23).) In the September 1, 1925 *Vogue*, Stewart's announced: "College Club Fashions, exclusive with Stewart & Co. will be exhibited by us at the leading colleges," moderately priced between $15-$40. Stewart's noted, "Paris and Fifth Avenue Fashion Book sent on request." (HB8/24)

The Sports Shop for Women – An exclusive shop that imported early Schiaparelli. A English hand-woven grey tweed Schiap ensemble was featured by *Vogue* in October, 1928.

Tailored Woman (632 Fifth Ave) – An exclusive import/design shop. "The shop that puts LINE, WORKMANSHIP and GOOD TASTE above everything is naturally the port of call for copies—exact in very detail—of the more subtle Paris models most shops necessarily ignore." "Patou-inspired" day dress, $78.50; "Chanel" print ensemble, $118. (V4/28)

Tappe (Herman Patrick Tappe - 57th St.) – This famous importer/designer was often featured in *Vogue*. A fashion commentator and illustrator, Tappe was noted for hats as well as gowns.

Thurn (15E. 52nd St) – "Exclusive Fashions for Women." A prominent import/design shop. Noted in a 1928 *Vogue*: "Announcing a new collection of ORIGINAL models!"

Wanamaker's (Broadway & 9th) – Philadelphia based John Wanamaker opened a New York store in 1896; they offered fine Parisian couture as well as their own creations. Wanamaker fashions for misses' were labeled "Mimi": "Mimi was designed with a keen appreciation for the many and varied activities in the day of a modern young woman…chosen from the best of Paris designers after a careful study of smart young women's tastes." (V10/28)

Fashion Glossary

Adrian, Gilbert, 1903-59: Designed costumes for Broadway shows until 1925, when he went to Hollywood. From 1926-28 he worked for DeMille, then MGM; he designed some of Rudolph Valentino's wardrobes.

Agnes: Famous French milliner, located at 6 rue St. Florentin, Paris

Antoine (Hairdresser): Antoine claimed to be the inventor of the famous "Bob," cutting the hair of French actress Eve Lavalliere in 1910 in this short, sassy style. He worked in both Paris, and New York (at Saks). He also claims credit for the even shorter twenties "Shingle" hairdo.

Argyle (Argyll): Sporty, diamond patterned, originally worn by Scottish clan Argyle.

Armscye: sleeve opening, armhole.

Art Gout Beaute: Exclusive French *pochoir* magazine published between 1920-1933.

Augustabernard: Parisian couturiere who opened in 1919 at 3 rue du Faubourg St. Honore. She was noted for tasteful yet cutting edge fashions in pale pastels. She retired in 1934.

Baker, Josephine (1906-75): Queen of Parisian nightclub entertainers, Josephine left home as a young teenager to join a touring group, "TOBA." In 1925, she joined the Revue Negre and sailed for Paris where she became a star at such glittering clubs as the Casino de Paris and the famous Folies-Bergere.

Barbier, George, 1882-1932: Famous French illustrator for such magazines as *Gazette du bon ton, Vogue*, et al.

Batik: method of wax printing where wax is applied to areas of fabric to prevent those areas from taking dye. Popular in the twenties, it enjoyed a huge revival in the sixties and seventies.

Beer: Prominent couture house established by Gustave Beer, a German designer who was the first to open on Place Vendome in 1905. Beer was known for "conservative elegance." The house merged with Drecoll in 1929.

Benito, Edouard: Famous Spanish illustrator for *Gazette du bon ton, Vogue, Harper's Bazar*, and others.

Bertha: A large cape collar that had been a nineteenth century favorite; it was revived to become very popular during the second half of the twenties through the mid-thirties.

Boa: Fluffy neck scarf of feathers, fur or fabric; often with tassel ends.

Boue Soeurs: Established in 1899 by the two sisters, Sylvie Boue Montegut and Baronne Jeanne (Boue) d'Etreillis, the House of Boue Soeurs at 9 rue de la Paix advertised "Robes (gowns), Manteaux (coats) and Lingerie "bearing the cachet of exclusiveness and originality and of surpassing beauty...". They were noted for their signature ribbon roses, for lavish use of embroidery and lace – and for their gold and silver lamés and metallic laces. In the twenties, Boue Soeurs had a New York branch at 13 West 56th Street in New York.

Boutet de Monvel, Barnard: Talented fashion illustrator—a fellow Zouave officer of Patou, he often illustrated Patou fashions.

Boutiques: Became very trendy in the twenties as couturiers opened small branches in popular resorts, selling accessories, sportswear, jewelry, and ready-to-wear.

Braque, Georges: Cubist artist, he met Picasso in 1907; both helped develop the art form known as Cubism.

Callot Soeurs: A top couture house established in 1895 by the daughters of a Paris antique dealer: Marie Callot Gerber, Marthe Callot Bertrand, and Regina Callot Chantrelle (Marie, the eldest, was the designer). Around 1919, they moved to 9-11 avenue Matignon where they remained until 1928, when Mme. Gerber's son took over and moved to 41 avenue Montaigne. Callot Soeurs is famed for work with antique fabrics, laces, and ribbons; for their exceptional robes de style and Oriental gowns—as well as for gowns with moderne cubist themes. Vionnet, who trained at Callot, noted that "...without the example of Callot Soeurs, I would have continued to make Fords... because of them I have been able to make Rolls Royces!" The House closed in 1937.

Cardigan: Originally a long sleeved braid-trimmed military jacket which buttoned up the front. It was named for James Thomas Brudenell, the 7th Earl of Cardigan, who led the famous Charge of the Light Brigade in the 1850s during the Crimean War. In the twenties, the classic cardigan gained couture cachet as a sweater that was extremely popular for sports wear.

Carnegie, Hattie: As a young girl, Henrietta Kanengeiser left Vienna with her family and moved to America; they "Americanized" their name to Carnegie after the steel magnate. At fifteen, Hattie got a job in Macy's Millinery Department; by 1909, she and a friend had opened their own millinery shop. In 1918, she presented her first collection; during the twenties she imported French couture as well as her own designs. She employed Claire McCardell, Pauline Trigere, James Galanos, Travis Banton.

Cascade: a rippling ruffle or frill, vertically placed.

Irene Castle, 1893-1969: Irene and her husband, Vernon, became a world famous dance team in the teens—the toast of Paris, as well as America. During the teens, Irene helped popularize shorter skirts when she took up her own for dancing. She was one of the first women to bob her hair, and to adapt men's wear for women's sports clothes.

Chemise: A straight, slip-like undergarment worn next to the body, beneath a corset, since Medieval times. During the twenties it referred to a dress with a straight silhouette, as "Simple" in line as its ancient ancestor.

Chanel, Gabrielle ("Coco"), 1883-1971: Considered by many to be the most influential couturier of the twenties, Chanel's clothes "fit" the decade—simple yet elegant, comfortable and easy-to-wear. She was the epitome of the boyish, independent *la Garconne*—and was an avid advocate of the era's straight "chemise" dress (she created her version ca. 1914.) Chanel was born August 19, 1883; she was twelve when her mother died and her father placed her in a convent—then disappeared from her life. At eighteen, she left the convent and got a job as a tailor's assistant in Auvernois. Nights she sang at a local nightclub—her favorite song, a sultry "Ko-Ko-Ri-Ko" earned her the famous nickname, "Coco." In the nightclub, she met Etienne Balsan, a dashing cavalry officer. His friends admired the hats she'd designed for herself, and by 1908, she was selling hats from Balsan's Paris apartment. In 1910, Balsan's friend, polo player Arthur "Boy" Capel, became her new amour and set her up in a shop on the rue Cambon. With a goal of "liberating" the female body, she started designing clothing with simpler, straight lines and shorter hemlines. Since her lease didn't permit her to sell couture dresses, she started making dresses of jersey, a clinging knit fabric then commonly used for undergarments. Around 1913, following the beau monde, she opened a boutique in Deauville, followed by another in Biarritz in 1915. During the war, she also moved to a larger establishment—still on the rue Cambon, but across from the Ritz Hotel. By the mid-teens, when her "simple" jersey fashions were creating quite a stir, she introduced her famous "little black dress"—a "uniform" for afternoon into evening. She was devastated when Capel was killed in a car accident in 1919.

During the twenties, the flamboyant Chanel typified the new *garconne*—her lifestyle was bold and unconventional, and everything she did made news! In the early twenties, her affair with Russian Grand Duke Dimetri inspired her lavishly embroidered "Russian" styles. Anticipating the pants-for-women trend, as early as 1920, she was borrowing from men's wear to show wide-leg "yachting pants" ensembles for women. She was famous for her evening gowns, lavish but with much more simple lines; her beaded dresses were often constructed in the round (with one seam rather than two). She was also noted for unusual combinations of fabrics, and for matching coat linings to dresses. By mid-decade she was embroiled in a torrid affair with the Duke of Westminster, and producing chic tailored tweeds with "mannish" English lines. Chanel also claimed as her own "bobbed hair" and the "suntan!" She closed at the start of WWII in 1939. In 1954, at age 71, she made a remarkable comeback, showing her beloved classic suits.

Cheruit, Madeleine: Opened ca. 1906, by 1914, Cheruit was famed for walking suits, cinema capes, and full-skirted *robe de style* or "fantasy dresses." In 1925, she was lauded for her spectacular hand-painted Cubist dresses. Cheruit closed in 1935.

Cocktail Dress: When prohibition made the "cocktail" a popular drink, a short, informal dress worn for cocktails was born. The "Little Black Dress" which could be dressed up or down with various accessories became a favorite Cocktail Dress.

Co-Respondent Shoe (Spectator Shoe): a sporty oxford trimmed with perforations, generally in white and black or brown; and often pointed "Wingtip" style on the toe.

Crepe: A fabric with a slightly crinkley or puckery texture, in silk, rayon or wool. In the twenties, both "Georgette" crepe and "satin-backed crepe" were favored. Also see "Georgette."

Crepe de Chine: Originally silk from China, a luxurious, lightweight silk.

Cuban Heels: A practical, short, thick heel popularly worn with '20s sportswear named for the boots worn by Gauchos.

Cubism: Ultra "modern" abstract art movement beginning at the turn of the twentieth century, championed by such artists as Georges Braque and Pablo Picasso. Its streamlined, geometric lines inspired many couturiers of the twenties.

Dache, Lilly, 1904-89: Famous milliner, trained with Reboux. In 1924, she was briefly employed by Macy's; that same year she bought out The Bonnet Shop, launching her career.

Dali, Salvador, 1904-89: A noted cubist artist, in the second half of the twenties, Dali was spearheading the Surrealist movement, painting bold, fantastic scenes. During the thirties, he designed surrealist fabrics for Schiaparelli.

Delaunay, Sonia: Famous cubist artist, her paintings are noted for geometric designs in vivid primary colors. She produced bold, cubist designs for textiles, and received acclaim for patchwork coats she produced with Jacques Heim.

Delman Shoes: (Herman B. Delman). Shoe manufacturer noted for very stylish, high quality shoes; after WWI, Delman opened shops in New York on Madison Avenue, and in Hollywood.

Doeuillet: Couture house established in 1900 by Georges Doeuillet after he trained at Callot Soeurs. Doeuillet introduced the famous "barrel" silhouette in 1917 that endured into the early twenties. In the twenties, Doeuillet was located at 24 Place Vendome. In 1929, after Jacques Doucet's death, Doeuillet merged with Maison Doucet and closed in the late '30s.

Dolman Sleeve: Sleeve cut as part of bodice with no armscyes, often wide at the top and tapering to a tight wrist.

Doucet, Jacques, 1853-1929: Doucet was founded in 1824 as a lace and lingerie shop owned by Jacques Doucet's grandmother. A couturier considered to be as important as Worth, Jacques Doucet opened Maison Doucet ca. 1875. The house was known for its sumptuous, elegant designs, and clients included the world's rich and famous—royalty, actresses, and socialites. During the twenties, Doucet was considered a venerable, traditional house, located at 21 rue de la Paix. On Doucet's death in 1929, the house merged with Doueillet.

Drecoll: A popular couture house noted for luxurious though conservative fashions, originally founded in 1902 in Vienna by Baron Christoff von Drecoll; the Paris branch was opened in 1905 under the direction of designer Besancon de Wagner. In 1929, Drecoll merged with Beer, then in 1931 with Agnes, which continued until 1963.

Dryden, Helen: One of the twenties best illustrators, noted for her exquisite *Vogue* covers.

Dufy, Raoul: Artist who also designed stunning art deco fabrics for Paul Poiret; he also designed for Bianchini-Ferier, the French textile manufacturer.

Duncan, Isadora: famous dancer who scandalized society around the turn of the twentieth century by performing in scanty, flowing Grecian style robes, uncorseted and barefoot. Associated with the dress reform movement, she favored Fortuny gowns!

Duvetyn: A smooth, soft, velvety fabric.

Eric (Carl Erickson), 1891-1958: Famous illustrator who worked for *Gazette du Bon Ton*, and was one of *Vogue's* chief artists until the 1950s.

Erte, 1892-1990: Russian artist and designer, Romain de Tirtoff. Worked with Daighilev on designs for the Ballet Russes; from 1916-26 illustrated for *Harper's Bazar*. Erte designed many of Josephine Baker's exotic costumes, and also sets for Folies-Bergere and Ziegfeld Follies. From 1925, he also worked on several Hollywood films.

Eton Crop: Very short, straight hairdo named for prestigious British public school, Eton College.

Fagoting (faggoting): A vertical or crisscrossed decorative embroidery or filling placed between an open seam; see hemstitching.

Faille: Lightweight silk or rayon fabric with a fine ribbed effect.

Fair Isle: Sweater originating from the Scottish island of Fair Isle, with geometric or jacquard type designs. Especially popular for golf, it was a sportswear favorite, popularized by the Prince of Wales. It was worn by both men and women.

Fedora: Originally man's sporty hat from Tyrol; it has a tapering center-creased crown with two "pinches" on either side. Very popular in the '20s, the classic "snap-brim" fedora's brim that tipped smartly down in the front. Named after the 1882 Sardou play, *Fedora*, this sporty hat was soon adopted by women.

Flapper: Term used around the turn of the century referring to a young pre-teen or teenage girl. During the twenties, it described the "New Woman" who bobbed her hair, wore short skirts, makeup, rolled her hose, and danced the Charleston till the wee hours.

Flounces (Ruffles): Pieces of fabric of various widths, bias, circular cut or straight, often pleated or shirred at the top, used to add flare to garments.

Fortuny, Mariano, 1871-1949: Renaissance man, artist, and textile magician, Fortuny was the originator of the famed pleated Delphos and Peplos dresses and stenciled silk and velvet capes. In the twenties, Fortuny's Paris establishment was located at 67 Rue Pierre-Charron cor. Champs-Elysees. (See pgs. 226-229)

Gabardine: Sturdy fabric with a fine diagonal ribbed weave, in wool, silk, cotton or synthetics—used in suits, coats, dresses, slacks.

Garbo, Greta, 1905-90: Swedish actress who began her career in Sweden in the early 1920s. In 1925 she came to Hollywood to work for MGM. Her beauty – and independent attitude – influenced women, helping turn the boyish flapper into the sophisticated woman of the thirties.

Garconne: French version of "flapper," taken from the 1922 novel, *La Garconne*, by Victor Margueritte, about a liberated woman. Coco Chanel typified the *garconne*, both in her designs and her personal life.

Gazette du Bon Ton: Lucien Vogel's superb French fashion magazine, published from 1912-1925, famous for its hand-stenciled *pochoir* plates of couture designs. *Pochoir* prints, especially from the *Gazette*, are avidly sought after by today's collectors.

Georgette: Very lightweight, translucent fabric in silk or rayon with a slight puckery texture. A favorite fabric of the twenties, it was often beaded in deco designs, or printed in floral or geometric designs.

Girdle: A briefer version of the corset, waist to hip length, with elastic panels and attached "supporters" (garters) to secure stockings. Or, a tight swathed or draped belt, extremely popular during the second half of the decade.

Godet, Gore: Tapering, triangular-shaped inserts, narrow at the top and wide at the bottom, employed to provide ease of motion ... and Flare!

Grosgrain: Silk or rayon ribbon with a pronounced rib, often used in millinery, and skirt's waistbands.

Haberdashery: A retail men's wear/accessories shop.

Handkerchief Hem: a full skirt hem ending in triangular points, especially popular for afternoon and evening dresses of the late teens through the twenties.

Harper's Bazar (*Bazaar* after '29): A prestigious American fashion magazine originally published by the Harper Bros. in 1867; it was taken over by Hearst in 1913.

Hartnell, Norman: English designer who had his first showing in 1927; Hartnell became the Royal family's official dressmaker.

Hemstitching: decorative vertical embroidery or stitches to fill an open seam. See fagoting.

Homburg (English, Trilby): A man's felt hat with a center crease and narrow, rolled brim.

Iribe, Paul: Artist best known for his fabulous art deco *pochoir* illustrations in *Les Robes de Paul Poiret*, published in 1908.

Jabot: originally a lace or fabric frill at the neckline of a dress; during the twenties, it referred to a large vertical ruffle or flounce.

James, Charles, 1906-78: Famous designer who began as a Chicago milliner in 1926, under the name "Charles Bucheron." Ca. 1928, he moved to New York, began designing clothing, and showing his first collection.

Jane Regny: A popular couture house in the twenties, especially noted for sports wear—very modern, futuristic sweater ensembles and beachwear. Located at 11 rue de la Boetie.

Jenny: Couture house opened in 1909 by Jenny Sacerdote; Jenny moved to the Champs Elysees in 1915. The house was known for elaborate beaded evening gowns as well as very chic "simple" sports wear. Jenny closed in 1938.

Jersey: a very flexible knit fabric in a tricot stitch, in silk, wool, cotton or rayon. It was named for the Isle of Jersey in the English Channel, where it was knitted by women for fishermen and sailors. A comfortable fabric, it was popularly used for undergarments. It became a fashionable favorite in the mid-teens when Coco Chanel began creating "simpler" fashions of jersey.

Jodhpurs (Breeches): Popular pants used for horseback riding and by aviators. Tight at the waist, they ballooned at the hips, and narrowed at the knees, were tightly "step" buttoned. Named for a state in northern India, they were originally worn by British troops in the nineteenth century.

Knife pleats: sharp, narrow vertical pleats especially popular during the twenties.

Lady Duff Gordon: See Lucile

Lalique, Rene, 1860-1945: Famous artist noted for fabulous designs in jewelry and glass sculptures. He opened in 1885, and designed for Cartier and Bucheron; he created jewelry for Sarah Bernhardt's plays.

Lamé: Heavy, shiny cloth woven with metallic gold or silver threads, very popular for twenties evening fashions.

Lanvin, Jeanne, 1867-1946: One of the most famous of the haute couture designers, Lanvin opened a millinery shop at 11 rue du Faubourg Saint-Honore in 1890. She began creating clothes for her younger sister and daughter so lovely that clients began requesting dresses for their daughters; by 1909 she was designing her famous mother/daughter fashions. Just before WWI, ca. 1914, she introduced the full-skirted eighteenth century-inspired "*robe de style,*" which would remain a "youthful" favorite for afternoon and evening throughout the twenties and thirties. Also ca. 1914, she created her version of the straight chemise dress, later to become *the* silhouette of the twenties. In the twenties, Lanvin Couture was located at 22 Faubourg St. Honore, and Lanvin Sport at 15 Faubourg St. Honore; she also opened branches in Biarritz, Cannes, and Nice. Lanvin introduced My Sin perfume in 1925, followed by Arpege in 1927. In 1926, she became the first to open a men's section. Her house was noted for its up-to-date yet romantic creations, for its lavish use of exquisite embroideries, and for the robin's egg blue color known as "Lanvin Blue." On her death in 1946, Castillo became premier couturier; followed in 1963 by Jules Francois Crahay. In 1997, Claude Montana began designing for the House of Lanvin.

Lawn: Sheer, translucent cotton fabric named for the French town of Laon.

Legroux Soeurs: Couture house founded in 1917 by sisters (soeurs) Heloise and Germaine Legroux. The house was in business until the 1950s.

Lelong, Lucien, 1889-1958: Prominent couturier who opened his couture house after WWI in 1919, at 374 rue St. Honore. Lelong was among the first to open resort branches in Monte Carlo in Biarritz. The house was noted for modern, "youthful" creations, impeccable workmanship, and luxurious fabrics. See pg. 200.

Lenglen, Suzanne, 1899-1938: Champion French tennis player who won at Wimbledon from 1919-26. A champion also of briefer, easier to wear sports clothing, she created a sensation when she abandoned her garter belt and rolled her stockings over elastic garters. Patou designed her chic pleated skirts and sweaters. Millions of women also adopted the famous bandeau headband she wore to accent her ensemble.

Lenief: Couture house opened in 1923; often featured in *Vogue* and *Harper's Bazar,* Lenief was located at 374 rue St. Honore, Paris.

Lepape, Georges, 1877-1971: One of the most talented and prolific of all the *pochoir* artists. In 1911, he illustrated Paul Poiret's famous second *pochoir* book, *Les Choses de Paul Poiret.* He worked for *Gazette du Bon Ton, Vogue* and *Harper's Bazar,* illustrating creations for many prominent couturiers.

Liberty of London: World famous London department store from the mid-nineteenth century on, especially known for silks imported from the Orient, flowing Grecian "aesthetic" dresses, luxurious lingerie, and many other unique items.

Linen: Fabric made from fibers of the flax plant. Linen was a favorite of the ancient Egyptians—remnants have been found in tombs that are over 5,000 years old. Linen is finished in many textures, from tightly woven to a fine gauze or mesh.

Lisle: Knitted cotton fiber used for stockings. It took its name for the French town of Lille, the place it originated.

Little Black Dress: A versatile classic dress introduced during the twenties; designed to go from day into evening, it could be dressed up or down—beloved of the new "cocktail" set. Though the "little black dress" is synonymous with Chanel, many other couturiers had versions.

Louis Heel: One of the twenties favorite heels for shoes, the graceful Louis heel narrows in the middle, flares out at the bottom. Originally named for the France's Sun King, Louis XIV (1643-1715), it was very popular during the eighteenth century.

Louiseboulanger, 1878-1950: Noted couturiere who opened her house at Champs Elysees, 3 rue de Berri ca. 1926, after working at Cheruit and Callot. She was noted for "pouf" frocks (fitted around the torso and draped to bustle effects), for bias cuts, and "peacock" tails.

Lucile (Lady Duff Gordon), 1863-1935: English couturiere, Lady Duff Gordon after her 1900 marriage to Sir Cosmo Duff Gordon. Lucile had branches in Paris, London, New York, and Chicago, and was noted for her luxurious evening gowns, tea gowns, and lingerie. Such notables as actress Sarah Bernhardt and dancer/fashion icon Irene Castle patronized Lucile. Her sister, author Elinor Glynn, coined the famous twenties term "IT," meaning sex appeal! Lady Duff Gordon and her husband, Cosmo, were survivors of the 1912 *Titanic* disaster; they were in Lifeboat 1, which carried only twelve people despite having a capacity for forty—their lifeboat did not return to attempt to rescue any of those still in the water. Questioned later by the Wreck Commissioner's Inquiry*, Lady Duff Gordon testified: "It [the Titanic] is such an enormous boat; none of us know what the suction may be if she is a goner."

In an interview in the *New York Sunday American*, she'd been quoted as saying: "An awful silence seemed to hang over everything, and then from the water all about were the *Titanic* had been arose a bedlam of shrieks and cries... And it was at least an hour before the awful chorus of shrieks ceased, gradually dying into a moan of despair" (she denied saying this at the Inquiry). The Duff-Gordons were the only passengers questioned. During the twenties, Lucile's Paris house was located at 11 rue de Penthievre, Paris, advertising "exclusive designs now under the personal direction of Monsieur Decio Rossi." *See details at titanicinquiry.org

Madeleine et Madeleine: A prominent couture house founded in 1919, and very popular in the twenties. In 1926, the house merged with Anna, the creator of the avant-garde "le smoking" women's tuxedo suit.

Maillot: extremely form-fitting knit fabric, similar to tricot, sometimes used for bathing suits in the twenties.

Mainbocher, 1891-1976: American designer Main Rousseau Bocher, originally from Chicago, in 1922 illustrated for *Harper's Bazar*; from 1923-29 was the editor of French *Vogue*. Combining his name to "Mainbocher," he opened his couture house in Paris in 1930 and became the first successful American couturier, famous for dressing the Duchess of Windsor.

Marcel Wave: A twenties favorite hairstyle with art deco lines, it consisted of a series of waves rather than curls, produced with multi-layered curved curling tongs. It was originally designed in 1872 by French hairdresser Marcel Grateau.

Martial et Armand: Popular twenties couture house located at 10 Place Vendome, 13 rue de la Paix, with a branch in London.

Martin, Charles, 1848-1934: Famous artist who illustrated for the prestigious *pochoir Gazette du Bon Ton, Vogue*, and *Harper's Bazar*.

Marty, Andre, 1882-1974: Very well known artist, illustrating for the *Gazette, Vogue*, and *Harpers Bazar*.

Mary Janes: A favorite shoe style for women and girls, generally with a low or small heel and fastened with a strap over the instep. Popularly worn for day or sports wear in leather, patent or canvas.

Mary Nowitzky: A couture house located at 832 rue des Petits Champs (Place Vendome); very popular in the twenties for sports wear, particularly swim wear and accessories.

Moiré: A rather stiff, heavy fabric, usually silk, with a wavy pattern in shades of the same color (also known as "watered silk").

Molyneux, Captain Edward, 1891-1974: Famed Irish couturier, who began his career by winning a contest sponsored by Lucile, where he trained. He was a captain during WWI, when he was blinded in one eye; he opened canteens in London and Paris and established a camp for war wounded. After the war, in 1919, he opened his own couture house at 14 rue Royale and was noted for exquisitely "simple" creations, including beaded chemise dresses and "unequaled" lounging pajamas. He soon established branches in Cannes, Biarritz, London, and Monte Carlo. The house closed in 1950, taken over by Jacques Griffe.

Mondrian, Piet, 1872-1944: Holland born artist Piet Mondrian took up Cubism in 1917; he was to become one of the world's foremost Cubist painters.

Mousseline: Slightly stiff, lightweight fabric in silk, wool or cotton.

Muslin: A plainly woven cotton fabric originally named for the Middle Eastern city of Mosul, and fashionable since the late eighteenth century's "empire" gowns. Popular in different weights for dresses, blouses, undergarments, and linens.

Negligee: A loose, flowing informal robe, worn at home in the boudoir between clothing changes; also see "tea gown."

Norfolk Jacket: A sporty tweed jacket originating in the nineteenth century, named for the English Duke of Norfolk. Originally men's wear, it was soon adapted for women and children. It was either self-belted only in back, or the belt encircled the waist; it featured roomy patch pockets and box pleats. During the twenties, it was a favorite paired with knickers for all types of sporting activities.

Nylon: A synthetic fabric developed by DuPont scientist Dr. Wallace H. Carothers who began research in 1927; it was not introduced by DuPont until 1938, when it was first used for nylon hosiery.

Organdy (Organdie): A very sheer but stiff translucent cotton fabric, similar to voile, and very popular for summer day and afternoon dresses in the twenties.

Oxford Bags: Wide-legged trousers immortalized by John Held Jr.'s illustrations of the "Sheiks" of the twenties. They were introduced by students at Oxford University, who began to wear them over the knickers that were banned. "Bags" often measured 20-24 inches around the cuff.

Paillettes (Sequins, Spangles): Shiny, usually circular disks pierced to stitch on evening/afternoon garments. Twenties paillettes or sequins were often gelatin based, and can be irreparably damaged by washing, dry cleaning, and extremes of heat or cold.

Pajamas (English, Pyjamas): pants and top sets worn by men, women, and children for sleep wear. During the twenties, women's pajamas for "Lounging" and "Beach" also became the rage; beach pajamas were the first commonly worn pants for women to venture out in public.

Panniers: Horizontal, hooped "cages," very popular during the eighteenth century, worn under the "robes" or gowns of that era; they were revived in the twenties to emphasize some of the more dramatic *robe de style* gowns.

Patou, Jean, 1880-1936: "We are witnessing a renaissance..."! (Jean Patou). Jean Patou, considered one of the twenties top five couturiers, was a man of the twenties—tall, dark, and handsome, he was a lover of fast cars, fast women, and fabulous fashions! Unlike his rival, Chanel, who'd claimed to "dictate" fashions to her clients, Patou believed that "women should dominate their clothes rather than being couture clotheshorses"—clothing should reflect the wearer's personality. Patou opened his first house, "Maison Parry," in 1912, but closed during WWI, when he was a captain in the Zouaves. After the war, in 1919, he reopened as "Jean Patou" on the rue St. Florentin—an eighteenth century home originally built by Tallyrand for his mistress. He was extremely successful, creating the simple, classic clothing that became synonymous with the modern woman of the twenties. He promoted a return to the natural waistline as early as 1925, and is credited with establishing the longer hemline that would lead to the look of the thirties. He was famous for his elegant evening gowns, chic day frocks, and especially sports clothes. He was the first to introduce departments solely for sports, and was especially noted for his cubist sweaters, inspired by such artists as Braque and Picasso, and for knit bathing suits adapted for sea water. He introduced the couture monogram. Patou had branches at Monte Carlo, Biarritz, Deauville, and Venice. (See pg. 224 in *Roaring '20s Fashions: Jazz*.)

Peplum: A short ruffle or flounce at the bottom of a bodice used to emphasize the hips and make the waist look smaller.

Permanent (Permanent Wave): Developed in 1904 by Karl Nessler (later changed to Charles Nestle), permanents became very popular during the twenties after a steam process was developed.

Perugia, Andre, 1893-1977: Premier shoemaker whose famed creations spanned many decades; Perugia created shoes for such famous couturiers as Poiret, Fath, and Givenchy.

Picot edging: A narrow band with tiny loops on either side—a twenties favorite used to finish edges.

Plus-four Knickers: A sports craze during the second half of the twenties introduced by the fashionable Prince of Wales; plus-fours were very baggy knickers worn for sports such as golf and cycling; they were cut so full they extended about four inches below the cuffed knees. (There were also "plus-eights.")

Poiret, Paul, 1879-1944: "I am merely the first to perceive women's secret desires and fulfill them in advance..." (Paul Poiret, self-proclaimed "King of Fashion.") Today, if not the "King," he might be considered the "Father" of modern fashion, as the revolutionary fashions he initiated paved the way for the styles of the future. He demolished the Edwardian hourglass silhouette by promoting slimmer yet opulent styles that presaged the chemise dresses of the twenties. His creations were often modeled by his striking, though then unfashionably, slender wife, Denise. Orientalism, a favorite theme, was reflected in his coats and gowns as well as his famous turbans. Entering the world of fashion at the age of eighteen, Poiret sold a dozen sketches to Cheruit, and then approached Doucet, where he worked from around 1897 to 1900; he later declared that at Doucet, "I learned everything." He briefly worked at Worth before opening his own couture house in September 1904 at 5 Rue Auber. He was so successful that in 1906 he moved to a three-story mansion at 37 rue Pasquier; and from 1909-1926 to an eighteenth century mansion at avenue d'Antin & Faubourg St. Honore (where he briefly opened a nightclub, the Oasis, in 1919). From 1926 until 1929, with his popularity waning, Maison Poiret was located at 43 Avenue Victor-Emmanuel III (1 rond-Point des Champs-Elysees).

Shortly after the turn of the twentieth century, Poiret set out to abolish the cruel corsets demanded by the Edwardian "S" silhouette, which he felt was contrary to the laws of nature "...on one side the bust, and on the other the whole of the rear end, so that women were divided in two...". In October 1908, Poiret presented his revolutionary "Empire" or "Grecian" gowns in a *pochoir* booklet, *Les robes de Paul Poiret*, illustrated by Paul Iribe, which was followed in February 1911 by *Les Choses de Paul Poiret*, illustrated by Georges Lepape. In May 1908, *Vogue's* Paris correspondent announced: "The fashionable figure is growing straighter and straighter, less bust, less hips, waist and a wonderful long, slender suppleness about the limbs... the petticoat is obsolete, prehistoric. How slim, how graceful, how elegant women look!" Poiret claimed the modern brassiere or "cache-corset," the famous "hobble skirt" (1910), and promoted pants for women. At his famous Persian "Thousand and Second Night" party held on June 24, 1911, Denise created a sensation when she stepped from a gilded cage in a harem costume of filmy chiffon pantaloons under a wired lampshade tunic and turban with tall aigrette. In his 1911 *Les Choses*, Poiret showed four stunning pantaloon outfits, including a pants dress for gardening and one for tennis as "*Fashions of Tomorrow*." And, though his "jupe culotte" pantdresses that followed were considered scandalous, they paved the way to pants for women. Poiret collaborated with many artists; Raoul Dufy designed incredible art deco "fantasy" prints for him and Andre Perugia designed shoes to compliment his fashions. Poiret established two enterprises named for his daughters—his perfume establishment "Rosine," after his eldest daughter, and his design house "Martine," after his youngest. Though one of the top designers of all time, Poiret's time was brief; he was a casualty of WWI—by the time the war was over, his fame had begun to wane as women increasingly demanded the even "Simpler" styles of couturiers like Chanel, Patou, and Vionnet. In 1929, he reluctantly closed the doors of his couture house.

Pongee: A favorite fabric of the twenties, with slightly irregular texture, available in different weights. Silk Pongee was used for women's dresses, blouses, and lingerie; pongee was also advertised in both silk and cotton for men's shirts. The word "pongee" originates from the Chinese "pen-chi," meaning "hand-loomed."

Premet: Successful French couture house, established by Mme. Premet in 1911 and popular with twenties new woman or "*garconne*." Madame Gres, later known as "Alix" trained at Premet. During the twenties, Premet was located at 8 Place Vendome; the house closed ca. 1930.

Pret-a-porter: French term for ready-to-wear or off the rack clothing.

Prince of Wales, 1894-1972: The male Fashion Icon of the twenties, he popularized such fashions as baggy "plus-four" knickers, golf caps, tweed suits, and Glen Urquhart plaids. Prince of Wales, 1910-36, he was to become King Edward VII, but abdicated in November 1936 to marry "The woman I love...", Wallis Warfield Simpson, an American divorcee.

Pringle of Scotland: Established in 1815, in the twenties and thirties, Pringle was noted for their cashmere sweaters in Scottish argyle patterns and cardigan twinsets.

Raglan: Type of sleeve named for the British Lord Raglan, who commanded the famous Charge of the Light Brigade during the Crimean War of the 1850s. The raglan sleeve cut in one with the bodice, so there is no armscye seam connecting the shoulders and arms.

Rayon: The first widely used synthetic fabric made of cellulose in several different finishes. It was named in 1924 by Kenneth Lord Sr., and was formerly known as "artificial silk." During the second half of the twenties, it became popular for dresses, skirts, and blouses as well as stockings and lingerie. Couturiers such as Lanvin and Poiret touted rayon in period magazine advertisements.

Reboux, Caroline, 1837-1927: Easily one of the world's top milliners from the mid-nineteenth century until her death. During the twenties, Reboux was one of the chief promoters of the famous cloche hat.

Redfern, 1853-1929: English couture house famed for fine tailoring and traditional designs. Redfern was originally established in 1841 at Cowes on the Isle of Wight, making yachting clothes. During the Victorian era, The House of Redfern was noted for smart sports clothes; in the 1880s, John Redfern created the famous clingy wool jersey dress designed for Lillie ("The Jersey Lily") Langtry. In the 1880s, Redfern opened a Paris branch; others were located in London and New York. In the twenties, Redfern was still a noted, though conservative, house located at 242 rue de Rivoli, Paris, with branches in Deauville and Nice. The house closed in the late twenties.

Robe de style: A popular alternative to the twenties tubular silhouette, the *robe de style* was a romantic, full-skirted favorite for afternoon and evening inspired by the eighteenth century robes favored by Marie Antoinette. Couturiere Jeanne Lanvin was its chief promoter, having first showed the style in the mid-teens; many other couturiers followed with their own versions.

Rochas, Marcel, 1902-55: Well known couturier who opened his establishment in 1924; Rochas was an innovative couturier who remained popular up to the 1950s.

Rouff, Maggy, 1896-1971: A popular designer whose parents directed Maison Drecoll; she opened her own establishment in 1928.

Sautoir: A long necklace or rope of pearls, very popular during the twenties for afternoon and evening wear.

Schiaparelli, Elsa, 1890-1973: One of the most famous designers of all time, "Schiap" opened "Pour le Sport" in 1927. Her success was assured with the introduction of her *Trompe l'oeil* Bow sweater, ca. 1928. Her clothes were witty but wild, elegant and eccentric, often influenced by cubist and surrealist art. See pages 156, 157, 176.

Shirring: parallel rows of gathered stitching, employed both to provide ease of motion and to accent feminine curves. Similar to "smocking," which has a more honeycomb-effect stitch.

Snow, Carmel, 1887-1961: Fashion editor of *Vogue* from 1923 to 1932, when she became editor of *Vogue's* arch rival, *Harper's Bazar*, until her retirement in 1958.

Surplice: Diagonal wrap or crossover closure very popular in the teens and twenties.

Surrealism: An abstract, fantasy art form which gained popularity during the second half of the twenties, promoted by artists like Salvador Dali, Picasso, and John Miro.

Tailleur: A feminine tailored suit.

Tango Dress: Originally described a teens dress either draped for fullness or slit up the side to facilitate easy movement when dancing the then daring "Tango." The term was used through the early twenties.

Tea Gown: A frothy, flowing at-home lounging gown popular since the Victorian era, traditionally worn during tea time, before dressing formally for the evening. During the second half of the twenties, tea gowns began to be replaced by the racier "lounging pajamas."

Tea Dress or Frock: A dress worn to an afternoon event, an afternoon "tea" party, or tea dance.

Trompe l'oeil ("fool the eye"): A design created to resemble an object. In 1928, Schiaparelli's *trompe l'oeil* sweater created a sensation, with a large *trompe l'peil* bow knitted into the sweater, rather than having an added on separate bow.

Tulle: A very fine and fragile net, usually silk or cotton. It was first made during the second half of the eighteenth century in Nottingham, England, on a stocking machine, and became popular on headdresses, veils, tunics, and gown accents. Made of sturdier nylon since ca. 1950.

Vionnet, Madeleine, 1876-1975: "You must dress a body in a fabric, not construct a dress into which the body is expected to fit." (Madeleine Vionnet) Vionnet is hailed as one of the most talented and innovative designers in the history of haute couture. Though not as flamboyant as Poiret or Chanel, she was one of the first to design simpler, more natural clothing for women; she developed the bias cut, and, like Poiret, fought to abolish the corset (at age 79, she told an interviewer: "...it was I who got rid of corsets, in 1907, while I was at Doucet, I discarded corsets"). Vionnet married in 1894 at age eighteen; she had a daughter who died very young and divorced in 1898. She worked briefly in London before returning to Paris in 1900 to become design assistant to Mme. Gerber at Callot Soeurs—while at Callot Soeurs, she was particularly known for her lovely lingerie. Ca. 1907, she left Callot and worked at Doucet for five years before opening her own couture house at 222 de Rivoli in 1912. Shortly after WWI, she began experimenting with her revolutionary "bias cut," creating clothes that caressed the body rather than forced it into an artificial silhouette. In 1922-23, she moved to 50 avenue Montaigne, Paris. Vionnet retired in 1939. See pg. 173.

Vicose rayon: most common type of rayon, patented in 1892 by Beadle, Bevan, and Cross, three English chemists.

Voile: A sheer, soft, translucent fabric, similar to organdy, but without organdy's stiffness. Most often made in cotton fibers, but also in silk, wool or synthetics.

Volants: Ruffles or flounces often used on twenties dresses, particularly evening gowns.

Weighted Silk (Shredded Silk): Weighted Silk is silk fabric that has had metallic particles added in the finishing process, which lent more body to the fabric; silks were "weighted" with metallic salts, usually tin or iron. This was a process that was used from the mid-eighteenth century up to the mid-twentieth century; it's heyday was ca. 1890-1930. These metallic salts eventually broke down fibers, creating long, shredded tears (think "ripped to shreds"). Though it was most often used in linings, it was also used for the outer part of garments. Needless to say, it's impossible to repair, and if it touches other non-weighted parts of the garment, it may damage them as well.

Worth: Couture house founded in 1858 by the "Father of Haute Couture," Charles Frederick Worth. His sons took over the House of Worth on his death in 1895, Jean-Philippe becoming the premier designer, and Gaston the business manager. In the early twenties, Jean-Philippe retired and Gaston's son Jean-Charles became the new couturier. During the twenties, Worth was considered one of the more traditional, conservative houses—located at 7 rue de la Paix in Paris, with branches in London, Biarritz, and Cannes. Worth merged with Paquin in 1954.

Zipper (Zip): A fastener for clothing and accessories. In 1851 Elias Howe patented his "Automatic Continuous Clothing Closure," which was followed in 1893 by Whitcomb L. Judson's "Clasp Locker" that used an intricate hook and eye system. In 1913, Gordon Sundback, an employee of Judson's Universal Fastener Co., developed a version using interlocking metal teeth known as a "hookless fastener;" it was used by the military during WWI. In the early 1920s, B.F. Goodrich ordered Sundback's hookless fasteners for their rubber galoshes or "Mystic Boots," and noting the sound made when the fastener was opened and closed, Goodrich christened it the "Zipper." By the second half of the twenties, zippers were used mainly on items like boots, luggage, and purses. In 1935, Schiaparelli shocked the world of haute couture with her "Fashion Zippers," and in 1934, Lord Mountbaten coaxed the Prince of Wales to try trousers with zipper flies, but it wasn't until the late '30s than zippers came into common use as fastenings for clothing.

Bibliography

Books

1920s Fashions from B. Altman & Company. Mineola, NY: Dover Publications, 1999.

A Singular Elegance: The Photographs of Baron Adolph DeMeyer. Exhibit sponsored by *Harper's Bazaar.* San Francisco: Chronicle Books, 1994.

American Heritage. *American Heritage History of the 20s & 30s.* New York: American Heritage Publishing Co., Inc., 1970.

Armstrong, Nancy. *The Book of Fans.* New York: Mayflower Books.

Baker, Jean-Claude, and Chris Chase. *Josephine, The Hungry Heart.* New York: Cooper Square Press ed., 2001.

Baron, Stanley, with Jacques Damase. *Sonia Delaunay, The Life of an Artist.* London: Thames and Hudson Ltd., 1995.

Bata Shoe Museum. *All About Shoes: Footwear Through the Ages.* Toronto: Bata Limited, 1994.

Batterberry, Michael and Ariane. *Fashion, The Mirror of History.* New York: Greenwich House, 1997.

Battersby, Martin. *Art Deco Fashion, French Designers 1908-1925.* London: Academy Editions, 1974.

Battersby, Martin. *The Decorative Twenties.* New York: Collier Books, 1975.

Blum, Daniel. *Pictorial History of the Silent Screen.* New York: Grosset & Dunlap, 1953.

Blum, Dilys E. *Ahead of Fashion: Hats of the 20th Century.* Philadelphia Museum of Art Bulletin, 1993.

Blum, Stella, ed. *Eighteenth Century French Fashion Plates.* New York, Dover Publications, 1982.

Bowman, Sara. *A Fashion for Extravagance, Art Deco Fabrics and Fashions.* New York: E.P. Dutton, 1985.

Bradfield, Nancy. *Costume in Detail: 1730-1930.* New York: Costume & Fashion Press, 1997.

Brough, James. *The Prince & The Lily.* New York: Coward, McCann & Geoghegan Inc., 1975.

Davenport, Millia. *Book of Costume, Volume II.* New York: Crown Publishers, 1948.

de Buzzaccarini, Vittoria. *Elegance and Style, Two Hundred Years Of Men's Fashions.* Milan: Lupetti & Co., 1992.

de Osma, Guillermo. *Fortuny, The Life and Work of Mariano Fortuny.* New York: Rizzoli, 1985.

DePauw, Linda Grant, and Conover Hunt. *Remember the Ladies, Women in America 1750-1815.* New York: Viking Press, 1976.

Deslandres, Yvonne. *Poiret, Paul Poiret 1879-1944.* New York: Rizzoli, 1987.

Druesedow, Jean L. *In Style, Celebrating Fifty Years of the Costume Institute.* New York: Metropolitan Museum of Art, 1987.

Etherington-Smith, Meredith. *Patou.* New York: St. Martin's/Marek, 1983.

Fitzgerald, F. Scott. *Novels and Stories 1920-1922* (Library of America): *This Side of Paradise* (1920); *Flappers and Philosophers* (1920); short stories including "Dalyrimple Goes Wrong," "Bernice Bobs Her Hair," and "The Ice Palace"; *The Beautiful and the Damned* (1922); Tales of the Jazz Age short stories including "May Day" and "A Diamond as Big as the Ritz."

Fitzgerald, F. Scott. *The Great Gatsby.* New York: Charles Scribner's Sons, 1925.

Gernsheim, Alison. *Fashion and Reality, 1840-1914.* London: Faber and Faber, 1963.

Ginsburg, Madeleine. *Paris Fashions: The Art Deco Style of the 1920s.* London: Bracken Books, 1989.

Glennon, Lorraine, Editor in Chief. *The 20th Century.* North Deighton, MA.: JG Press, 2000.

Goldthorpe, Caroline. *From Queen to Empress.* New York: Metropolitan Museum of Art, 1988.

Griffith, Richard, and Arthur Mayer. *The Movies.* New York: Simon and Schuster, 1957.

Howell, Georgina. *In Vogue.* New York: Schocken Books, 1976.

Kamitsis, Lydia. *Vionnet.* Paris: Editions Assouline, 1996.

Kyoto Museum. *Fashion (A History from the 18th to the 20th Century).* Taschen Press.

Kyoto Museum. *Revolution in Fashion 1715-1815.* New York: Abbeville Press, 1989.

Laver, James. *Costume & Fashion, A Concise History.* New York: Oxford University Press, 1982.

le Bourhis, Katell, ed. *The Age of Napoleon.* New York: Metropolitan Museum of Art, 1989.

Lencek, Lena, and Gedeon Bosker. *Making Waves, Swimsuits and the Undressing of America.* San Francisco: Chronicle Books, 1989.

Lynam, Ruth, Ed. *Couture, An Illustrated History of the Great Paris Designers and Their Creations.* New York: Doubleday & Company, Inc., 1972.

Martin, Richard, and Harold Koda. *Bare Witness.* New York: Metropolitan Museum of Art, 1996.

Martin, Richard, and Harold Koda. *Bloom.* New York: Metropolitan Museum of Art, 1995.

Martin, Richard, and Harold Koda. *Haute Couture.* New York: Metropolitan Museum of Art, 1995.

Martin, Richard, and Harold Koda. *Orientalism.* New York: Metropolitan Museum of Art, 1994.

Martin, Richard, and Harold Koda. *Splash! A History of Swimwear.* New York: Rizzoli, 1990.

Martin, Richard. *Cubism and Fashion*. New York: Metropolitan Museum of Art, 1998.

Martin, Richard. *Fashion and Surrealism*. New York: Rizzoli, 1987.

Milbank, Caroline Rennolds. *Couture, The Great Designers*. New York: Stewart, Tabori & Chang, Inc., 1985.

Moore, Doris Langley. *Fashion Through Fashion Plates 1771-1970*. New York: Clarkson N. Potter, Inc., 1971.

Morgan, Sarah. *Art Deco, The European Style*. New York: Gallery Books, 1990.

Mulvagh, Jane. *Vogue History of 20th Century Fashion*. London: Viking, 1988.

O'Keeffe, Linda. *Shoes, A Celebration of Pumps, Sandals, Slippers & More*. New York: Workman Publishing, 1996.

Olian, JoAnne, ed. *Authentic French Fashions of the Twenties*. New York: Dover Publications, 1990.

Parrot, Nicole. *Mannequins*. New York: St. Martin's Press, 1982.

Payne, Blanche. *History of Costume*. New York: Harper & Row, 1965.

Piña, Leslie, and Donald-Brian Johnson. *Whiting & Davis Purses*. Atglen, PA: Schiffer Publishing, Ltd., 2002.

Pratt, Lucy, and Linda Woolley. *Shoes*. London: Victoria and Albert Museum Fashion Accessories, 1999.

Robinson, Julian. *The Fine Art of Fashion, an Illustrated History*. New York/London: Bartley & Jensen.

Robinson, Julian. *The Golden Age of Style, Art Deco Fashion Illustration*. New York: Gallery Books, 1976.

Robinson, Julian. *The Brilliance of Art Deco*. New York/London: Bartley & Jensen.

Rothstein, Natalie, Ed. *Four Hundred Years of Fashion*. London: Victoria and Albert Museum, 1984.

Schoeffler, O.E. *Esquire's Encyclopedia of 20th Century Men's Fashions*. New York: McGraw-Hill, 1973.

Time-Life Books. *This Fabulous Century, 1920-1930*. Time-Life, Inc., 1969.

Tozer, Jane, and Sarah Levitt. *Fabric of Society, A Century of People and Their Clothes 1770-1970*. Carno, Powys, Wales: Laura Ashley, Ltd., 1983.

White, Palmer. *Poiret*. New York: Clarkson N. Potter, Inc., 1973.

Wilcox, R. Turner. *The Dictionary of Costume*. New York: Charles Scribner's Sons, 1958.

Wilcox, R. Turner. *The Mode in Costume*. New York: Charles Scribner's Sons, 1958.

Wood, Barry James. *Show Windows, 75 Years of the Art of Display*. New York: Congdon & Weed, 1982.

Periodicals (These refer to complete magazines, not fashion plates):

Art Gout Beaute: June 1922; October 1927; May 1928.

Butterick Quarterly: Spring 1920; Spring 1922; Summer 1924; Autumn 1925; Spring 1926.

Delineator, The: May 1921; March 1922.

Fashion Quarterly, Ladies' Home Journal: Winter 1922.

Fashionable Dress: October 1922; June 1926.

Flapper, The (magazine): May to December 1922.

Harper's Bazar: April 1923; May 1923; September 1923; August 1924; January 1925; October 1926; October 1927.

Illustrated Milliner: September 1923.

L'Illustration, Exposition des Arts Decoratifs: Aout (April) 1925.

Ladies' Home Journal: July 1920; October 1920; November 1920.

Milliner, The: May 1925; August 1925.

Mode Pratique: March 1924.

Pictorial Review Fashion Book: Spring 1921; Winter 1922-23; Summer 1925.

Vogue Fashion Bi-Monthly: June/July 1927.

Vogue Pattern Book: August/September 1927; October/November 1927; December 1927/January 1928; August/September 1929.

Vogue: July 15, 1921; February 1, 1922; June 1, 1922; April 15, 1923; February 15, 1925; September 1, 1925; April 1, 1926; June 15, 1926; September 15, 1926; October 1, 1926; January 15, 1927; July 1, 1927; September 1, 1927; October 1, 1927; April 1, 1928; March 2, 1929; June 1, 1928; October 13, 1928; January 5, 1929.

Catalogs:

Bellas Hess: Fall/Winter 1920-21; Fall/Winter 1921-22; Spring/Summer 1925; Fall/Winter 1925-26; Spring/Summer 1926.

Chicago Mail Order: Spring/Summer 1922; Spring/Summer 1923; Fall/Winter 1927/28; Fall/Winter 1928-29; Fall/Winter 1929-30.

National Bellas Hess: Spring/Summer 1928; Fall/winter 1929-30.

National Style Book: Spring/Summer 1920; Spring/Summer 1922; Spring/Summer 1923; Spring/Summer 1925; Fall/Winter 1924-25; Spring/Summer 1927; Fall/Winter 1926-27.

Pierre Imans: Catalogue of Mannequins, 1927.

Index

Roaring 20s Fashions: Jazz. Susan Langley. Dubbed "The Jazz Age" by F. Scott Fitzgerald, the 1920s were characterized as a decade of frenetic fun. In the fashion world, clothes began to lose the last vestiges of the fussy, frilly Edwardian era as they grew more svelte and "simple." This wonderful, in-depth look at the styles of the Jazz Age and the people who wore them covers the first half of the 1920s — years that served as a prelude to "The Party of the Century," as Fitzgerald called part two of this free-wheeling decade. A combination of vintage images, professional photographs of existing garments, and period artists' illustrations vividly display clothing and accessories for men, women, and children worn from 1920 through 1924. Clothing for all occasions is featured, including evening wear, day wear, the all-important sports fashions, lingerie, and even wedding attire. Fascinating timelines place the fashions in their proper setting, describing each year's film, music, literary, and couture trends. Among the book's many highlights are rare French pochoir fashion plates and photos of authentic signed haute couture gowns by Patou and Fortuny. This informative and visually engaging book will delight fashion and history connoisseurs alike. A companion volume covers fashions from the years 1925 to 1929.

Size: 8 1/2" x 11"   560 color & 123 b/w photos   248pp.
ISBN: 0-7643-2319-9   hard cover $39.95